UNSEALED

An Unconventional Story of Love and Friendship

K. M. LANGDON

MOTUS PUBLISHING

TORONTO, CANADA

Motus Publishing
1120 Finch Avenue West, Suite 701-1556
Toronto, Ontario, M3J 3H7

Copyright © 2016 by Motus Publishing. All rights reserved.

No part of this publication may be reproduced, distributed, or transmitted in any form, including photocopying, recording, or any other method whatsoever without the prior written permission of the publisher, except in the case of brief quotations embodied in critical reviews and certain other noncommercial uses permitted by copyright law. For permission requests, write to the publisher at the address above or by email at motuspublishing@gmail.com.

Though inspired by true events, this book is a work of fiction. The story, names, characters, and incidents portrayed are fictitious. No identification with actual persons, places, buildings, and/or products is intended or should be inferred.

~

Editing by Jessica Wright

Cover Design by Warren Keefe

Interior Design by Cory Visser

Author headshot by Tanya Smith Photography

~

All communications regarding book purchases, special discounts for bulk orders, and booking K. M. Langdon as a speaker at your event, contact motuspublishing@gmail.com.

Printed in Canada

10 9 8 7 6 5 4 3 2 1

ISBN 978-0-9953038-0-5
ISBN (ebook) 978-0-9953038-1-2

"Be kind for everyone you meet is fighting a hard battle."

- John Watson

To first loves

Prologue

When our relationship ended, everyone asked, "Did you see it coming?" Though it was masked with concern, the tone was always accusatory and bewildered. I could see the thought process in their eyes. "There must have been warning signs… You can't have been totally surprised… You could have avoided this."

I've thought long and hard about this possibility. I've relived every good day and bad, every passionate kiss and every screaming fight. I've analyzed every romantic gesture and every cutting word. I don't think I could have avoided this. I don't think I would have. Maybe, on some level, I did know. Maybe I knew we would end in an explosion of emotions, truths, and long-buried memories. But where they're wrong is that I would never have guessed why. I would never have believed why. But, even if I had guessed, I know I wouldn't have left. I wouldn't have avoided it. He confronted this head on, and I don't think there's a person out there who could convince me that it would have been best to let him do it alone.

- Kara

PROLOGUE

The sideways stares, the calls of protest as parents pulled their children tight to them, the anonymous bibles left on my doorstep – I saw them. I got the message loud and clear. I just wish that they'd seen that I was just being me; the guy who signed away his life to protect their country. But they never did. The worst were the young hicks who came into the bar from the small towns surrounding Nashville. They thought the muscles they'd gained hauling hay and building fences could teach me a lesson about what's "proper" in this country, my country. I've had to teach a few of them a good lesson instead – that my muscles are still bigger than theirs. And that I have a lot more anger bottled up in me than they do.

The confrontations don't hurt my feelings like they used to. What hurts the most now is when people, most often my friends and family, say, "This isn't you, man. Why don't you just go back to being your old self?"

"This is me now," I tell them. I don't know why they can't see it. I'm still me. I still love to drink and watch football with a big, fat dip in my lip. I might change again, might look a little different in another little while. I'm just trying to figure it all out. But, right now, for forever, I'm still me. Why doesn't anyone see that?

- Liam

PROLOGUE

KARA EDWARDS

Competitive, outgoing, and talented, Kara Edwards grew up in a supportive upper-middle class home in Toronto, Canada and excelled in almost every area of her life. She maintained her status on the honor roll throughout high school and had a budding social life while competing at the national level in 3-Day Eventing, the most demanding and dangerous equestrian sport. She did this while traveling around the USA and Canada for competitions all year long. On the first day of a competition, she and her horse would perform in front of judges and show their control and unison by transitioning through several ballet-style movements. On the second day, her inner daredevil would come out and the pair would gallop fast and hard around a three to four mile course jumping solid fences built from logs and stone and running through water and over bridges to showcase their speed, endurance, jumping ability, and bravery. On the third and final day, the pair took on a phase called "show jumping" during which she and her horse would jump around a stadium with fences that could fall down at the slightest touch. This day allowed the horse and rider combinations to demonstrate their suppleness, obedience, fitness, and athleticism, which was difficult after the day before. With its roots in military training, 3-Day Eventing is a sport that tests the horse and rider to the maximum of their physical and mental abilities. Kara's affection for "difficult" or "problem horses" and for taking any amount of the verbal abuse that so many top riding coaches are known to dish out without blinking an eye, gave her a reputation for being strong and tough. Her soft approach to training her big, and somewhat bull-headed, horses let people see her kind and gentle heart. The ease with which she walked into a party, without makeup or fancy hair, and could befriend anyone around her showed a confidence that many adolescent girls could only wish they had. She was fit and naturally pretty, with long brown hair and a flirty smile.

PROLOGUE

These traits, along with the drive of an athlete, allowed her to overcome many of life's challenges with little effort.

However, like most people, she had a side of herself that she hid from everyone. She was shy and insecure about who she was deep down. She was scared of a lot – of not being good enough, of failing her family, her coach, and even her horse. She was never afraid of being hurt or falling down, but her fear of not succeeding – and what others would think of her failure to succeed – held her back from pushing her talent to its fullest potential.

In between riding, school, and seeing her friends, she wrote. It was her way of letting out the side of her that no one else knew. She wrote about achieving dreams. She wrote about the injustices she saw in every day life. She wrote about the stories of love and loss, betrayal and angst that she imagined the strangers all around her went through. She wrote about feelings she knew nothing of and that she was too afraid to acknowledge within herself. Writing was her way of experiencing life in a different way. However, she never told anyone outside of her family about her aspirations of being a writer or how she could so easily lose herself in the fictional worlds she created. Once she grew up and started university, she kept that dream to herself because she realized that the reality of becoming an author was difficult and sprinkled with roadblocks. She found that when she did open up and talk about publishing a book and, maybe, one day winning a Pulitzer or some other prestigious recognition award, boys' eyes would often glaze over and girls would look for someone less "artsy" to talk to. So, instead, she kept these dreams close to her heart and talked to others about parties, boys, the latest music, and movies. They never knew that she liked to write stories about ending horse slaughter, seeing the signs of abuse in children and animals, and of seeking to understand people thinking of suicide. She had no first-hand experience with these things, but she wanted to help give a voice

PROLOGUE

to those who did. It gave her strength and confidence to feel like she was doing something that mattered. However, because she stopped telling others about this side of her, people only saw a popular girl who loved to laugh, enjoyed a party, but never fell in love or took life too seriously.

Throughout undergrad, almost all of Kara's friends found "love" two, three, four times at least. Some even found the real thing. Kara never came close. An avid reader, Kara often found herself enthralled in fantasy worlds filled with adventure, love, seduction, and heartbreak. In real life, she never found a man who made her weak in the knees or forced her to let down her walls. She never felt that she could be entirely herself with any guy she met, so she could never really fall in love. She watched her friends find boyfriend after boyfriend and let themselves fall harder and harder each time, letting the guys into their hearts completely, only to pick themselves back up again and again when the relationships ended. Something deep within her prevented her from opening up and finding love the same way. She knew how to play the game, and she enjoyed the chase, but she never found anyone who challenged her to let down her walls, or cared enough about her to do so. Her façade was exhausting to hold up, so every relationship ended quickly with Kara too tired or too bored to fight for it to continue. So instead, she found love in her dreams and lived it through her stories, while enjoying her college years with countless nights of beer pong, hard-bodied athletes, and long nights of studying.

At 22 and at the end of a fun and academically-tiring four years, she landed herself a position in the graduate English program at San Diego State University.

PROLOGUE

LIAM SUNDRY

Liam Sundry had always been a dude. When people asked him to describe himself, Liam always replied with a shrug and said, "I'm a dude."

Growing up on the outskirts of Nashville, Tennessee, Liam had a lot of freedom at a young age. While his parents taught him right from wrong, and to always accept people despite their differences, they pretty much let him roam free and do what he wanted. Working in farmers' fields during sticky hot summers, cooling off with beer that his friends' older siblings had bought them, and fast rides in someone's borrowed pick up, he figured himself a man long before other boys his age considered themselves teenagers. From the time he was 12, he always had a girl on his arm. He had an easy smile and natural charm that let him have two, three, and sometimes four girlfriends at a time without breaking a sweat. Earning the coveted spot as captain of the football team in high school only increased the number of girls who were eager to win his affections and, as he got older, he learned that it was easy to convince them that this was best done naked. He always had something, or someone, to do on a Friday night, but his boys always came first. They'd go out into a field somewhere to drink beer and shoot the cans, crank their country CDs up loud, and pack their lips full of Copenhagen Straight – a man's dip.

Liam loved the gym, loved his dip, and loved his girls. That's what he told people and it was true. But what he never told them was that he didn't just love girls for their bodies, but for the way they laughed and how they smelled when he picked them up for a date. He didn't tell people that sometimes he envied the way their hair blew in the hot summer wind. And those weren't even his biggest secrets. There was one secret that Liam carried with him. One that he never planned to tell anyone because if he told someone then it would've been real, and he couldn't accept that while continuing to live large

PROLOGUE

the way he did. Eventually though, this was the secret that pushed him to the other side of the tracks.

Christian. The thought of him popped into Liam's head at the most inconvenient of times. As a young boy, Liam was best friends with Christian's younger brother. Because they lived just a few houses down from him, and Christian was old enough to watch Liam and his friend, Liam spent much of his spare time at their house. When Liam was over, Christian was always more than happy to babysit, and often sent his parents out to dinner so they he could be alone with them. However, shortly after the adults left, Christian would always ask Liam to help him with something in his room. For a long time, they just played together – cards, board games, action figures, or whatever else Christian had lying around. As a small fourth-grader, Liam was unprepared when Christian made an advance at him. Nervously, Liam did as he was told, even though felt wrong to touch Christian where he wanted, and it felt dirty to have Christian touch him where only he touched himself.

As time passed and Liam's friend circle grew and he saw his once best friend less and less. His parents believed he was old enough to take care of himself so they didn't care if he had a babysitter anymore, and he was never pressured to go visit. Instead, he spent much of his time with his football friends, his cousin Billy, or with girls. However, the memories of that night with Christian never left his mind. The more football he played, the bigger he got. And the older he got, the angrier he got. The combination made him into a great fighter so now when he came across Christian in the streets, Christian couldn't intimidate him like he used to.

As time went by, a darkness grew in Liam. He always liked the way girls' bodies felt under his big, rough hands. He liked the softness of their skin, the firmness of their breasts, the way he could cup their asses into his hands and lift them up. But some part of him never felt

PROLOGUE

quite satisfied. At first, he tried hard to block out the feelings. He'd try to focus on whichever naked girl he had in front of him. At 16, Christian moved away and Liam started turning to drinking, smoking weed, and even doing cocaine to block out the memory, but nothing worked and he developed new, haunting thoughts that made him uncomfortable. He loved sex with girls. He didn't think he was gay – he didn't want to have sex with men or anything. But there was something that never felt complete in him with the way he was living his life. He started dating a coke-addicted high school dropout. His friends, who saw Liam less and less, nicknamed her Caligula and, more than occasionally, Liam called her that too. She was pretty, but had hit her prime early. However, Liam was content enough with her looks, and more pleased that she spread her legs for him any time and place that he wanted with no work on his part.

By 17, Liam had done more drugs than he'd ever planned on. His grades dropped, he lost touch with most of his friends, and he got kicked off of the football team. He got in fights almost daily over the smallest of offenses, but still stuck up for others he saw getting harassed. His parents began to urge him to reach out to Christian and his old friends, wanting him to break up with Caligula, but while Caligula was the gateway to his new world, Christian was the fire behind him, pushing him farther and farther into it.

After high school graduation and a little over three years of working, Liam knew it was time for a change. His old friends had given up their old ways and were either in college or training for their careers, but he knew those kinds of careers weren't for him. He knew he had to get away and make something of himself. He needed to respect himself, he needed a challenge, and he needed to be a *man*. So when he turned 21 he joined the Navy. He knew that being in the Navy would force him to give up drinking and drugs, as well as the lifestyle he was now accustomed to, and he both needed and wanted

PROLOGUE

that. He needed to lack the time to relive the memories and reoccurring thoughts that he had been trying so hard to escape and he couldn't think of anything more meaningful than protecting his country. So he'd broken up with Caligula, trained hard, and joined up.

"I'm here to serve my country, sir. I'd like to become a Navy SEAL," he'd told the officer.

One year later, after going through basic naval training, he was in San Diego, California – the home of the Navy SEALs – and gearing up for Hell Week.

One

Stepping off the plane, Kara let the heat seep into her bones. Breathing in the new air, she felt the kind of excitement that only new beginnings could offer. In a jean skirt and white tank top, her long brown hair cascaded down her already tanned back in beach waves, held off her face by a pair of sunglasses. With the number of a pro-surfer from her flight tucked into her pocket, she felt the promise of an exciting new life.

She grabbed a cab to her new apartment, one that she'd found online – just close enough to campus that she could walk, but far enough that she didn't feel she'd be overwhelmed by campus events. She looked happily out the window, welcoming the warm air and hot sun on her face, and at the palm trees and sidewalks full of chiseled, tanned bodies running, skateboarding, and casually hanging out with friends. She couldn't wait to get to the beach to start making friends, but she first had to attend orientation.

Though she considered herself past undergraduate immaturity, she hadn't quite reached a Master's level of maturity where beach parties didn't outweigh the excitement of academia. Orientation was exactly the level of boring that Kara expected – meeting professors, listening to their areas of study, and an awkward mix-and-mingle event with all 12 students. It might have been more exciting if Kara had seen anyone that looked like her or the kind of fun-loving, Bay Street-bound people she was used to. Back in Canada, Bay Street was the closest Kara could get to Wall Street and was where the majority of her friends from undergrad had found jobs. She enjoyed partaking in the extravagant parties that the future lawyers and investment bankers put on in their free time. She knew if she could find people like that in San Diego she'd click with them immediately, but there was no one like that at orientation. All of the other students looked to be sun-deprived and far too interested in the program director's area of study – war poetry. In her mind, war poetry was far too depressing to dwell on. Though she herself was a "book nerd" at heart and could become enthralled in her studies like the rest, she was used to portraying herself as a less-than-serious party girl, and wasn't quite ready to shed that shell. She hadn't told anyone, but she was incredibly nervous that all the socially awkward men and women with unkempt hair around her would see her as an imposter in their intellectually superior world. While intelligent, she'd partied harder than she'd studied throughout the past four years of undergrad, resulting in many of her early grades being lower than she'd ever experienced before going to university. To protect herself from academic embarrassment, she held onto her superficial mask and let herself act as though she'd prefer to spend her afternoon acquainting herself with the men of San Diego's beaches more than learning about the program.

Ducking out of the mix-and-mingle event before it even began, she bumped into a large chest smelling of Boss cologne and cigars.

"Woah, excuse me," said the man in a deep Californian surfer drawl. "Leaving so soon?"

Kara looked up and saw the owner of the large chest. He was staring down at her, a goofy expression on his face. His actual appearance was slightly at odds with the height and solidity that his chest and voice had suggested. He was lean and soft, resembling an athlete who had been too busy with books and work to keep up with spending hours in the gym, but his skin still had the tan of an active outdoorsman and his warm smile gave the impression that he could burst into laughter at any moment. Catching a glimpse of his flip-flops and Margaritaville t-shirt, she liked him immediately. "Well, unfortunately, I just remembered that I have something to do. I just moved here, you see, so I have a ton of errands to run," she replied, fumbling over her excuse because she was a little embarrassed about her lack of interest in the program's opening event.

"Doesn't look like my scene either," he chuckled, a deep *huh-huh-huh* sound. "I'll head out with you."

As he turned and walked away, she didn't think he would be the man who she hoped would steal her heart in California, but she noticed that he had his own unique, and somewhat comforting, charm. He was gangly, all legs and arms, but he moved with purpose. His personality seemed to mimic the Golden Coast's signature surfer vibe, but there was also something a little bit different about him too. She followed him out of the building and, as they reached the sunny outdoors, he turned and grinned at her while he stopped his too-long arms from swinging in time with his legs by hooking each thumb into his pockets.

"You from Canada, then? I can tell by your accent. I love Canada. Great hockey, and great fries."

Kara laughed. "Yep, it's a great country. Long winters though. I can't wait to enjoy the sun and palm trees here." She looked at him with a slightly confused expression and asked, "Are you a hockey fan? I didn't expect to meet many of those down here."

"Ah, yes. I'm a big hockey fan. I used to spend summers, Thanksgiving, and Christmas vacations on my grandparents' farm in the northeast, and they love hockey. They don't like L.A. too much, so we always went to visit them. We went to Montreal once too and ate poutine – it was one of the most delicious meals of my life. I was a pretty young kid then, but I still remember."

She started walking towards the parking lot but noticed that he made no move to follow. Instead, he grinned at her and asked, "Wanna get a beer? You must drink a lot of beer up there."

"Sure," she answered. Kara felt immediately comfortable around him and was eager to make a new friend. She loved country music, so she felt sure she'd like anyone who liked Jimmy Buffet enough to sport his t-shirt to the first day of school.

Sitting at a bar near campus, they chatted about home, her distaste for cold winters and his nostalgia for white Christmases, his love of hockey and her mere tolerance of the sport, and their shared excitement of living in the craft beer capital of the USA. His name was Michael, and he absolutely did not like being called Mike. He was easy going, loved to laugh, enjoyed sports, and was easy to feel comfortable around. He reminded her of her friends at home, only quirkier and with a bit of West Coast chill. As they packed up to leave, Kara asked what his plans were for the evening, and had to work hard to stifle a giggle as he talked excitedly about the typewriter he had bought specifically for his move. He liked to write short stories and was working on a novel, and preferred to do it in the way that all the past greats had done.

"When I get home tonight, before we get too much school work, I'm going to pour a tumbler of scotch, light a candle, and channel Hemingway while I type. It's a restored 1915 Underwood. Have you seen how beautiful those babies are? It looks and feels just like how I always imagined the machines the great American writers would have used," Michael gushed. His cheeks were blushing red, and his eyes were light with barely contained excitement and pride.

Kara laughed. "You talk about your typewriter like most guys talk about girls," she said with a toying grin. While she was mocking him, he intrigued her. He was athletic, confident, and artistic. He even admitted to having a geeky side. And, most interestingly, he was comfortable with it all. In fact, he seemed proud of it. They reached the parking lot and he offered her a ride home. He handed her the only helmet and asked, "Ever been on a bike?"

With her eyes as wide as a shocked schoolgirl and the slight shaking of her hands as she did up her helmet, the answer was easy for him to guess. "Just hold on tight and, please, lean into the turns," he winked before he took her arms and wrapped them around his waist.

Once at home and readying for bed, Kara thought about Michael working with a glass of scotch beside him, alone at home on a Friday night, writing furiously about something deep and intelligent. He'd talked of sports games and kegger parties, so she knew they shared the same kind of undergraduate experience, but he was different. She, too, liked to write and create characters to tell stories, but she always kept this to herself, like a dirty little secret. Michael, on the other hand, seemed to embrace it, which only made him more interesting.

Turning off her lights, she promised to try and let herself be unique too. *What better time or place to do it? New place, new me*, she thought to herself. *And, maybe, new love*, she added hopefully.

<u>Kara</u>

>After orientation, I'm still worried about the program and proving that I'm smart enough to be here. But I'm not worried about

meeting people to be friends with anymore. Grad school doesn't seem like high school, or even undergrad. My program seems to have people of all ages and from all over the country. Everyone has a different background with different experiences. I met one guy from L.A. who, aside from his surfer drawl, is a lot like me. He likes to have fun, drink beer, and go to parties, but he also likes to writes stories, watch old movies, and quote Hemingway.

 It's scary as hell. I don't have horseback riding or my friends from horseback riding to fall back on. No one here has the same kind of drive for a corporate future that everyone I know back home does. Here, everyone is intellectual, a little bit geeky, and totally comfortable with it. I feel like the outsider. Going forward, I have to remember to be *me*. I have to accept them for being *them* too. I can feel it... This is where *my* story is going to start. I just hope I can let it.

Two

In Coronado, Liam Sundry was in celebration mode. After a week of no sleep, 132 hours of running, carrying logs, doing pushups, laying in the ocean with nothing but their noses showing, and pushing through the pain of exhausted and frozen muscles to race against each other in the military crawl races, Liam and his friends had graduated from Navy SEAL Hell Week.

On average, only about 25% of SEAL candidates make it through the five-and-a-half days of mental and physical testing with extreme sleep deprivation, which is intended to push each candidate past his limits and allow only those who have the determination and mental power to continue fighting into BUD/S SEAL training. Without any sleep, candidates are expected to perform under harsh conditions, in great physical pain, and while completely exhausted, with commanding officers constantly yelling harsh verbal abuse intended to degrade and test mental fortitude. "You worthless piece of shit! You're doing those pushups like a fucking faggot!" rang in every candidate's ears long after the week was finished. The honor of becoming a Navy SEAL is bestowed on only the most deserving applicants and is earned through extremely hard work, extreme toughness, and enormous amounts of sweat and pain. Hell Week is just the tip of the iceberg. It is designed to wean out all those who want the honor but do not want to, or cannot, endure the pain required. Most of the young men that Liam had befriended during his time in the regular Navy didn't make it past the second or third day, but that didn't matter by the end of the week. He'd become much closer with those he had graduated with. They had become his brothers. He had two staph infections – one in his hip and one in his leg. His friend Jones had a broken arm, Matthews had a gash on his jaw, Stevens had a sprained ankle, and the rest of the men scattered around were nursing other injuries, aches, or pains. They had all gone to hell and back together, and survived.

After hot showers and medically supervised sleep (men had been known to be so sleep deprived that they'd attempt suicide during their first night of sleep in a week), Liam and his friends were now celebrating at a local Mexican restaurant with, what they believed to be, the best tacos in Coronado. They were comparing battle scars and downing beers and shots while often declaring to each other, "I'd take a bullet for you, man! And I'd never leave ya behind." With every round, these promises grew louder and louder so that any local passersby knew another Hell Week must have wrapped up.

Liam looked around him as he waited at the bar for another beer, which was, in Coronado tradition, on the house. He appreciated the beer and the congratulations that came with each new bottle. He'd earned it. They all had. Seeing his new friends laughing, drinking, and holding their hurt limbs out of the way of those stumbling past, he felt more content than he ever had in his life. He was consumed by it all, and that felt good. He wasn't the strongest or the most skilled fighter. Nor was he the smartest or the fastest. It was a mish-mash group of people who, he realized, likely wouldn't have been friends in other circumstances. There were men from Ivy League colleges and some with nothing more than a high school degree, like himself. There was an ex-professional fighter, a poet, and a tech-genius who taught himself about technology and the digital world after leaving his Amish community. They were all different and they all had their pasts. But, the Hell Week experience and the dedication they all had to serving their country as Navy SEALs kept them together. He could see the same hungry need in their eyes that he had in his. As they had stood waist-deep in the ocean with wet sand that had infiltrated their uniforms chaffing their private parts and the cold ocean whipping around them in the darkness of 3am, he'd seen what separated those standing around him now from those who had walked out of the ocean, quit, and gone home to dry beds and loving wives with soft touches. All that any of them had wanted to do was leave – walk out of the ocean and return to their quarters to dry off, warm up, and shut their eyes like so many of the other Hell Week candidates had. However, no matter how much pain they felt or how severe their exhaustion was, no one with him in this bar had quit. Liam could see his own blind and stubborn determination reflected in their eyes. For the men at this bar, there was no other option than to make it through. There was no other option but to succeed.

Thinking back to the pain he had tried so hard to block out, he remembered his leg with the staph infection and all the times that his throat and chest had tightened up and cut off his airflow for some unknown cause – a new allergy, exhaustion, pain, or all three. When he remembered how he had to fight through the threat of blackness that encroached on his normally perfect vision, he was proud. He would not let anything stand in the way of him becoming a Navy SEAL. He told himself that his body would just have to learn to adapt. He fought hard to continue running and swimming and crawling without any of the training officers seeing him struggle. He knew others had done the same and that it was possible to overcome any obstacle. He was fairly certain the ex-fighter had faced a similar challenge because he had seen in him the same flash of fear that he'd felt before his gaze hardened with determination on several occasions.

These are my people, he thought. *I've finally found my people.* He looked around at all the tired yet determined faces and he felt safe for the first time in a very long time. *With them, with this job, I can move forward. I am a man. Only a real man can be a part of BUD/S and become a Navy SEAL.* He smiled to himself as he sipped his beer. *I can finally move forward*, he thought.

As the night went on and the sun went down, his comrades started taking out their cell phones to call their girlfriends, wives, or just any girl with a warm bed and open legs. He didn't have any of those. His ex, who he still thought of as Caligula, had sent him numerous texts during Hell Week and he could probably have had Skype sex with her, but he didn't want that. He was happy leaving her at home. He was becoming a new man, a better man, without her. There was always the option of one of the frog hogs that followed the SEALs around town, he could have had any of them easily, but he didn't want that either. He wanted a real woman now. He wanted someone he'd have a future with. He wanted a girl that a soon-to-be United States Navy SEAL deserved.

So, instead of calling anyone, Liam finished his beer, slapped a few of his buddies on the shoulders as a goodbye, and went back to his barracks alone to enjoy another long, uninterrupted, and dreamless sleep. This was the kind of peaceful sleep that only Hell Week and starting on the Navy SEAL career path had brought him.

Liam

My calf throbs. I can feel the bandage start to get wet with blood, and maybe more puss. It hurts, but the pain just reminds me of what I've survived, like a badge of honor. It makes me proud. After Hell Week ended, the Navy assigned a nurse to each of us who was supposed to check us over, ensure that we made it to our appointment with the base doctor, and then look after us overnight to make sure we didn't try and kill ourselves in our sleep. Apparently that happens sometimes.

My nurse found two staph infections – one on my hip and one on my ass. Each was a lump the size of a golf ball, filled with blood, puss, and sand. I had sand everywhere. I can still feel the grains between my teeth, even though I've brushed them 20 times since. And it's still in my eyes. The grains scrape my eyeballs every time I blink. It's fucking annoying but I can't get it all out. The damn sand made my infections gooey so the nurse had to squeeze all the shit out of me. The staph infection on my leg, though, was missed. I should have been mad. My friends from home told me so anyway. After all I had been put through, they said, the nurse should have at least done her job right. I didn't see it that way. I took care of it myself, with the brand new knife I earned by graduating Hell Week, and it was nothing compared to what I had gone through that week. Plus, it gave me a reason to christen my knife. I couldn't have thought of a more fitting way to do so either. It's a badass knife – big, serrated, and can cut through anything. With just a slip of my hand, I could have cut through my calf muscle. But I didn't. My hand was perfectly steady and I didn't even have a drink before doing it. I just poured some alcohol on the blade and cut away at the thick, black scab on the underside of my calf. Then I carved out what looked like a small serving of cottage cheese, bandaged it up, and went out drinking. It was nothing, really. I'll be doing crazier shit in the field. Plus, it isn't the kind of thing a woman would do, is it?

Everyone seems to have a scar coming from this week. Jones has a broken arm; Matthews has a gash on his jaw that's still swollen from impact or infection, I'm not sure which; Stevens has a busted ankle that he's been using to get sympathy from the frog hogs; and Gonzales' shoulder is hanging at an odd angle. Everyone's knuckles and elbows are bright red – raw from the chafing of ocean water and wet sand. Hallows, who was tyke-sized for what he'd managed to do this week, was holding his shirt off his chest the whole night at the bar. His nipples must be worse than mine. The mixture of sand and sweat is a lethal combination for those little patches of sensitive skin. Gonzales actually whispered to me that he had put bandages on his – SpongeBob Square Pants, to be exact. His five-year-old nephew had given them to him before starting Hell Week. He'd wondered whether this would help or hurt his game with whichever girl he went home with tonight.

Three

At SDSU, Kara was sitting in her first class of graduate school. Her professor was an older man with wild grey eyebrows and earnest eyes that made her think of a very approachable, yet very mad, scientist. She read his profile on the school website before coming to class and had been intimidated. He was a very smart man and seemed to be one of the most respected academics in the field. She refreshed her mind by re-reading all of her old notes from her undergrad classes, but her stomach still knotted when she saw the 30% next to "class participation" on the marking rubric. Even with her newfound goal to find comfort in her own academic skin, she was still terrified of not measuring up to her peers.

As always, she answered nerves with ditzy-sounding humor. When it came to be her turn to tell the class who she was and why she'd wanted to join this particular program, she said, "Hi everyone, I'm Kara. I'm from Toronto, Canada. I used to compete in horseback riding. I love to make up stories and write them down, I have degrees in English and Philosophy, and writing is present in all three. I joined this program for several reasons, with the most important being the men. I've always had a thing for California guys…" While she grinned jokingly with her last remark, she was scolding herself internally for not stepping up to the serious nature of Master's programs. She didn't want the class to think she was a ditz.

Thankfully, the class seemed to take her comment for what she had intended – a joke.

"Well, that might have been the most honest answer of today," said the professor, blinking his eyes a few times under his bushy brows and looking somewhat perplexed. She scolded herself for falling back into her old ways.

Kara breathed a sigh of relief when the class moved on.

The girl next to her leaned over and whispered, "If you like Cali guys, you are really going to love Coronado. It's where all the SEALs are. We'll go this weekend and try to catch them on their run down the beach – it's fantastic," she breathed, a little too hard. She wrote down her name, thankfully, because Kara hadn't paid attention to her introduction to the class.

Franceen: (619) 555-2943

Kara eyed her up and down sideways. She was short and stocky, with arm muscles that could intimidate many men, but she had a cross around her neck and a friendly smile, so Kara figured a day out with her might be fun. Kara had never subscribed to the military fantasy that so many women, particularly those she'd met in the USA, seemed to share, but she figured it would be fun to go out and test out the San Diego nightlife.

* * *

That weekend, Kara and Franceen got ready together at Kara's apartment. Franceen lived on campus and shared an already small room with a fairly antisocial undergrad. They'd recruited a few other girls from the program to come, as well as Michael, who was likely to become the English program's token male.

Franceen had a thing for Michael, Kara was sure. She always acted schoolgirl-silly around him – twirling her hair, batting her eyelashes, and giggling at all his jokes. He was too good, too cool, for her, Kara thought, but he seemed to lap the attention up like a kitten with warm milk. He never reciprocated, just smiled his goofy grin and watched her.

They were going out to Pacific Beach. They had tanned on the beach in Coronado during the day in hopes that they would see the SEALs on their morning run but had missed them. A girl in the second year of the program, Tiffany, was more into chasing men than Kara had accidentally let herself seem. In fact, she was what Kara would later learn was called a "frog hog," or a SEAL-chaser. Tiffany told them that Blake's Tavern in Pacific Beach was the place to go if they wanted to actually meet the SEALs or SEAL candidates, or any other Special Forces trainees. Of course, they'd have to deal with a large number of drunk and skimpily clad college girls who had the same idea, Tiffany said. But, as they readied, the girls realized that Tiffany was actually one of those girls in the barely-there dresses that squeezed their tiny figures into voluptuous curves and caught the attention of most men.

For her first night out in San Diego, Kara chose a short pair of cutoff jean shorts and a simple white strapless top that, when paired with flip-flops, looked more beach-ready than bar-ready. She left her face bare of makeup except for a little bit of mascara and kept her hair salty and wavy from the beach. She was tired and fairly certain that the likelihood of her meeting someone worthwhile at this kind of bar with these kinds of girls was very low. So, she spared herself the hard work of primping and sat quietly with her drink while the other girls got ready.

Franceen wore ripped jeans with a one-shoulder white tank that accentuated her arm muscles more than Kara would have allowed for herself, but tried to soften the look with plenty of makeup and big Texas-style hair. Talia, a highly sarcastic tattoo model with a part-time job working with disabled children, a lover of poetry, and the top student in the second-year class, wore a simple cotton dress. She spent most of the time the other girls used to get ready to joke, in detail, about all the things she'd like to do to one of the chiseled "SEAL babies," as she liked to call the candidates. Kara liked her.

In the middle of one particularly steamy X-rated description, Franceen turned the music down and asked all the girls to put down their drinks. She checked the door quickly to ensure that Michael was still in the pool area chatting with some other tenants who were having a BBQ party. Her face was serious, and a little embarrassed, when she turned back to the girls. "I need to tell you all something. I think it's important that you know because, well, I need to know how to play the Michael situation."

The girls all waited, unsure whether to be concerned or annoyed with the interruption.

"I'm a little inexperienced with men... And by that, I mean that I haven't really dated much so I don't know what to do now." Franceen let her words sink in for a few moments before beginning again. The other girls were fighting the urge to look at one another in confusion, not understanding what they were supposed to do with this information. "You've all probably guessed that I like Michael, and I can tell he really likes me too. And then he said to me today, 'Maybe you can even stay over tonight.' Which would be great, I want to wake up in his arms. But, the way he looked me up and down while he said it suggests he doesn't want to just sleep. And I don't know how to tell him that I'm 28 and still new to the dating game."

Her question was met with silence. No one knew exactly what response was expected or needed.

"Do you have to tell him? If you do, I guess you could tell him that you don't date unless you see the guy as marriage material?" offered Kara.

"No, that puts way too much pressure on him," refuted Tiffany.

"Why don't you just not tell him?" asked Talia. "It isn't really his business who or what you've done before. He probably doesn't care."

"You could just take it slow and hang out as friends first?" Kara suggested.

Franceen looked embarrassed. "Well, I may have slipped him a very suggestive note."

"How suggestive…?" asked Tiffany.

"Well, I may have detailed everything I wanted to do to him and everything I wanted him to do to me…" said Franceen, her cheeks blushing red. "And, no, I don't normally do this type of thing, but I wanted him to think that I'm sexy and experienced so I Googled and found some very *50 Shades of Grey*-type notes and copied them. I'm pretty confident I can fool him if I keep reading, but I can't learn enough in time to embody those things tonight."

No one really knew how to respond, or what kind of response she needed. Finally, Talia broke the silence and said, "Well, if you want him, you're just going to have to go for it. Don't let him think you're something you're not. Just go with the flow. He seems like a good guy." With that, Talia turned the music back on and continued to paint her nails.

Franceen still looked uncertain and, despite that Kara thought Franceen might be a little too immature to become a close friend, she said, "Hey, if tonight isn't the night for whatever reason, you can always sleep on my futon and we'll go for brunch in the morning. We can rehash the night over some pancakes and bacon."

It wasn't long before the girls, with Michael in tow, were at Blake's Tavern, a casual pub only steps from the beach. There were so many hard bodies and drunk college girls crammed into the space that the group considered turning back and trying a different bar. But Talia pushed through the crowd towards the back of the bar. She was letting no one stand between her and the breathing room that the only vacant table in the whole place could provide. Once they reached the back they all folded into a tiny booth, with Michael cushioned between the wall and Franceen – it was clear she was letting no one else near him.

Before sitting down, Kara looked around and saw a group of young, very well-muscled men near the bar. She grabbed Tiffany's hand and stopped her from grinding on a young boy who looked no older than 18, and headed for the bar. "Military," Kara said, glancing quickly in the direction of the men she had spotted.

Tiffany looked over and, apparently, liked what she saw. She quickly fixed her dress, pulled out her lip-gloss, and strutted to the bar. Tossing her hair as she reached the closest man, she asked him if he'd like to buy her a drink. That would be the last time that Kara saw her before they left the bar for the night. Normally, Kara would've been a bit annoyed that her friend had left her so quickly, but someone in the corner had caught her eye.

A young military man with a shaved head and bulging arm muscles was sitting on a stool with his back to the bar while talking with friends. As he was laughing at something one of his friends had said, he turned his head and glanced around the bar. That's when

Kara spotted him. For years after this moment the two would disagree over how they met. Kara would insist that the world stopped turning, everything but his face blurred, and that their eyes connected – sealing their fate. She wouldn't remember what he was wearing or who he was talking to, but she would remember having the strongest need to go right up to him. And she did. She walked up to him, extended her hand, and said, "Hi, I'm Kara" with her most flirtatious smile. However, in all later discussions, Liam would remember making the first move. He'd remember seeing her talking to a friend of his and being envious that he hadn't gotten to her first. He'd remember watching her laugh and thinking that her smile was the most beautiful thing he'd ever seen. He'd also remember how he'd been admiring her body and imagining how soft her skin would be. He had wanted to see her long brown hair all messed up, her makeup smudged, with nothing but a smile on as the morning sun shone in the window. With all that, he decided to walk right up to her, cut his friend off, and tell her that she was the most beautiful girl in the bar. Whichever version was true, from that point on Kara and Liam were an item.

After a night of too many shots, dancing, and exchanging life stories, last call arrived and the group started to search for a taxi. Although Kara never invited him back to her apartment, Liam started to look for a cab with them. Though unsure if she liked his confidence, Kara wasn't ready to let him go so she held onto his hand – rough, weathered, and strong. She had thought he might've been cocky and dumb, judging by his bulging muscles, tattoos, and an intimidatingly bald head, but he wasn't. He was witty, kind, and only borderline cocky. She suspected his confidence is what made him able to do his job, rather than a result of his job. Michael and Franceen were also coupled off, holding hands and whispering in each other's ears. Because they couldn't all fit into one cab, the four of them shared one while Talia and Tiffany took another. Michael's house was the first stop. When he climbed out alone, Kara looked at Franceen quizzically.

"His roommates ended up coming home early," she explained. "So I'm coming to your place."

Kara's eyes widened in surprise as she looked at Liam, who was sitting next to her with his hand on her thigh, when she realized that both he and Franceen might be expecting to stay the night at her place.

"It's okay, darlin'. I was just coming along for the ride. I want to take you out on a proper date before I even think about inviting myself over."

Michael was still standing outside the car, leaning in the window to whisper his drunk goodbyes to Franceen when Liam interrupted and said, "Hey man, how about we take these girls both on proper dates tomorrow? We could go for a few margaritas and some dinner in Old Town."

Michael considered for a moment. "Sure, that sounds good. Does 7pm work for all of you?"

With that, their date was set. Liam stayed in the cab all the way to Kara's, kissed her goodnight, and went back to base. As she readied for bed, Franceen chattered on and on about everything that Michael had said to her, overanalyzing every detail. She digressed quickly, and was soon examining every piece of evidence she had, real or imagined, that said Michael liked her, reveling in the fact that she'd found a man. However, Kara wasn't listening. All she could think about was Liam. She'd never really understood the military fantasy, but now she did. Liam was smart, funny, incredibly fit, tough, intelligent, and incredibly brave for being willing to put his life in danger as a soldier. There was much more to his bravery though, and Kara would often witness this characteristic in play in all areas of his life, with her admiration growing each time.

Liam

I'm going to marry that girl. I thought it yesterday in the cab as I rode back to base and I know it now after taking her out on a proper dinner date. She's got something special – a spark or something. Something in her literally shines when she laughs. Everyone else sees it too, I can tell. As she walked back from the bathroom, I watched every man's head turn. I don't even think she noticed. She just kept her eyes on me or down at the ground pretending she was trying not to trip over the chairs. All throughout dinner, I just kept getting lost in her eyes. I couldn't stop my hands from running up her thigh, just to see her eyes widen a little every time. She'd try hard not to blush and to act unaffected, but she couldn't help herself. She'd stutter and get all tongue-tied. She comes across as so confident and outgoing, so I really like that I can shake her up a little bit. It's cute. You can tell that she's classy, too, by the way she talks and how she wouldn't let me make out with her at the table. She wanted to, it was pretty obvious in the way she looked at me, but she wouldn't. So, it was really unexpected when she asked me back to her place so that we could hang out in the hot tub. I actually jumped at the chance. As soon as she said, "Want to come back to my place?" I was on my feet.

I would have been fine to wait. Most girls like her would have made me work for it. But I guess she really liked me, too. What I really couldn't believe was when her friend Franceen added, "The hot tub sounds like a great idea. Michael and I would love to come too." I didn't want her to ruin our first night together. She talks too much and even though she's short, she has huge arm muscles that I couldn't imagine looking good in a bikini. Over dinner, she kept slapping me on the shoulder like a bro and I could just feel myself cringing. Between her constant chatter and the way she treats me like a buddy instead of a friend's boyfriend (or date), I feel less like a man around her, and I need to be all man for Kara. In the end, I decided to only look at Kara and to pretend no one else was sitting in the hot tub, and it worked just fine.

Kara straddled me, kissing my lips, my neck, whispering things in my ear. Sexy things. Because of the steam from the hot tub it easy to pretend we were the only ones there. Eventually, she told me she wanted to go upstairs. I couldn't wait to get to her room because I didn't want her to rethink her decision. So, I carried her there. We stayed locked up in her room all night, entirely forgetting about the other two. In the morning, while she slept, I went to her kitchen to make breakfast. I was naked because I'd forgotten that we weren't alone and I'd been hoping for a naked breakfast with her in bed, but then I saw Franceen and Michael tangled in some sheets on Kara's futon. I didn't want to cook with them sleeping there. So, instead, I grabbed a box of granola bars that was left on the counter and a magnet from her fridge that was shaped like a Hawaiian flower and returned to the room. I had to make do with the circumstances, and I hoped that she'd find the gesture sweet.

<u>Kara</u>

He opened doors for me, paid the check, and never took his eyes off of me. He asked me all about myself, my friends and family, my studies, and he actually listened. He was a gentleman, mostly. But I kind of liked that he was confident and cocky enough to be sliding his hand up my thigh and was wanting to make out with me throughout dinner, all the while looking at me with a boyish grin. He'd lean in for a kiss and I would have to push him back, reminding him that we were at dinner. He'd just wink and say, "Just a little make out real quick. No one will see." That made me laugh.

I like him. I like him a lot. I'm still getting used to his bald head and the fact that he perpetually has a fat wad of dip in his bottom lip, but this feels real. While we were out, he'd taken the time to get to know Michael and Franceen enough so that it was a comfortable double date, but he never made me doubt that he was there for me, and only me. Even when the waitress blatantly hit on him, he made me feel special. She never asked for *my* order or if *I* needed a refill. Liam always had to remind her. She also had a way of showing up exactly when he'd try to kiss me. Normally, I probably would have been a little jealous, or at least annoyed. But he handled it so well, never letting anyone doubt that he was interested in only me, which made me feel *more* confident. After hanging out with him, I felt so sexy that the words just slipped out, surprising even me, *"Want to come back to my place?"* I was so nervous. I felt so innocent and unsure. I hoped he couldn't tell, but I knew that he could. As soon as I uttered those seven words he hopped to his feet and called for our waitress, even though Michael and Franceen were still working on their drinks.

"Can I get you anything else, sir?" the waitress asked, leaning in to let her chest look him right in the eyes.

"Just the bill, please. Unless my girl wants some dessert?" He looked at me questioningly. I shook my head and let my hand rest on his thigh.

"Just the bill," he told her.

She kept at it. "Are you sure there's nothing I can get for you? Another drink?"

"Nope. I want to get going. I'm going to take this girl home," he said, looking at me with a big, boyish grin.

The waitress sighed with annoyance but finally gave in and brought us the bill. After looking at it quickly, Liam chuckled.

"What is it?" I asked.

"Well, she only charged us for your dinner, for starters."

I looked at the bill. He was right. Only my drinks and my meal were listed. That wasn't all. She'd also written her name – Carli – with a heart and what I could only presume was her phone number. I read it aloud to him in a tone that clearly mocked her, but felt a little uneasy. I mean, he was obviously on a date with *me*. Who did she think she was? Liam didn't let me dwell for too long, though. He just said, "That's frog hogs for ya darlin'." Then he put down the cash, left the receipt, and we walked out of the restaurant with his arm around me, jingling the keys to his Chevy truck happily in his hand.

The rest of the night was perfect. It didn't even matter that my white guest sheets were in dire need of a wash or that Franceen and Michael didn't leave my living room until 1pm the next day. Liam brought me breakfast in bed. Granted, it was a box of granola bars that I'd bought the day before. Given the situation, though, I couldn't blame him. And, he brought me a "flower" as well, after waking me with a kiss. We just spent all morning in bed. A part of me wanted him to leave, and I told him so. I felt cramped with everyone staying in my apartment for so long. He just grinned easily at me, ignoring my comment, and asked me more questions about myself. Eventually, I didn't want him to leave anymore.

We laughed, we napped, and we ate. I wasn't able to stop looking at him. He might be the hottest guy I've ever seen. There's just something about him, and something about the way he calls me "darlin'" or "baby" that makes my stomach flutter. I traced over his scars with my finger and he told me about his crazy childhood antics, and of the hell he endured during training. In return, he traced my scars and I told him of my years as a competitive equestrian and my many falls.

This is something different. Being with him… It's just different. It's better. It's easier. And those butterflies everyone always talks about? They haven't stopped. I'm pretty excited to see where this relationship takes me.

Four

After their first date, Liam and Kara spent all of their spare time together. Liam called her every day on lunch. He went over to her apartment every weekend and spare weeknight. He listened to her. He found that he genuinely cared about her and his secret felt lighter the closer he felt to her. The shy part of Kara faded as Liam's predictability grew. He never failed to call. He never failed to make her feel wanted. Regardless of how many hours his commanding officers made him run, no matter how many dives he had to go on, no matter how many miles he had to swim in the cold Pacific Ocean, he never let her feel neglected. Any spare moment he had, he texted. He called. He told her that he was putting her first, and then he did.

Not long after, Kara and Liam were a package deal. She went to every BUD/S party in Pacific Beach and he accompanied her to every academic event that he could. She went and drank Bud Light with young, blonde co-eds who fawned over each BUD/S candidate in Liam's class, Liam included. Yet, Kara always watched with satisfaction as he ignored their advances and, instead, found her wherever she might be in the room. And she got to know his friends who, to her surprise, were so much more than just muscle. He got to know everyone in her graduate program. He became friends with them. He discussed ideas and debated with them. He showed each of her classmates that he wasn't going to be satisfied with the SEAL stereotype of an ignorant playboy and, instead, that he was intelligent, interesting, and entirely devoted to Kara. He knew what they expected of him as a young, attractive, soon-to-be Navy SEAL, and he did everything he needed to in order to prove them wrong. Kara dreaded the nights he had to spend away for training or watch duty. She wanted his arms around her every night and wanted to wake up to him every morning. He felt the same. His hard, small bed in the barracks couldn't live up to being entwined with Kara. It wasn't all about comfort either. They both actually feared the nights that had to be spent apart. Kara's picturesque apartment complex, with manicured lawns and palm trees surrounding a large pool area, was also home to several rougher characters that had taken a particular disliking to her, the only Canadian there, and harassed her whenever Liam's truck wasn't in the parking lot.

    Liam had always suffered from vivid nightmares containing some of his deepest fears and had always thought that they would vanish when he found the right girl. For him, Kara was the right girl. However, his nightmares didn't vanish. They had actually grown to be worse. He saw himself not only with long hair, but also in dresses and high heels. His nightmares were worst when he was alone and surrounded by the ultra-masculine, and often right wing-minded, men that lived with him in the barracks sanctioned for those in BUD/S. When he woke up and saw Kara's naked body covered only by a thin sheet next to his, he was able to dismiss his dreams as nothing but nightmares. When he felt turned on at the sight of her, when he felt his love for her swell in his heart, he could push those feelings down deep inside him. However, when he woke up in the dark next to men he could never really talk to, or trust with this secret, buried fears, the feelings only became more and more real and weighed heavily on his chest long into the following day and night. So, both Liam and Kara struggled through the nights until they could be together again.

One particularly sleepless week, Kara's friends encouraged her to tell Liam about the harassment she was receiving from her neighbors. Never wanting to appear at all weak or unable to take care of herself, especially to someone she considered to be so brave and self-sufficient, Kara had been hiding the situation from him.

"Why don't you just tell him?" an exasperated Franceen asked one day after gushing to Kara about Michael as they lay on the Coronado beach, only to find Kara half-asleep with her sunglasses on.

Kara just groaned.

"You know he'd find a way to fix it," Talia pushed. "He'd take care of it. For God's sakes, you're a zombie these days." She poked Kara to make sure that she was still listening. "And you won't let us come out with paintball guns to scare them off, so this is pretty much your only option left."

Since arriving in San Diego, Kara had learned that there were several individuals in her apartment complex who, she could only assume, didn't care for Canadians and that had taken to staring at her for too long as she passed by. Additionally, her car had been vandalized several times each week – soda, urine, paint, and an unknown paste often coated her car in the mornings. Somehow, they had also figured out which apartment number was hers. She was woken up at all hours of the night by threats being shouted at her and loud bangs on her walls. Sometimes, she could hear their voices float up from the courtyard into her open window and would be privy to their discussions filled with their distaste for Canadians but how they would be willing to make exceptions for her "sexy" body.

Kara giggled. "I'm fine. It's fine. They'll get bored of picking on me soon. Liam's got enough on his plate right now. It's all he can do to stay awake for our dates. He's so tired and stressed from training, plus he's got his second phase test coming up, I don't want to be added to that list," Kara replied. "It's the hardest test, he says. People have actually been seriously injured during it. Plus, the guy at the car wash is giving me free candies now. He says he's never seen someone wash so much urine and graffiti off of one car, so there are perks to this situation," she joked tiredly.

"Ha, well, at least there's an upside." Franceen looked serious for a moment and then added, "You should tell him. He's your boyfriend. It's his job to look after you. Don't you think he's going to start wondering why you look like you're pulling all-nighters every night?"

"I'm a grad student. What else would he expect from me?" Kara just smiled and turned over, signaling the end of the conversation. She knew she that should tell Liam and that he would somehow fix it. But she didn't want him to feel like he had to take care of her. She'd ridden horses with men more foul-mouthed and less sympathetic than many sailors; had ridden through broken bones and torn ligaments; and had always faced her fears without telling a soul what she was afraid of, and she was proud of that. So instead, she decided to put off telling Liam and vowed to finally go to the Muay Thai gym near her yoga studio to sign up for some lessons and to ask the coach for some specific self-defense tips.

Unfortunately, later that evening she found she had little choice but to tell Liam what was going on. She planned to go to bed early and, to help, she had some hops tea that a hippy herbalist in Ocean Beach had strongly recommended for relaxation and sleep. With the hope that she could finally sleep through even the loudest banging, she put earplugs in and wore a headband over top for added sound protection. At around 1:30am, she was sadly disappointed when she was woken up by the loud, thundering banging she had grown so accustomed to hearing and that still made her hide under her blankets like a child. She pulled the covers up to her chin and waited for it to stop. She heard some yelling so she took out her earplugs to see what they were saying tonight. Lately, they'd really taken to calling her a communist or a socialist, which she assumed resulted from the Canadian license plates on her car, and very detailed descriptions of all the sexual things they could, and would, do to her if they ever caught her alone. She didn't know if they actually hated Canada or if her license plate had singled her out, making her an easier target because she wasn't from San Diego. Either way, she was growing weary of them making her life hell. However, when she took out her earplugs, she didn't hear the same hate-filled yells that she was expecting. Instead she heard Liam calling her name.

She jumped quickly out of bed, slightly regretting her choice of pajamas and her decision to opt out of a shower that night. She hadn't expected to see him until the weekend and it was only Wednesday. He had 20-hour workdays scheduled for the entire week, so he'd planned to stay overnight in the barracks. She opened the door and he picked her up, still in his crisp, rough camouflage uniform. He kissed her lips as he spun her around, letting himself into the apartment.

"Hey baby, surprised?" He grinned at her.

"What are you doing here? I thought you had work!" giggled Kara as he kissed her again and tickled her cheek with his fresh stubble.

"I do. I've only got about an hour before I have to head back, but I couldn't go an entire week without seeing you, darlin'." He searched her eyes, hoping he'd see that she felt the same. He didn't add that he couldn't go another night surrounded by the other men with no one to clear his mind. No one else in the program seemed to have another side, a softer side, which needed to be hidden. The men in BUD/S were strong, driven, and simple. Even the few with artistic hobbies, like the youngest guy in the group that wrote poetry, never seemed to be ashamed of their softer sides. He never saw any of them show anything similar to the shame he felt for his secrets. But, then again, his secrets were a little harder to confess.

"Perfect. You must be wanting to get to bed, then," she said coyly, as she pulled him towards her room by his belt.

Liam laughed. "Girl! I'm exhausted. If I go to sleep now, I won't get up until tomorrow night. I was thinking more of a date, like frozen yogurt. There's a place open across the street."

Before she could protest, he gave her one of his sweatshirts that he'd brought in from his truck and pulled her out the door.

They ate their frozen yogurt sitting on the curb outside of the store. They were the only customers of the only store open in the plaza, so the parking lot was dark and abandoned. It was quiet except for the shouts of drunks from a pub across the street and neither spoke much. Kara was tired and drained, and finally felt relaxed now that Liam was beside her. She loved his salty smell, which was probably a mix of sweat and ocean water, and how solid he felt against her. She felt so safe tucked under his arm that her eyes began to close as she ate. Liam was mentally and physically exhausted and barely felt connected to his body anymore. Between the lack of sleep, the unforgiving workouts, and his nightmares, he could do little more than put his arm around Kara and take a few moments of comfort in her nearness. Though neither said it aloud, both thought, *I wish we could just stay in this moment forever.*

As they arrived back at her apartment building, Liam insisted on walking Kara back to her room before driving to the base. That suited Kara because she wasn't ready to let go of his hand yet. As they turned down her hallway, they were met with loud shouts and bangs. Liam tensed and muttered, "What the hell?" But Kara knew exactly what was happening.

As they reached her door, they could see the source of the noise quite clearly. They were very obviously new recruits into the military; they still had tan lines from their new crew cuts and could not have been over 22 years old. Kara noticed with gratitude and pride that Liam had put himself casually between her and the two men, but still hadn't let go of her hand.

"Hey fellas, how can we help y'all?" Liam asked in a friendly tone. He didn't sound threatening, but Kara could feel the warning in his voice. The two boys eyed him up and down but didn't say anything. "Y'all got the right apartment?" Liam asked.

Again, he was met with a few moments of silence as the two boys, obviously drunk, stared back at him, assessing their options. Liam just looked at them levelly until one answered, "Yeah, course we do. That girl you're bangin' there, she's a fuckin' Canadian slut! Don't ya know? She's been askin' fer it. We were jus' takin' her up on what she's been offerin'."

Liam just looked at him, expressionless.

"C'mon, man. Ya know. You's sleepin' with her, which is fine. She's hot. But you should know that she runs around more than half naked when yer not here. She puts on them little shorts and goes runnin' all around the area here, gettin' sweaty, and then she goes to stretch and do her yoga by the water. All she's got on top is a little sports bra. Now, come on, that's jus' askin' fer attention. But when we whistle or call out to her, she just ignores us or shoots us a dirty look. She's a fuckin' Canadian slut and a snob. That bitch gotta learn some manners. You how how it is with these girls."

"No, actually, I don't know *how it is*. This is my girl, my little Canadian, and this is our apartment. I don't care what she wears to work out. It's hot here. But I know she's definitely not trying to invite you for anything. It ain't even an invite to me when I work out with her. It's what she wants to wear and it's what she's comfortable in. That's her right. There ain't anything this girl can do that would give you any right to any part of her. And hell, if all she shot you was a dirty look for harassing her like you do, you boys got off easy. If you ever even so much as utter the words 'she owes me' or look at her with anything other than complete respect again, I'll be sending a hell of a lot more than just a dirty look your way." Liam's body was tensed, his muscles were visible, and his eyes were dark, but his tone was calm and firm, leaving little room for rebuttal.

The two boys eyed him carefully, assessing the situation they'd gotten into. While there was two of them, Liam's expression was ominous and daring. Kara watched carefully, nervous of a fight. She knew that in Southern California everyone seemed to be able to guess which branch of military a person was in based on haircut, build, and demeanor. These boys were new to the military, and drunk, but Liam had the no nonsense confidence and muscled build of a Navy SEAL, and she knew few would willingly get into an altercation with one of them.

After about a minute of Liam calmly letting the boys size him up, he said, "Alright. Why don't y'all let us enjoy the rest of our night and be on your way."

Finally, the chatty one ended their conversation. "Uh, yeah, wrong apartment. Sorry 'bout that. Y'all have a good night." The two walked off quickly down the hall, throwing quick glances at Liam over their shoulders.

Liam turned to Kara with concern in his eyes. "Babe, are you okay? Does that happen a lot?" He pulled her close to him and hugged her, kissing the top of her head.

"Not anymore," she replied with a grateful smile into his chest.

From that point on, she completely dropped her guard with him. She'd never felt safer and she didn't feel the need to protect herself anymore – from letting him see her weaknesses or from anyone else. Liam always seemed to be there. Whether they were leaving a bar with friends and some drunk frat boys decided to grope her, some young army men wanted to show off their strength by tossing her between a group of them while pulling at her clothes, or when she was nervous about walking through a bad part of town, Liam was always there and handled it. Soon, she felt like she walked in a bubble. The moment she felt something might be off about a situation, Liam seemed to appear at her side and, all of a sudden, drunken idiots and thugs treated her with nothing but indifference. Kara started to see Liam in a whole new light. She started to love his bald head, boulder-like shoulders, and the tattooed bald eagle that decorated his forearm. She loved dating a soon-to-be Navy SEAL and was proud to be the girl on his arm.

Liam noticed all of the changes with Kara. She had opened up to him and she seemed freer and more comfortable. He could see the change in the way she looked at him. He felt it in him too. Trust. He'd never felt that with another girl. He'd been cheated on and had games played with him. He'd just learned to date without even thinking about trust. But, with her, he realized the difference. Looking into her eyes, she made him feel like the only man in the world, and he liked that. So he refused to let anything happen to her. It didn't matter if they were out together or if he was with friends miles away, if he felt that she might need him or want him beside her, he went to her.

They continued this way for months. Liam knew he was in love with her. He had known he would be from the first time he met her, but Kara had never been in love before and wasn't quite sure what it felt like. He knew she was scared and too insecure about her inexperience to ever say those three words first. So, he waited for the right moment.

Soon after, a little boy, with an unbarred admiration of Liam's job, gave him that opportunity. For brunch one morning, Kara and Liam went to their favorite little burrito shack in Coronado. With barely any seating room inside or out, Kara and Liam were waiting on the sidewalk for their order when a little blonde boy with wide blue eyes ran up to them and tugged on Liam's shirt.

"Excuse me, sir," he said to Liam. His eyes were brimming with excitement.

Liam looked down and grinned at him. "What can I do for ya, little man?"

"Well, I was wondering…" he said, sounding out won-der-ing in three clear syllables. "Are you a Navy SEAL?"

He looked back nervously at his father who was a couple of steps behind him, watching with a proud and humored smile. His father nodded encouragingly. Kara saw that Liam was barely containing his pride – he didn't like to show off – but his smile was beaming as he looked down at the boy. "I will be one day," he told him. "I'm in BUD/S right now."

"I'm going to be a Navy SEAL too!" exclaimed the little boy. "I just need to get bigger."

Liam chuckled and knelt down to look him in the eye. "Well, let's feel how those muscles are coming along."

The boy flexed his arm so hard that his face contorted. Liam squeezed his arm gently and said, "Wow, you've got some guns, my man. You keep workin' hard at it and you'll make a good SEAL."

The little boy's smile stretched wide across his face. He stood tall, put his hand to his brow, and saluted Liam. Liam's eyes showed how touched he was, and told Kara that he was stifling a chuckle, but his face was serious as he stood and saluted the boy back.

Kara watched the exchange and listened as Liam politely declined the father's offer to buy their lunches. Her heart swelled. She felt proud to be standing next to him. She thought about how he knew exactly what to say to the little boy to make him smile. She thought about all the people in Coronado who shook his hand and thanked him for his service, and the pride that showed in his eyes when they did. He was working hard to achieve his dream. He had passion. He cared about people. He cared about her. It was then that she realized she loved him, and had for a while.

"So how about that, huh? Cute kid," Liam said to her as he pulled her into his arms.

"Yeah…" she added. She looked him in the eyes and wanted to tell him how she felt, but couldn't. She couldn't find the words. So instead she just kissed him and said, "You're pretty great too."

Liam saw the want in her eyes. He knew what she wanted to say. Seeing his opportunity, he told her how he felt.

"I love you, Kara." He kissed her so deeply that she could only mumble those three words as she said them right back to him.

Liam

I've done the falling fast and hard thing. I've felt passion and I've felt desire. None of that is new to me. With Kara, though, there's something more. It took me a while to figure out what it was but, finally, I realized that I feel safe. I want her, need her even, but I admire her too. She's strong, smart, and self-sufficient. I don't worry about her like I've had to worry about other girls. In fact, I think she worries more about me. She tries hard to support me and to make me believe in possibility. Possibility has always scared me. Where I come from, we learn not to dream too big. We work hard to achieve what we can, but we see the limitations long before we let our minds dream. That's what the SEALs teach you too. You think about fighting for your country. You think about fighting alongside your brothers. You don't think or dream about anything else, which is probably because you might not be around to see those dreams come true. But I've never thought about life in any other way. I've never thought that I was missing anything. I thought it was practical, the way life was. But she's different. She dreams first and figures the rest out later. It's contagious. Being with her, I want to work harder, be better, and make myself more successful so that we can have the kind of life that she deserves. I've never felt this way before. Positivity radiates from her like the sour stench of addiction radiated from my ex-girlfriend. The man I used to be would've run away from this kind of pressure. I never dreamed of being more than where I came from. But with her, it's not as scary. With her, I believe I can make it, that I *can* be so much more.

Kara

I've never met a man like him. With him, I feel passion and love and admiration all while feeling completely and entirely safe. Last week, he took me on a date at 2am because that was the only time that he had free before the weekend. When he could have been sleeping, should have been sleeping, he wasn't. He wanted to spend time with me.

UNSEALED

He surprises me every time we're together. Whether it's putting an end to the harassment I've been facing in my apartment building or stopping to help someone with their grocery bags, he's always doing something. I don't know if it's that he was raised as a Southern gentleman or if this is just him, but I suspect it's the latter. I was walking to my building this morning and the homeless guy that lives outside in the alley next to a bar on the way there stopped me. I was nervous at first, judging him by his stench and ripped clothing, but then he spoke.

"Are you Liam's girlfriend?" he asked me.

"Yes..." I replied warily.

"Tell him thank you for me, would you? I wasn't in a proper state last night and I never thanked him."

"Sure, I'll thank him for you. What for?" I asked, somewhat skeptical.

"He dropped another sandwich off for me. He asked to stay for a beer too. I wasn't in good shape, see, so he was checkin' in like he always does and I just yelled at him. I didn't want company so I never thanked him."

"Checking in on you?" I asked. Liam had never mentioned anything like that to me.

"Yeah. He's a real good guy. I used to serve, see, so I called to him one time when he was walking by. We got to talkin'. No one ever talks to me. It was nice. He took me for a bite to eat inside the bar and got me a nice big bottle of water. I didn't really want water at the time, just some money, you know? But it was good of him. And he's been stopping by ever since."

My heart swelled hearing this story. I was so proud to be associated with Liam. I texted him after I left the man to ask why he had never mentioned anything. All he said was, "What's to tell? I just stop by sometimes. It's no big deal."

It isn't about bragging or "doing something good." He just does these things because that's who he is, and I admire that.

Five

After days of drills that included running 10 or more miles on the beach as a warm up, followed by push-ups and pull-ups and squats, followed by swims that were sometimes twice as long as their runs, Liam and the rest of his team often finished their days with some sort of classroom work. Whether the work was for tactical, cultural, or strategic learning, the effect was the same – Liam was mentally and physically exhausted. He had never been more dedicated to something in his life, but the anger, sadness, and impatience that he felt at not being able to go abroad to help sooner, along with the physical testing, was tougher than anything he had encountered before. On his time off, he learned to appreciate the one piece of advice that a commanding officer had given him early on:

"Dude, this job will get ya. No matter how big, strong, driven, or how good of a shot you are, it'll break you down if you can't turn work off and live your life outside of duty. Whether that's a party, your woman, your kids – whatever, I don't care. Just don't forget to live. Otherwise, you'll never see a team," he'd said.

It seemed simple to Liam at the time. *What else would I do?* he thought, as he headed off to the first of many BUD/S parties that were held at the start of first phase. As the weeks went by, though, he learned what the officer had meant. It was easy to be consumed by the training – the exhaustion, the stress, and the fear of failure – it built up in all of the candidates. Those who couldn't handle the build up, who couldn't let go for long enough to relax and reset, they didn't make it through. Those were the candidates that were sent back to the ships to work – sweeping, cooking, or to some other quiet job that was the antithesis of the SEAL program. Liam was determined that he was not going to have that happen to him. He relaxed. He turned his brain off of work, left his stress about training and testing at the base, and he went home to Kara. Every weekend, every moment of his time off, he spent with her, and it only made him perform better. After one particularly stressful week, he longed for some time off with just her, her hot tub, and a few margaritas. One Friday afternoon, after work, he stopped at Vons to pick up limes, margarita mix, and a fifth of tequila. With his swim trunks in his gym bag, he was ready to see her. That was, until he got a text at the checkout counter.

Caligula: Hey sweetie, I just landed in San Diego. I'm waiting for my bags. Come get me?

Liam: What? Are you serious?

Caligula: You didn't leave me much choice.

Liam: What do you mean? When I said, "We're over. I'm in love with someone else," I meant it.

Caligula: We both know it isn't over. I'm the one for you. You're just too stupid to realize it.

Liam: No. Go home. I'm with Kara now. I don't love you anymore.

Caligula: Baby, I'm here now. You might as well come spend the weekend with me. My flight home doesn't leave until Sunday… And if you don't then I'll tell your new girlfriend about that time I dressed up your passed-out body in my clothes and how turned on you were when you woke up and realized what I'd done.

Liam groaned. "Fucking bitch," he said to himself, shocking the cashier. *What choice do I have?* he thought.

Liam: Fine. I'll be there in a couple of hours. Get yourself a hotel. You're not coming to base with me.

Liam

With her grey-green eyes looking up at me through her long, dark lashes, I couldn't even think about telling her. I love her. She loves me. We just told each other a week ago. How can I say that to her and then tell her that I'm going to be spending the rest of the weekend with my ex-girlfriend in a hotel? Caligula is an awful girl. I'm not even sure my friends remember her real name. And now she's taking advantage of me. She knew some of my secrets and tempted me with drugs to make them go away. Then she mocked me, dressed me up in her clothes, and told me I was "pretty." She somehow knew what was deep inside of me and pulled it out, waving it around like a flag of inadequacy during our relationship.

But, if I say "no" to her now then she'll hate me. And worst, she'll tell Kara about what she used to do to me. Plus, she flew across the country to see me. How can I turn her away? On the other hand, Kara will hate me if I tell her that I'm going. She'll stop trusting me. She might even break up with me. I texted my friends immediately and every single one of them told me not to go and to stay with Kara all weekend. I know I should. I know they're right. I love Kara. I want to be with Kara. I *do not* want to be with Caligula. I don't even care to see her again. Why can't I just stay at Kara's? It's the right choice, the easiest choice. I just really don't want Caligula to hate me so much that she'd expose my secrets. And I just can't have somebody really hate me. I hate myself enough without that. I hate myself for hiding all my fantasies and nightmares from Kara. If I just told her already then I wouldn't need to worry about Caligula blackmailing me right now. But I can't stand the thought of making Kara hate me. Losing her isn't an option. I'm just going to have to risk it and tell her that I'm seeing Caligula this weekend. If I don't give in to Caligula, then Kara will only hate me more if Caligula outs me. I'll just have to smooth it everything over later.

I just *can't* say "no."

Kara

The last week had been great. Liam's work schedule was lighter, so we actually spent every evening and night together. As cheesy as it sounds, he makes me feel complete. Life is better with him beside me. He makes me feel more confident and more beautiful. I actually woke up one morning to a delivery man knocking on my door with a bouquet of white lilies and a simple note that said, "I'm so blessed to have met you, baby. Love, Liam." I don't know how he knew that they were my favorite, but he did. When I'm with him, all I want to do is be with him. When I'm not, all I can think about is when I get to see him. I can't focus on schoolwork, or anything really, but I'm so happy that I don't care. But then he told me on Friday night that he was going to spend the weekend in a hotel with his ex-girlfriend. I said "okay" when he told me. I didn't give him a hard time. I trusted him. Or at least I thought I did. He said he'd call each day, but he didn't. I tried to stay distracted. I went to a party at his BUD/S training buddy's apartment. His friends there were supportive of my anger but they still tried to placate me. They insisted that he wasn't cheating on me. But would they really tell me if he was? I mean, he was with an ex-girlfriend in a hotel and not calling me. What was I supposed to think?

I know I should break up with him. If this happened to any of my friends, I wouldn't be able to understand why they didn't walk away. I just can't let go, not yet. I need him to tell her that he's picked me. Then I feel like I'll be fine. I think that it will matter more if he wants me for a lifetime. But I don't know what he told her or why he *had* to see her. And I feel like I don't know how to believe him anymore.

He called me Sunday night and said, "Baby, you're like a brand new book. She's an old, tattered book that's been read a hundred times over. I know how that story ends. I've only just cracked the first chapter of our book, and I can't wait to see how this one ends. I hope you'll let me."

It was cheesy and could so easily have been phony. But his voice sounded sincere. I told myself that it was his voice that made me want to stay. I was so happy to hear it that tears actually rolled down my cheeks. He'd picked me. He wanted me. He promised me she was gone. I'm happy, of course. I love him and I want him too. There's just a little part of my heart that still feels broken and a little protective voice that's telling me to pull back. But, it's too late. I've decided that I'm all in. Let's just hope that this becomes a small blip in a lifetime of months like the ones we've just had.

Please... Please let him always want me. I can't imagine feeling this way again.

Six

Liam

Ice, so much ice, and so many cold winds, un-showered men, and lonely nights in the wilderness spent thinking about how hungry we were for real food – that's survival training. While she partied in Pacific Beach and decompressed before starting the second semester of her Master's program, I spent the month freezing my ass off in the Alaskan woods, hunting what little food there was, and huddling for warmth in my lean-to constructed from nothing but a tarp and some branches. When the skies opened up and snowed too heavily for us to make a fire to cook what little dinner we could find, we went to sleep hungry, tired, and alone. We rarely got a night off, but when we did we were almost too tired to make the most of it. It didn't seem fair that all my friends who flunked BUD/S got to spend the so-called San Diego "winter" partying with her and all of the other co-eds. As I shut my eyes to rest, I could see them dancing with her, lying on the beach with her, taking shots with her. In reality, she probably wasn't hanging out with any of my friends, which actually scared me more – the unknown men who could've been making moves on her without me there to defend her. I just wanted her bikini-clad body in my arms. Not only did I hate thinking about who she could've been dancing with, but all that time alone gave me too much time to think about what it would mean for me if it didn't work out with her and about who I really am.

We'd had a couple of relaxing weeks together after her finals, just the two of us. Things were a little rough after the Caligula situation. Kara backed off, distrust showing in her eyes and passive aggressive comments escaping her lips like darts. She wasn't herself. She wasn't letting herself be all-in in our relationship like she used to. Then, one day around Christmas, it was like she made a choice. She settled whatever dispute she had going on in her head. She became the old Kara, loving and carefree, with an even more fiery devotion. She made it clear to me, and to everyone else, that she wasn't going anywhere. We went to the beach, even though the California-natives thought it was cold, and we went in the ocean to crash waves. She felt weightless with the power of the ocean underneath her and I felt how easy it would be for her to be swept away from me. I felt how easy it would be for her to be taken in by some other life, by some other man. But then she wrapped her arms around my neck and gripped tightly while looking into my eyes, laughing as the current tried to tear her body from mine. It was as though she mocked it for even trying. She was *mine*.

I tried to remember that feeling the whole time I was in Alaska. It didn't matter where she was or who she was with, at least it shouldn't have. She trusted me now. I still trusted her. I just didn't trust myself. Alone, in the middle of Alaska, I had time to think about all those things I worked so hard to not think about. When I'm with her, I can push those thoughts aside and focus on her warm, soft skin or her infectious giggle. If she had been with me in Alaska, I wouldn't have had to think about the fact that I stole my favorite pair of her underwear and I wouldn't have had to contemplate what that meant about me. I hate the part of me that keeps forcing me to do and think these things. All I want to do is love her, and only think about her, but when I'm alone, like when I was in Alaska with all those men, I couldn't. All I wanted was for everything else to just go away and to be with her. When I'm with her, I actually believe that it could all go away and be okay. But because we were apart I couldn't help but worry about what she was doing with all of her spare time since she was probably spending it on the beach, in a bikini, with plenty of other hard-bodied men who weren't stuck in sun-less Alaska. I can't lose her. I don't know what will happen to me if I lose her.

Kara

Liam was coming home and planning to stay with me in my new Ocean Beach apartment while he looked for somewhere else to live. However, with Michael just down the road, and plenty of space, I had a strong feeling that Liam would probably end up living with me. Most of his other friends found places before they'd left and, since he hadn't, he must've at least thought about the possibility of us living together when he got back. We never officially talked about it, even though we spend all of our time with each other, and I thought it would be nice to surprise him with the possibility. And so I gave him a key.

I left a white envelope with "LIAM" written in large letters tucked under the doormat. Then I texted him the address and waited. My heart was beating so fast that I couldn't sit still so I cleaned while I waited. I'd already done every dish, scrubbed every surface, vacuumed the rugs, and lit candles for a fresh scent, but I needed to keep myself busy. A month isn't a long time, but who knows what happened while he was up there. Maybe he didn't miss me as much as I missed him. Maybe he met another girl. Maybe he still wanted to have his own space. I really didn't know. All I knew was that I wanted to wake up to him every morning and go to bed with him every night. The thought that he might not feel the same way was terrifying to me. Michael and Franceen, who were the closest to me of all my friends in San Diego, couldn't keep my mind occupied, and they had escaped to a beachside hotel up the coast for the weekend. So I was left with no one to talk me through my panic. I just worried. What if he didn't see the envelope? I debated whether it would be better to just call him and tell him my plan, but where was the romance in that? I knew he'd check the envelope. He always brought up packages for my neighbors when they were left outside of my last apartment. It's who he is.

Finally, I heard the key in the lock and hid. I wanted to really surprise him, so I hid myself in the coat closet and waited for him to come inside.

"Babe? You here?" he called. I heard him drop a heavy bag. "Where are you?" I could hear him kicking his boots off and knew he'd come to the closet next. As he slid open the door, I couldn't help myself from smiling and tried not to jump on him before he actually saw me. I wanted to see him startle.

I should have known better, because he just looked up at me calmly, with nothing but happiness in his eyes. You can't surprise a

SEAL, or even a SEAL-in-training. He grinned his easy grin and eyed me up and down.

"Well ain't you a sight for sore eyes. Let's get you outta that closet now, girl," he said as he scooped me up by my waist and pulled me out into the living room. He spun me around while I squeezed him tightly in my arms. I breathed in his salty, sweaty smell. He smelled cold, as though the fresh Alaskan air was still seeping from his pores, his body felt thinner, and he was far less tanned than when he'd left, but it felt so good to have him in my arms. He set me down in front of him and cupped my face in his hands.

"God, I've missed you," he whispered before kissing me. We stood there for a moment or two before he pulled back and said with a joking twitch of his lip, "I hope you've left me at least a little room in the closet." He picked up his bag and motioned for me to show him the way to *our* room.

Seven

Later that night, Liam was barbecuing their dinner while Kara poured them each a large glass of wine. She curled her tanned legs onto one of the lounge chairs she'd bought for their patio and asked, "So, tell me about Alaska. What was it like?"

Liam took a big sip as he flipped their steaks over. "It was alright. It's beautiful country up there, but it was cold as hell." He took another sip. "How was your 'winter' here? Meet anyone special?" He had a joking half-smile on his face, but his eyes held concern.

Kara looked confused for a second before deciding that he was joking. "Ah, you know, all the same PB frat boy types." She coyly popped a grape from their appetizer dish into her mouth. "No one quite like you, though."

He smiled at her. "I could have cheated, you know. There was a girl in town who was pretty into me. She kept trying to sell me coke and then would ask me back to her place."

Kara waited for the punch line, but none came. Liam sat calmly in front of her making cheese and cracker sandwiches while he let the steaks sit. "But… You didn't, right?"

"Huh? Oh, of course not, baby. You know I wouldn't do that to you."

"Then why bring it up?" Kara was hurt. It was something she worried about but never once thought would actually have crossed his mind.

"I don't know. I just thought it was funny. You know, like, I could have cheated up there and you'd never know." He looked at her calmly, as though he didn't realize how his words sounded to her. In his mind, he thought, *Just like you could have been cheating on me here and I'd never know. It's impossible to know what someone else is doing or thinking.*

"But, you didn't, right?" she asked again. Deep down she knew he wouldn't cheat on her, but part of her had to be skeptical. It was an odd topic to bring up.

"Babe, of course not. Don't worry so much. Here's your steak." He placed the smaller of the two perfectly cooked steaks on her plate and raised his glass. "Here's to being home with my baby." He smiled at her, the same way he always did, and Kara saw the love in his eyes where concern had dwelled just a few moments before. She pushed her insecurities down and raised her glass to him in return.

"Here's to you never having to go away again." She clinked her glass against his and gave him a quick kiss. "At least until you're an actual SEAL."

Liam

I'm not sure why I brought up that story. Maybe it was the rush of testosterone it gave me. The look of insecurity it brought to Kara's eyes made me feel like a man. It's messed up, I know, because it didn't even happen. Sure, there was a girl that was interested in me but I spent my nights avoiding her until I needed to use her feelings for me to score some cocaine at a discounted price. She was a coked out Anchorage townie and I had no interest in pursuing someone like that when I had my girl waiting for me back home. However, being so stressed out and having coke so easily available was a lethal combination and I fell back into some old habits. That didn't mean I wanted her though. But for some reason I still told Kara a different story. I wanted to make her uneasy because it made me feel better. It made me feel like a man after I'd had to sneak some of her panties back into her drawer while she went to the bathroom. That's the kind of story SEALs are supposed to tell and so that's the story I told. And I buried the panty story deep in the back of my mind.

Eight

Over the next few weeks, a slight change in Liam became evident. While he normally left his fire at work, he started having little explosions of anger at home. Sometimes it was over a scuff on his boot and his temper would be confined to the mat he sat on to polish his boots, but sometimes it was over something Kara had done – left the milk out, woken him from a nap, stretched out his shirts too much by constantly tugging at the sleeves when she borrowed them.

He'd taken to smoking weed and drinking too much Jack Daniels at night. After feeling the release from his inner stresses that cocaine had given him in Alaska, Liam picked up on old habits, dabbling in more frequent cocaine use. Kara suspected that he sometimes drove under the influence of one drug or another, but she hoped it was just her paranoia. However, she did know that he went to the gym under the influence and that, recently, he could only have sex under the influence. Luckily, Kara knew that he still took his job far too seriously to ever work under the influence. The drastic shift in his attitude, and especially his inability to perform in bed without being intoxicated in some way, wore on Kara no matter how understanding she tried to be.

Trying to keep the judgment out of her voice, Kara started to try asking him to do various activities with her – hiking, surfing, training with her at the Muay Thai gym – but she asked that he be sober. He'd always respond defensively, saying, "Don't worry so much, babe. I'm just de-stressing. It's no big deal, but I need to let loose sometimes."

So, he'd go on these dates with her but rarely left his pipe or his drugs at home. For a while, Kara kept quiet about these changes. She started to feel self-conscious about them and she didn't want anyone's opinion of her impressive and charming Navy SEAL boyfriend to change. She didn't even confide in her closest friends. Every once in a while Michael would cock his eyebrow if Liam was yelling cusswords at her, or Franceen would ask, "Are you going to let him say that to you?" In response, Kara would simply shrug her shoulders as if to say, "What can you do?" In her mind, he wasn't always bad. He just had bad days. Kara let him have his bad days, turned the other cheek when he lashed out, and relished his good days.

Then, one day, she finally got tired of covering it up. He'd woken her with kisses and then left her wrapped in their crisp white sheets with the promise of breakfast in bed. She stayed there for a while, stuck in the moments before. He hadn't paid her that much attention in weeks and she was savoring it. She remembered where his lips had moved up her stomach, from her belly button to her breasts. He'd taken each softly in his mouth before dragging his lips along her collarbone, then kissing her neck and nibbling at her ear. He'd focused on her that morning, entirely sober, and he made sure that she enjoyed every second of it. Eventually, her stomach began to rumble so she tugged at the sheet and wrapped it around her loosely to shield herself from the wall of windows lining the east side of their apartment.

"Babe?" she called as she left the bedroom. Their kitchen was fairly small and in direct view of her bedroom. When she didn't see him there, she wondered if he might have left to pick up Denny's from a few blocks down – he loved their oversize breakfasts. But there were eggs and bacon and all the fixings for chicken fried steak lying out on the counter. He was never one to eat for health, just for his taste buds.

She glanced around the rest of their 850-square foot apartment and still didn't see him until she heard a cough coming from the patio. Her heart sank. She knew what that cough meant.

"Babe? What are you doing out here? I thought you were making us breakfast," she leaned against the side of the partially opened sliding door with her long hair falling in loose waves around her shoulders and breasts. She looked down at him, huddled over a small table where he was rolling another joint. He had gained weight with all the testosterone pills he'd started adding to his daily diet. His arms and shoulders contained more than their normal amount of muscle. With his head kept closely shaved and the tattoo on his forearm constantly exposed now that no shirts could fit over that part of his body, he was actually quite intimidating. She smiled to herself because she knew there was a soft side to him, regardless of how grumpy he could be.

"I will. Just gonna smoke first," he replied gruffly without looking up.

Her heart sank. She hoped that the morning surprise was indicative of a positive change back to the life they used to have. "It's okay, I'll just start everything. I'm hungry."

Kara went back to the kitchen, leaving Liam to smoke outside. While he clearly wanted chicken fried steak with bacon and eggs, she didn't know how to make it. Instead, she decided to make some caramelized onions to have with the eggs and bacon. Caramelized onions were her favorite breakfast treat.

She sliced the onions thinly and, perhaps, chopped a few too many because the sauté pan was filled to the brim. She added a hunk of butter and covered the pan with tin foil. Then, she went back to their bedroom to change into some clothes and to tidy the laundry that had been strewn across the room over the course of the week.

She must have been in there longer than she thought because she came to when she heard Liam yell, "What the hell is this!"

She ran into the kitchen. "What?"

"All these fucking onions in here. I told you that I was going to make breakfast for us and now you fucking burnt this pan to shit and I can tell you I ain't fucking cleaning it." He picked up the pan with the now crisply blackened onions and chucked it hard into the sink. It sizzled loudly.

"Shit, I totally forgot about the onions. It's okay though. I have other pans you can use." Kara smiled sweetly at him. She'd grown used to his outbursts now and expected this one to subside as quickly as it came up.

"Don't tell me to fucking relax. I was going to make breakfast and it would have tasted a hell of a lot better than whatever shit you tried to make. How can you *forget* about what you're cooking? How fucking stupid can you be?" He glared at her over the counter. "You're getting your Master's and you can't even handle cooking? Fucking embarrassing." His knuckles were white where he clenched the edge of the counter.

"What the hell are you so mad about? Let's just go out for breakfast then." Kara glared back at him. "You need to calm down. You're being an asshole right now." Her voice was growing louder too.

"Don't tell me to calm down. I'll say whatever the hell I want." He grabbed the bottle of Jack from their freezer while accidentally knocking his body against hers and she was shoved back into the counter. He went back out to the porch, slamming the sliding door behind him. He sat heavily into the patio chair and soon there was the familiar skunky smell of weed wafting into the apartment.

Her hands started to shake. Whether it was from anger, surprise, or fear, she didn't know. But she was willing to bet it was a mixture of all three. She didn't know what to say to him, but she needed to talk to someone. So she called her closest guy friend, Jay, from home.

She suspected she was overreacting. She'd become more prone to it after becoming accustomed to how Liam had treated her when they first met. Jay always told her the truth and she hoped that he would set her straight again. She called him hoping he would talk her down so that she and Liam could get their day back on track.

Unfortunately, that was exactly what he told her *not* to do. After relaying the story, Jay's usually laidback and comforting tone turned hard as he said, "Kara, no guy should ever act like that towards you. Do you hear me? Never. You need to cut him loose right now. You go out there and break up with him because this is a bad sign. If he's doing this now, he's got some serious problems and you need to get out." His tone was fierce.

Immediately, Kara felt guilty. *Did I exaggerate the story?* she wondered to herself. *I must have. He's not a bad guy. And now Jay hates him before he even gets to meet him. I shouldn't have said anything.*

"Kara? Promise me you'll break up with him," Jay's voice broke through her thoughts. She wasn't going to break up with him. She knew she probably never would. In her heart, she knew he was reacting to something else and that his outbursts weren't about her, and she wanted to stay and be there for him.

"Hm? Well he's really not a bad guy. I think he's just stressed with work…" Kara let her voice trail off.

"You deserve so much more than that. You have to realize that."

"I love him, Jay. I'm sure it'll get better. He's got a stressful job," she said with a sigh. *It has to get better,* she thought. "Don't worry. I was just venting. He's usually really sweet." She made her voice sound light, confident.

Jay sighed heavily. She knew he was unhappy with her response.

"Fine. Just know that you didn't do anything wrong," Jay told her before they hung up.

She knew he was right but she still felt guilty for venting about Liam. Jay hadn't given her the reaction she'd hoped for and she decided to go outside and apologize to Liam. As she watched him smoking, his back to her while he looked out at the surfers waiting for a wave, she felt a surge of love for him. Her heart swelled in her chest. She admired him. She loved him. She wanted to share that version of Liam with her friends, not the irrationally angry one who only came out sometimes. After that, she never shared any stories that showed him as anything other than perfect for her.

At the sound of the screen door closing, Liam turned to look at her. His eyes were dark and pained. The anger from before was replaced with something else, something dark and deeply personal. He reached an arm out to her, putting his joint out with the other. Her eyes welled up with tears. She went to him, tucking her body under his arm, taking in the solid warmth of his body. He held her tightly and kissed the top of her head.

"I'm sorry, baby. I know I haven't been myself lately," he said softly. His voice was tight with emotion. "This isn't about you. I love you. You know that, right?"

"I love you, too," she said, looking up at him as the tears slid down her cheeks.

His eyes grew darker as he wiped her tears away with his thumb, his weathered skin rough against hers. She looked up at him and saw all of the pain that he was clearly trying to suppress etched into his face.

Liam

I thought it would be different this time. I thought it would be different with her. I thought, with the right girl, with a great girl, I would be finally be okay. The SEALs kick my ass all day, my shot is the best in my class, and I am squatting almost 600 pounds. After all that hard work, I go home to the best girl in the world – the hottest, smartest, funniest girl I've ever met. By all accounts, my life could not be better than it is right now. I should not be sad or angry, and I shouldn't be thinking about the things that I'm thinking about. It's wrong. I don't need to change anything.

I love the way my skin feels against hers. I love the way her hair gets messy and tangled, and how her eyes can't hide that they're completely satisfied. But, sometimes, I want to feel like that. Really, I want her to make me feel like that. There's an online store I found that sells that sort of thing. More than once I've filled up my shopping cart with all kinds of... toys... for her to use on me, but then I just can't hit the "Buy Now" button. I picture her face when she opens the box and the look of horror that would probably be painted all over it as it dawned on her what those items were for. So, I just daydream. In my mind, I hear other people tell me that my ass is sexy and that my thick pecks actually look like boobs since they are dotted with my big nipples. They tell me the things I think about Kara. They tell me things that make me feel as attractive and sexy as I think Kara is. Most importantly, everything I daydream about feels authentic. These people see the real me and they like the real me. It's freeing.

It's also ridiculous. It doesn't make sense. I love my girlfriend. I love her body. I love her personality. I love the way a vein actually pops out of her left temple when I really piss her off. I love how she can hold her own in any argument. I love having sex with her. I just… I guess I just need something different. For some reason, all of that isn't enough anymore. I want to look different. I want to be seen differently. I want her to look at me the way I look at her – with all of that same love, understanding, attraction, and maybe even a little bit of jealousy.

I'm trying to push it down like I always have, but it won't go away. The feelings just push back harder now. To be honest, it's scaring me a little. And then she looks me in the eye with those big, trusting, green eyes, those eyes full of hope for our future, and it scares me a lot. I want to protect her from all of the bad in the world, myself included. Her eyes are full of the innocence of first love. I want her to hold onto that forever. But how can I protect her from that when it's going to be me that ends up hurting her? If she ever finds out about these thoughts I'm having, it's going to break her heart. She'll probably feel like she isn't enough. I'd hate to do that to her because she's more than enough. I'm just fucked up. Then, she'll probably look at me with sadness, maybe pity, and I know I won't be her rock anymore. She might even look at me with disgust. I promised her that I'd always be there for her. I promised to always be strong and to protect her. Lately, I haven't been very good at that and, if she ever finds out what has been distracting me, it'll be even harder on her. She deserves more than me, more than what I'm becoming. I should let her go, but I can't. I refuse. Every time I snap at her, push her away in my frustration, she comes back stronger. I think she's trying to drown my problems with her love. She says she's going to "love the shit out of me" and I think she means it. She is trying to love this confusion out of me. It's both stressful and sweet. It feels good that she keeps trying but it's scaring me because my urges get stronger the more blatantly she shows how much she loves me.

She's never going to let me go, that much is clear, and I can't find it in me to let her go either. Something is going to happen. This secret can't stay inside of me forever. I just don't see any way out of our relationship. I don't want to end it. I don't want to live without her. I'm just not happy anymore. Frankly, if I can't be happy with her in my life and I know I can't be happy without her... Well, then I must not be destined for happiness.

Nine

Liam's phone rang, again. He felt it buzz inside the back pocket of his faded, torn jeans and pulled it out. Kara's smiling face looked back at him. He hit decline, again.

"You got somewhere to be, man?" his buddy chided him.

"Nah, just here," replied Liam.

He lied. In fact, he did have somewhere to be. At this moment, he was supposed to be at a movie with Kara. They'd planned this date night last week after a particularly big fight about his drinking and smoking. Kara felt that they weren't getting enough quality time and Liam felt backed into a corner because smoking and drinking were the only ways he could numb his feelings. So, they'd fought. He'd yelled, she'd cried. Her crying always broke his heart. The tears would come on suddenly, she'd lose the ability to formulate words, and then she'd be an utter mess in just a matter of seconds. She'd often try to continue their argument even though her lips would fail her and her eyes would give away every thought that needed to be voiced. Liam found it more sad than frustrating to watch her when she was like this, so he often gave in at this point. He promised her a night of no drinking, no drugs, just him and her going to dinner and a movie. That date was today. He had woken up next to her that morning, but hadn't responded to her calls or texts all day. Instead, he had started getting drunk and high with his friends as soon as he finished work at 4pm. By now, he'd already missed dinner, failed to tell her, and was about to miss the movie.

"You sure you can leave that wifey home alone for one night?" his old barracks roommate, Colin, teased.

Liam grinned. "Ya, I'm sure. I might just have to make one call first. You know how women get."

Colin slapped him on the shoulder, "Do I ever, bro… Do I ever."

Liam took his phone back out of the pocket that he'd shoved it in, willing it to stop ringing, wishing away the responsibilities he had with the girl on the other end. He tapped her name on his screen and put the phone to his ear as he sent a mocking eye roll towards his buddies. He was good at playing the role of a bro. He had mastered the art of hiding the way his stomach clenched and his palms sweated with the thought of a romantic date night without any booze while his mind was occupied of images of men, high heels, and tight skirts. He knew he was losing control and it frightened him.

"Hey babe, sorry I missed your call," he said.

"Where are you? I've been so worried! You were supposed to meet me here two hours ago," replied Kara, her voice moving quickly from worried and scared to angry and hurt.

"I'm going out with the boys tonight. I just need some man time, you know?"

"You're drunk already…" Kara's pained voice trailed off.

"I need to let loose tonight, babe. We'll hang out tomorrow." Without waiting for a reply, Liam hung up the phone.

Kara's heart hurt. Whether it was anger, disappointment, or embarrassment, she wasn't sure. But she turned her phone off to avoid being let down when he didn't call to apologize or to check in with her. She hated feeling forgotten, especially when it was drugs, alcohol, and horny SEAL candidates that had cleared his mind of her. Wiping off her makeup and unzipping her new dress, she climbed into bed alone.

* * *

The night was only just beginning for Liam. They were still at the first bar on their list with another few bumps of cocaine left in his pocket. His friends were drunk, ready to talk to girls, and excited to not talk about love, the future, girlfriends, or wives. Passing the third phase of BUD/S and Parachute School, and starting SEAL Qualification Training (SQT), had them excited and ready for the new phase of their futures. Soon, they would earn their tridents and be sent to a team. They felt that they had earned themselves a stress-free night filled with shots and girls – a night that would leave them in a hung over haze for the entire next day. Liam didn't only want to celebrate, but he needed this night to shut off the reeling thoughts in his head about women and dresses that left him wondering who he really was supposed to be.

The next day, Liam woke up at 2pm in Colin's guest bed without his phone, his wallet, his car keys, his car, or any memory of the night before. Kara was shaking him awake. He looked up at her through eyes blurred from lack of sleep and too much alcohol.

"What the hell happened to you last night? You didn't come home," she said angrily. "And I thought you said we would do something together today."

"Baby... Please don't. Not right now," he groaned groggily. "I had a really bad night."

She'd stormed into the guest bedroom at Colin's house ready for a fight – her mind had been spinning with arguments since the night before – but something made her stop. There was something different in his voice. *He sounds almost ... broken*, she thought as she eyed him closely. His eyes opened wider as if to plead with her. His body was still curled in the fetal position. She sat down on the bed with him and let her hand fall onto his back and rub in circular motions. He always felt soothed when she did that.

"What happened?" she asked.

"I-I... I don't know," he replied. He closed his eyes and clenched her hand tight. "I lost everything, baby. I lost my wallet, my phone, my keys. Hell, I even lost my truck. Babe, I don't even know where my truck is." He looked so broken, so in need of love and comfort, that Kara's heart broke. She'd never seen him like this. He drank and he got rowdy or he got angry, but he never lost control.

"Don't worry, sweetie. We'll figure it all out. How did you get here?" she asked.

He paused. "I think I took a cab. I-I was walking and all I remember is coming-to walking in a neighborhood I'd never seen, covered in dirt, and realizing that I had nothing with me. I think I convinced a cab driver to come here and... I don't know. I guess Colin must have paid. I was alone though... I remember that much."

She patted his back. "Why don't you get up so I can get you some food and we'll go find your car?" She kissed him on the forehead and stood up. "Let's go."

Liam groaned, but slowly shifted his body to the seated position. He swayed slightly with the effort. "Where's Colin? Maybe he knows what happened."

Kara shrugged. "Sleeping, maybe? His door was shut when I came in. He'd left the door unlocked." There was a pit in her stomach. This wasn't the same kind of "Oh-god-I-wish-I-remembered-what-I-did-last-night" kind of feeling that she and her roommates in undergrad used to moan about on Sunday mornings. This feeling played more like the start to one of the *Hangover* movies. *This is a big fuck up. This doesn't happen with just regular partying*, she thought.

"He's got to know what happened. Maybe I just got tired and left my car and keys at the bar and decided to hitch a ride a taxi…" his voice trailed off as he looked around the room. He doubted that was all that had happened. While he was in Colin's guest room, he had apparently left his pants elsewhere. He groaned and stumbled out into the living room wearing only his compression shorts and sporting a nasty purple bruise on the left side of his ribcage.

Colin met them in the kitchen, also in boxers. At six feet tall with 220 pounds of chiseled muscle, Colin looked like a typical SEAL or SEAL candidate. However, coupled with deep, dark eyes, espresso-colored skin, and the hint of a Southern drawl, Colin was even more sexually enticing to sorority girls and frog hogs alike, which resulted in his personality and moral compass being heavily underdeveloped after years of unsolicited admiration.

Coffee mug in hand, he leaned against the counter and looked at Kara and Liam with one eyebrow cocked.

"Hey man, so I guess you are alive," he said.

"What the hell happened last night? I don't remember a damn thing," Liam asked as he poured himself a cup of coffee.

"What happened is you got fucked up, man." Colin took a sip of his coffee. "You were fine at Tap House, but you got weird at Blake's Tavern. You got so angry all of a sudden. You tried to fight me and Gonzales, and pretty much any other dude who was at the bar. One guy even took you up on it," he said as he motioned towards Liam's bruised ribs. "He would have got you good too if it weren't for us. You weren't even fighting back. You just let him wail on you. It was like you wanted it."

Liam leaned heavily against the counter. "That's not like me at all," he said.

"Nah, man. That's not like you *at all*. We were pretty surprised. Figured you got some shit happening or somethin'."

Liam buried his face in his hands. "And then, well, how did I get home? Why did I take a cab?"

"You left early. You were piss drunk and raging out hard by 1am. I tried to take your keys off ya, but you threw a hard one at me. You got in your car and just drove off. We tried to talk you out of it, but you said you had to get out of there right away. And then you just sped off," said Colin, turning his head so that Liam could see where he hit him square in the jaw.

Liam's eyes were filled with a mixture of disbelief, pain, and regret. "Why didn't you stop me?" He kept his eyes on the countertop, his voice soft.

Colin looked unperturbed, as though they were simply talking about a disagreement at work. "It wasn't my business, man. You were fucking angry and mean, and I was just out to have a good time. I told you not to drive, but you didn't listen. That's on you."

Liam shook his head, not in disagreement but more out of disbelief. "But, man, we're brothers. We're teammates. You're supposed to have my back when shit's not right." Liam's voice was filled with lost hope and confusion. "Work can't know about this, buddy. Please."

"I needed to let off steam just as much as you, brotha, and I wasn't about to ruin my night cause you got some shit going on." Colin finished his coffee, put the mug in the sink, and headed back to his room without another word.

"Man, I just wish you'd have knocked me out or something," said Liam, more to himself than to Colin, who was clearly finished with the conversation.

Kara, who'd been standing quietly behind Liam throughout the exchange with Colin, let her hand rest on Liam's shoulder. "Let's go, babe. We'll fix this. Don't worry."

He rested his calloused, hard-worked hand on hers. "Okay," he said.

She smiled at him as she took his hand in hers to lead him to her car. "We'll find your car. It's probably parked close to the bar. You wouldn't let yourself drive when you were *that* messed up." She smiled comfortingly at him, trying to dissuade the worried frown from his face.

Liam

Blurry streetlights, angry yells, the crunch of metal, intense fear... I lied to her when I told her that I didn't remember anything. I remember things. I don't remember sequences or places or people, but I remember details. I remember running, fast. I remember feeling pain in my ribs and thinking I deserved it. I remember drinking, a lot. And I remember that voice in my head not getting any quieter. Instead, it just got louder and louder. The girl in me would not let herself get drowned out.

I know something bad happened. I know I fucked up. The sound of crunching metal and the crushing fear that goes with it is too real for me to fully believe that my truck is still innocently in the parking lot behind Blake's Tavern. Something bad happened with me in that car, I know it. I can't bring myself to tell Kara. It's so humiliating. I don't do this kind of thing. I like to drink and occasionally I'll get into a fight or two, but I don't get angry and drive drunk. I know I haven't been myself lately, but I don't fuck up like this. If the Navy finds out, there's no way they'll let me be a SEAL. My career will be finished. Kara's not the kind of girl to date a fucked up drunk, especially if I did something bad enough to go to jail. I don't know what I'm going to do. I had to get out with the boys to let off some steam because I just couldn't face a night with Kara alone without drinking or smoking to take the edge off, but now I wish I had just gone to the theater and eaten popcorn with her.

With all the thoughts going through my head, I just couldn't look her in the eye without any chemical help. Every time I see a hot guy or see Kara in her little jean skirt, the girl in my head whispers to me, *Wouldn't it be hot if he fucked you while you wore that jean skirt? He could just lift it up and pound you.* That shit is fucked up and, if Kara ever knew, it would absolutely break her heart. So, I went out to drown those thoughts. I went out to try and *kill* those thoughts. It was supposed to be a night to escape, to get back being to the man I'm working to become, and now look where that's gotten me.

I also remember calling someone. I think it was Kara. I wanted her to rescue me. I needed her to save me. I was so lost. But she didn't pick up. I called over and over again, but she never picked up. I don't blame her. I'd abandoned her, so she'd abandoned me. And now I'm in a whole worse mess of trouble. I can't help but wonder if the situation would have been better if she had picked up. I don't want to blame her, she has every right to be mad at me. I also can't help myself though. Maybe I wouldn't have all this shit to clean up if she had just rescued me. I need her to rescue me, not just from this, but from myself.

Kara

I don't know what to think. I'm hurt that he ditched our plans again, especially because this was going to be a night without the drugs and alcohol to let loose, but look where that pressure got him. Obviously, he needs the alcohol and drugs, but I just wish I knew *why*. I don't understand it. He isn't this guy. This isn't the guy I fell in love with. I love him just the same but, looking at him as he sits in the seat next to me, I don't see the old him. I don't see the man I can rely on, who has protected me from harassment, taught me what love is, and made me feel like the sexiest woman alive. Now, I have to guilt him into spending a night alone with me, and even then he can't manage it soberly. Now his shoulders are stooped, his are eyes worried, and his lips are tight. The confidence and self-assured, easy smile that is his trademark is so far buried beneath the mix of anger and frustration that has taken over his face lately.

I didn't know how to tell him, so I didn't. But while we drove around Pacific Beach, and he tried to piece together his night by looking at the bars and restaurants he could have passed, I felt too guilty to tell him one piece that he was missing – that he'd called me 10 times. He left me voicemails. Most of them were too garbled by noise and rustling to be understood, but his voice was clear enough in one to decipher his message. He had said, "Hi Kara, I know you're mad at me and I deserve that. I fucked up and I'm sorry. I don't know why I'm calling you now, then, except I don't know who else to call. I'm lost, baby. I'm so lost. I don't know how I got here. I'm not even in PB anymore. But, I don't have my keys or my car or my wallet. I don't know how to get home." He paused for about 10 seconds before continuing. "Baby, I need your help. Come save me, please. I want to come home."

He'd called me for help and I wasn't there. Being too angry with him for canceling our date, I turned off my phone. I never do that. I never let myself get so mad that I don't communicate. In reality, I usually want to talk *more* when I'm angry. There have been times when I've called him 20-30 times when I'm angry so that we can talk it out, or so that I can yell at him. I always have my phone on, but not last night. If I had, if I had controlled my anger, maybe his night wouldn't have gone quite so badly for him and I could have been there for him like I had promised I always would be. I feel like this is partly my fault and I don't have the guts to tell him. All I can do is try to help.

His truck wasn't at or around Blake's Tavern, but he was caught on camera leaving the lot at 2:30am. From there, he turned left and headed off the screen. Walking down the road, we saw a mailbox knocked down and run over, but no truck. Liam doesn't remember if he hit the mailbox, but it looks like he did. It's flat on the ground and the wood looks newly splintered. We chatted with the bartender at Blake's and his bar tab from the night before was over $100. It isn't a pricey joint with $2.00 shots being a normal occurrence, so $100 buys a lot of alcohol. No wonder he doesn't remember anything. He doesn't usually get that out of control and I find it difficult to believe that he'd let himself drink that much knowing that he had to drive home, but I guess I don't know anything about the stress he is under.

Ten

After three weeks of investigation, Liam was finally called to Captain's Mast. Once the police dropped the case and declined to press criminal charges for driving under the influence, punishment was in the hands of the Navy. With his white uniform pressed and cleaned, his boots shined so thoroughly that he could see his own reflection in them, and his head freshly shaved, Liam did his best to present himself as the kind of candidate worthy of their leniency. He walked onto the stage with his shoulders back and his body rigid in true military-form. He held his head high, but his eyes were contrite. He spoke with sincere regret, owned his mistakes, and apologized for bringing shame to his class and to the base. Every person standing on stage with him believed him. His commanding officers liked him and they saw the potential for a dedicated and talented SEAL in him, but they knew what had to be done. They couldn't have a candidate who acted so irresponsibly in public, regardless of whether it was intentional or not. That behavior was not up to SEAL standards. Many candidates in the audience also thought that the rigidity Liam's superiors' were showing on the matter was in response to the growing public impression that there was too much drinking and partying happening within the classes. While no one in the classes knew whether or not this was a normal punishment for breaking the rules of training, or if it was in response to public perception, many chose to believe that Liam's harsh punishment was one way that the Navy was trying to combat the sometimes tainted view of its candidates as rowdy, inappropriate, and drunken womanizers. Remembering the many times that they had acted inappropriately while off base, many of the younger men believed that Liam was being used as an example of the ramifications for partying too hard. However, many of the older, more seasoned Navy men believed that Liam's punishment was justified and was a direct response to him violating the military's code of ethics.

At Captain's Mast, the decision was made that Liam would not stay in his current training class, or in training at all. He was to be dropped from the program entirely and, likely, sent to work on a ship. Afterwards, Liam was told that there were a couple of officers who had argued on his behalf that a one-year suspension from the program should have sufficed, and that during which he should have been able to still work on the base to ensure his readiness to reapply the following year. However, that was a losing battle for them. The captain overseeing the case had no previous interactions with Liam, nor did he care about the individual over the success of the team. He looked at the big picture and made his decision based on the information he had. After listening to Liam speak, he'd taken a moment to think and confer, and then delivered the news that ended Liam's life as he'd known it. Liam was dropped from the SEAL program. He would be transferred to a ship once an appropriate availability came up and, until then, would work on menial tasks around the SEAL base.

Liam

All that pain, all that drive, all that work, it was all for nothing. I would have made it to graduation. The trident pin given to every SEAL upon graduation was within my sights.

I made it through the hardest parts of BUD/S and some of SQT without any problems. Everyone knew I would make it. It was within my reach. I couldn't wait to be on a SEAL team where I could go on actual missions, make a tangible difference, and be a real man. Now, all I've got is hate and shame.

Hate. I've never felt it like this before. Sure, I've hated myself for things I've thought or done, but not like this. I've been miserable during parts of SEAL training, been angry at friends or ex-girlfriends for things they've done, blamed Christian for what he did to me and how it made me feel. I've felt all of that and sometimes mistaken it for hate, but I've never felt hate like this. It's not even directed at anyone anymore. It's just emanating from my soul like a wildfire – and anyone and anything can be consumed by it. I hate my "friends" for not being there for me when I needed them and for not taking my keys away when it was obviously the right thing to do. I hate Kara for constantly judging me for how much I drink and smoke and how she won't even try to understand why I need these things. I hate feeling reliant on her for driving me to base in the mornings while my truck is still impounded as evidence. I hate my superiors for making an example out of me, especially when I know that they've fucked up in the past too. Everyone messes up sometimes. But, most of all, more than anything, I hate myself. With that realization comes a kind of brokenness I've never felt before.

Without the SEALs, I'm back to being the same confused screw-up everyone always thought I'd be in high school. I might be even worse. I had a shot at really making something of myself. I almost let myself achieve something great. I just had to screw it up because that's what I do. I let those thoughts take control over me. I drank. I smoked. I snorted. I took... well, God only knows what else to make me act the way I did that night. I tried to take back control of my mind but, by now, I should know that it doesn't work that way. Instead, I drove right into a nice old lady's mailbox. I could have stayed and tried to explain it to the police. I could have tried to convince them that it was a mistake. Instead, I took off and ran. I made myself look guilty. Maybe it was the best thing, in the end, because it sounds like I probably couldn't have passed any breathalyzer or drug test. But what if I could have talked my way out of it? I could have told them I'd been drugged or something. For how messed up I was, and how little I remember, I very well could have been. The cops here really do respect the SEALs, even if they haven't quite earned their tridents yet. Maybe, if I had tried, my career wouldn't be gone. Maybe I wouldn't have to ask my girlfriend to drive me to and from work, buy my lunches, buy our tickets to the movies, and cover our rent. Maybe then I would still feel remotely like a man. I might as well just give into the urges now. I don't deserve to call myself a man anymore. I don't even resemble a man anymore in my dreams. Maybe all of those thoughts have finally gotten the best of me.

* * *

Waiting for the day I was scheduled to appear at Captain's Mast where I was told whether or not I could continue in the SEAL training program was more than stressful. For three weeks, from the time of the incident to the day they dropped me, Kara had stepped up and taken care of the both of us. She'd paid for our groceries, she'd made our dinners, she'd driven us to the gym, and she'd helped me figure out my legal matters. She became my rock. Unfortunately, it wore on her too. She snapped at me more often and, when she was really angry, she'd shamelessly chide me for fucking up so badly. All of that wore on me and I'd yell back at her. The fighting was fueling a lot of my frustration towards our relationship. We didn't have that passionate spark that we used to have and I just couldn't get myself there anymore. Our sex life died for a while because I just didn't feel like a man anymore. I wasn't able to find our spark, or any spark. I'd just wanted to sleep, or drink, or both.

It was shit timing, but her parents had come to town on the exact day that I was dropped from the program. They'd invited us to dinner at a pretty fancy restaurant in Del Mar. Kara, knowing that I probably wouldn't be in good shape after Captain's Mast, had asked them that we all go out to dinner the next day instead. I'd told her that I was okay with that. In reality, I probably shouldn't have. I love her, though, and I wanted to meet her parents. I want to marry her someday and I wanted them to get to know me. I just wish they could have gotten to meet the old me – the confident, Navy SEAL candidate – not this mess that I've become.

The night before our dinner, the night I'd gotten dropped, we'd gone out to a friend's house and I'd gotten really drunk. It started out as a fun night. I look back at the photos we'd taken and we look happy. We look like the old us. Somewhere around my eighth or ninth drink, though, something changed. You can see it in the photos too. I'd gotten dark. I looked… off. After that, I'd started drinking fast and hard. Kara had tried to stop me. First she whispered in my ear, then she tried to drink some of my drinks, and finally she took me aside to beg me. She said that she didn't want me to be hung over when I met her parents, but it just pissed me off that she was trying to control me. So I drank more. I hate how she tries to mother me sometimes and thinks that she knows what is best for me. I'd just needed to drink. I'd had a really *bad* couple of days.

At some point, I'd passed out in someone's bed and I woke up to her bringing me a glass of water and some Advil. It was a nice gesture but for some reason it made me feel so much shame. I couldn't handle it. It was embarrassing, emasculating, and proof that I was a drunken failure. She didn't even trust me to take dinner with her parents seriously anymore. She tries to control me now and I can't take it. She's trying to make me into someone I used to be and, frankly, I'm just not him anymore. I don't really know who I am anymore, but it isn't him.

She was sitting on the bed next to me, her slender back facing towards my legs. I didn't even open my eyes because I knew what I would've see on her face – disappointment, hurt, anger – and I wouldn't have been able to take it. I couldn't handle feeling any more shame. So, I'd done something even worse. I'd taken both of my legs and quickly, smoothly, placed them on the small of her back and pushed out with enough force to send her tumbling from the bed.

I'd heard her fall against something, maybe the dresser. At first I'd felt a deep sense of satisfaction, but it was soon followed by an even more crushing shame than I'd felt when she'd first walked in.

"Get out," my voice started out quietly. "Get out of here you stupid cunt. Leave me alone!" My voice had escalated and was loud enough to almost scare her out of the room. Soon after, she said something in a tone that revealed her anger, hurt, and maybe even a little bit of disgust. At least that's what it had sounded like to me.

"What the hell, you asshole," she'd whispered fiercely. She never wanted anyone to know that we were fighting so she'd always whisper when people we knew were nearby. Michael, Franceen, and a few of her other grad school friends had been in the next room and we'd both known it. "Just fucking sleep, okay? You better be fine for tomorrow."

I needed to be alone. I should have apologized, but I just didn't want to. She couldn't possibly have understood how I'd felt at that moment. No one could have understood. I felt so completely and utterly alone and I was coping in the only way that I knew how. So, I didn't say anything; I'd just kept my eyes shut and hoped that I could soon fall into a deep, dreamless, comatose sleep.

"I know you had a rough day today and I feel for you. I love you, after all, and will always be here. But don't you ever call me a cunt again. Especially after everything we've been through these last couple of months." Her voice had still been a whisper, but it had become less angry and a little bit shaky.

I knew I had hurt her. I'd regretted my actions, I did, but some small part of me had felt a little bit of satisfaction for causing her even a fraction of the pain that I'd been feeling.

Kara shut the door quietly behind her and stopped to take a deep breath. Tears had sprung to her eyes, but she wasn't about to let anyone see them. Her friends were all in the next room, still laughing and drinking. She walked into the kitchen, took a drink from the fridge, and sat down to listen to Franceen's story about attending her first college party where she had misunderstood the intention behind a "cups" themed party. Rather than bringing anything besides a cup to drink out of, as the theme generally required, she'd worn an outfit made entirely out of cups that, she claimed, made her very popular with the athletes. Kara rolled her eyes in annoyance – all of Franceen's stories seemed far too outlandish to be credible.

Michael, who had the seat next to Kara, leaned in close and asked, "Is he okay? He seemed like he was in a rough mood."

"Ya, he's asleep now," she said, looking at him. It always felt nice to talk to Michael. He reminded her of her friends back home in Canada – a laidback "bro" with a kind heart. He'd grown close with Liam over the past seven months and had grown close with her while having had more than one all-night study session as they powered their way through the program. Since he knew them both, she felt that he understood her situation better than anyone and she didn't worry about tarnishing his view of Liam. She knew that he thought Liam was a good person. She also suspected that he was far less oblivious to the drama of their relationship than his increasingly self-involved girlfriend, Franceen. He often had kind words or a hug for Kara when she and Liam were having problems, but never pressured her for information or passed any judgment.

Michael searched her face. "Are you okay then?"

Kara was feeling weaker by the minute. She knew it was the stress of the past few months culminating in one day so she tried to be understanding but she couldn't. Something had broken and she'd felt herself start changing, wanting to control Liam and taking things more personally. She'd actually grown to expect his cutting words, which, somehow, only made them more hurtful. She had tried hard to hide her frustrations and to explain any explosive arguments that were overheard by Franceen, Michael, or any other visitors. Looking into Michael's eyes and seeing nothing but openness, Kara realized how tired she was of it all – the secrecy, the shame, the pain. So, she opened up for the first time since venting to Jay a few months before.

"He's just in such a bad place these days. He called me a 'cunt' in there and he literally kicked me off the bed… and all I did was bring him Advil," she said, keeping her voice low. She looked at him, locking her eyes on his. It felt good to see such clarity in someone's eyes. So often, now, she felt that the only eyes she looked deeply into contained dark secrets covered by anger, hate, and pain.

"Well, Liam… Liam's complicated, Kara. He might do that from time to time, but you know he loves you, right?" he said, squeezing her knee under the table while Franceen still stood a few feet away, enthralled with telling her story.

Franceen was saying something about the captain of the men's team being completely unable to contain his attraction to her as she danced around in her cup-dress. Had she been listening more carefully, Kara would have struggled to control the roll of her eyes. It seemed so banal compared to her life at the moment.

"Just remember that he loves you. You guys *fit*. He's just going through a rough patch right now," Michael said.

"I know. It's just… it's hard, you know? And it makes me so angry. He can be such an ass," she said with a small chuckle.

He smiled his crooked, toothy grin and chuckled. "Yep, he sure can. I don't get it because I sure can't imagine saying anything like that to you. But, that's Liam and it still doesn't mean that he doesn't care. He's got another side that none of us see. That's how he excelled throughout BUD/S. No ordinary man can do that." He paused, contemplating whether he should say his next words or not. "But, in case he doesn't realize it enough right now to tell you, or doesn't know how to tell you… He's lucky to have you. You're special and you deserve to be told as much."

Kara smiled. It felt good to be told that, really good. She felt lighter, freer, and a little bit more confident with just those few words. "Thanks," she said, a small smile playing on her lips. "That means a lot."

"No problem. Just don't forget it, okay?" he said before taking his hand off her leg. It left a warm, comforting feeling that Kara couldn't help but relish in. "I'll make sure he gets cleaned up and makes it to dinner with your parents. I've got nothing to do tomorrow. I can play Liam's nanny for a day and give you a break." He grinned jokingly. He didn't mean it as an offense towards Liam; it was just his way of letting Kara know that someone had noticed how hard she was trying to get Liam back on track.

"Thanks," she said again.

UNSEALED

Kara

Part of me doesn't really feel it anymore. The cutting words, the anger, the embarrassment, they all just go right through me. I don't mean that it is easier now or that it doesn't hurt, but it doesn't shock me anymore. It's become a constant presence in our relationship. He can say the sweetest words and then turn around and say words that cut me to the core. Our relationship is now one of extremes. At the beginning of this phase of his, when he'd yell cuss words at me or try to make me jealous with other girls, the words and actions would cut me like a knife. Now, I think that my heart must be totally cut up because I don't even flinch anymore. I soak in any complements he gives like a sponge absorbs water, but there's always an element of dread that comes in with them because I know there's a bad mood coming. The good, the bad... it's all the same now. They are entirely intertwined.

I still love him, I do. He isn't mean-hearted or an ass all of the time. I mean, when he met my parents and I saw how they fell in love with his personality, I saw the old him again. I remember falling hard for him when I saw his easy smile, his natural charm, and felt how much he cared about me, just like my parents did. He even took my hand in the car on our drive home and told me, while completely sober, "Babe, I love your family. I am so excited for the day that they'll become my family too." He smiled at me, then, and leaned in to kiss me more deeply than ever. It was honest, committed, and sincere. He was the Liam I'd fallen in love with. He was the Liam I wanted to marry.

After that dinner, I wanted to let myself believe that he was back to his old self. I held his hand and squeezed his forearm tightly, like I always did when we drove in his truck. I didn't want to let go. There was such comfort in sitting there with him in silence. But, then, he always disappoints me again. The memory of the night before was still fresh and sore. If he never drank or smoked or snorted again, I think we could be fine. It's when he does all of those things that the darkness in him comes out. When it does, I feel so alone. I don't talk about it with anyone, so I just paint a smile on my face and pretend that everything is fine. It's not, though. I'm broken, I think. A part of my heart feels permanently broken. When Michael put his hand on my leg and talked to me about how I was feeling, I felt something I hadn't felt in months. I felt *seen*. It felt good, so good, and that makes me feel so guilty.

I wish I didn't lash out at Liam all the time, but he makes me so mad. I wish I could just let go and help him heal in some other way, but I can't. I can see his life going up in a cloud of smoke. If he hadn't gotten kicked out for his drinking, he would have for his smoking. If he pulls any of this in the regular Navy, he'll probably get an automatic dishonorable discharge and then where will we be? Few reputable companies hire dishonorable discharges. Best case, he'll get an "other than honorable" discharge. But that's not a great option either. He was so stressed about the possibility of getting kicked out of the program that for a second I really thought that he might kill himself when the day came. He *was* that program. He lived it, breathed it, and very honestly I thought he might die without it. He'd told me of his plan to go to the gun range for target practice and to kill himself if he got dropped. He always said he was joking, but his eyes and demeanor were always a little too dark for me to completely believe him. And so I can't help but try to control him. I can't let him keep spiraling out of control.

He's trying now, that much I can see. It may not always seem like it, but I have to remind myself that healing always comes in baby steps. He surprised me once by waking me up early on a Saturday morning, backpacks filled with snacks and coffees in his hands, and said he was taking me to a rodeo in Temecula. He even took me dancing downtown with all of his old SEAL friends. He showed me off proudly, like he used to, and only had a couple of drinks. He twirled me around the dance floor and whispered sexy words in my ear. Even when his friends stole him away for a few minutes for shots at the bar, I caught him looking at me and he gave me a boyish wink.

It was hell for a while but he seems to be trying. Maybe meeting my parents shocked him into realizing that his life wasn't over even though he wasn't going to be a SEAL anymore.

Last night, wanting to do something special for him to show my appreciation, I asked for his deepest, darkest fantasy. I knew he had at least one secret that he kept locked away. He said he'd never told anyone, not even his past girlfriends. I thought, *If he can trust me enough to tell me that one fantasy, even if I just listen to him tell me what it is, he can see that I'm all-in and we can finally move forward.* So, I asked. Instead of being excited, he looked at me with a look of complete terror. I urged him, promising that I would not judge him. He'd half-heartedly grinned at me and agreed to share it. As the whispered words started to spill from his trembling lips, my stomach clenched. Not only did I not want to do it, or even think that I *could* do it, but I just wanted to hold him. I think I was silent for over a minute, and then I think I just nodded. I couldn't show how scared I was by his confession or the sick feeling that was building in my stomach. All I had wanted was to finally make him happy and, even if his fantasy never became a reality, I thought I could make him happy by simply showing him that I accepted this part of him that he so clearly was afraid to share. But hearing the words coming from his lips made me terrified that I would never be the person for him.

Eleven

While Kara expected her and Liam's relationship to grow stronger with the revelation of this fantasy, it actually had the opposite effect. For all the raw vulnerability Liam had showed as he revealed it, he woke up the next morning even more isolated and angry.

That morning was Kara's birthday. She knew that Liam wasn't a big birthday celebrant, and she wasn't either, but he had enjoyed the way she had doted on him for his birthday. She had served him breakfast in bed, baked him a birthday cake from scratch, and surprised him with a pair of tickets to the upcoming CMA Music Festival. She had tried hard to make him happy, so Kara expected to wake up to something similarly thoughtful from Liam on her birthday. Instead, she woke up to an empty apartment. He was nowhere to be found. He didn't have to work that day, so she assumed he had gone for groceries or to the gym. She had ensured that there were eggs, bacon, and ready-made biscuits in the fridge last night in hopes that he would bring her breakfast in bed, but Kara just figured he hadn't seen them.

She let herself wake up slowly. She felt lighter and more solid than she had in a long time after having had such an open and honest conversation with Liam. It never crossed her mind that he might be avoiding her because of it. She stayed in bed, annoyed, waiting to hear Liam's key in the lock. When he still hadn't returned two hours later, her hunger got the best of her and she finally brought herself into the kitchen. Disgruntled, she cooked her own birthday breakfast, complete with freshly brewed coffee and buttered cinnamon-swirl toast. She ate it alone, sitting on the balcony with *Friends* playing on her laptop. *Ironic, isn't it,* she thought to herself as the *Friends* theme song played. *These are going to be my friends today.* Michael and Franceen were at a conference in Las Vegas, her other friends were swamped with work, and she couldn't find her boyfriend.

Time ticked by. The clock in the top right corner of her Macbook started taunting her. With each inevitable glance, the time showed that another 10, 20, or 40 minutes had gone by with no text or phone call from Liam. Eventually, she shut her screen and pulled on her running shoes.

"I've got to get out of here," she muttered. *If I see another text message from someone asking what Liam did for my birthday, I'm going to scream, or maybe cry. It's after 6pm now and I haven't even heard from my boyfriend. How embarrassing is that?* she thought to herself.

She ran for two hours. She weaved through every street in her neighborhood. She ran along Sunset Cliffs Boulevard to Saratoga Avenue, then back along Bacon Street to Newport Avenue where she jumped onto the beach and ran until she couldn't move her legs anymore. The sun had set, the partygoers had started coming out in their evening outfits, and she could barely move her legs enough to get home. It had worked, though. She felt less stressed and less hurt by Liam. Running always made her feel better. Still, the closer she got to home, the more hope she had. Glimpses of a candlelit dinner flashed through her mind before she could shove them out. She knew better than to get her hopes up with Liam anymore, regardless of what had happened the night before. Still, some small part of her waited in expectation of something fabulous and heart-felt, something she could brag about to her friends.

She entered the apartment, equally excited at the prospect of a surprise celebration and full of fear that Liam would let her down again. She was met with silence. Everything was exactly as she had left it. Liam hadn't been home. She fought back tears. It was 11:30pm when Liam finally stumbled in. In her bed with the door shut, Kara wiped angrily at her eyes. She couldn't decide whether to be hurt and angry, or entirely numb. She knew better than to expect anything from him now. She heard the swish of his coat coming off followed by a bang which meant he either bumped into the chair or had aggressively thrown his jacket at it with his cellphone still in it. She heard more swishing, clanking, and the soft thud of shoes, jeans, a belt, and a shirt hitting the floor, getting closer to her door.

He opened the door. "Hey babe," he said before belching. "I'm so fucking tired. Move over."

She looked at him, her eyes wide in shock. She moved over to the far side of the bed against the window. She didn't take her eyes off of him, though. She didn't want to bring it up but she couldn't believe that he'd forgotten. She'd told him a few days ago and hinted that she was hoping for some time alone with him. It was also on Facebook.

He just curled up on his side, faced away from her, and closed his eyes. Kara felt speechless. *He really hasn't remembered. Or, worse, he doesn't care.*

"Hey, babe," she said, tentatively. "Did you remember that it's my birthday?" she asked.

She heard a groan, but Liam made no move to roll over. "Of course I did," he said.

"I thought I'd ask because you haven't said anything…" she let her voice trail off.

"Well, I just don't think a birthday is a big deal. It's pretty selfish to expect me to drop everything to celebrate something you didn't actually do anything to deserve," he said evenly. "If anything, this is a day for me to celebrate with your parents, not you."

She felt angry now. Hurt and *very* angry. He wasn't like this towards other people and he had talked about doing fun activities for her birthday until recently. She was too shocked to think of a smart retort, and all she could muster was a small, "What?"

"Come on. It's not always about you, princess, you know," he said, his tone icier now.

"Well, if it's about my parents and not me, did you get them a present?" she asked, knowing the answer.

"Nope," he said easily, allowing himself to sink deeper into his pillow.

Kara wasn't finished. She couldn't let it go, even though she knew she wouldn't get through to him tonight. "Well, aren't you going to say anything?" she asked, a hopeful undercurrent to her otherwise edgy tone.

"Fine. Happy fucking birthday, baby," he said, looking at her without any warmth in his eyes. He let his left arm lazily pat her on the hip before turning his head away. His breathing slowed shortly after, indicating that he'd passed out.

Kara lay awake for a few more hours, just staring at the ceiling, wishing he would wrap his arms around her, too exhausted from holding onto hope to wake him up, cause a scene, or even tell him that she was upset. She just wanted to be comforted by him. She wanted him to live up to her hopeful expectations and go back to being the man that she'd fallen in love with from the moment he'd smiled at her through the crowd at Blake's Tavern.

Liam

My gut wrenches every time I think about what I'd told her. I said those words. They mean something out in the open. What I want... no, what I *need*... from her isn't something that most men want. It might not even be something that any *man* wants. We had sat in front of her laptop until the early hours of the morning and we'd looked at blogs and forums that detailed this kind of... desire. It makes her nervous, I can tell. She tried hard to mask her concerns, but she's always been a bad liar. It probably disgusts her. Yes, she pretends to accept it, but she's definitely not into it. She's just being nice because she cares about me. I know her well enough to know that. But who can blame her for being turned off? It's wrong. I'm supposed to be the man in our relationship. I'm supposed to be normal.

All the forums we read put a positive light on it. I read comments posted by various military and other tough guys that had said it was relatively normal for a guy with my kind of male-centric line of work. Since anything not considered highly masculine is shunned at work, the people writing in the forums said that I needed to see, or feel, it elsewhere. "Everyone needs balance," they said. I want to believe them. I just don't. She doesn't either. It's abundantly clear in the way she looks at me before she undresses me now. In a way, she's self-conscious. It's almost like she doesn't trust me as much anymore. She always looks deep into my eyes, as though she's searching for something. I feel bad for causing that, but a part of me finally feels free.

Now that she knows this secret, I feel like I can really enjoy myself. Before, I could stroke her bare thighs, her firm ass, her slender back, and nothing would happen. She could kiss my lips, my neck… anywhere, but nothing would happen. I just couldn't get there. I feel free now that she knows, though, and can finally do my thing. I feel good again. More importantly, I feel *seen*. There's only one problem though. I'm not hiding my secret very well anymore. I gave her an inch and told her my secret, and now the rest of the walls I've built want to come crumbling down. I talk a lot about her clothes and admire her makeup. Sometimes, while she's asleep, I dress up and, even though I try to put things back exactly where I got them, I don't always get it right. Plus, sometimes when I put her clothes back, they're a little stretched out. For some reason though, she hasn't questioned me about it. She's either going to be really confused by all of these little details or she's going to fit all the puzzle pieces together, which would probably make her hate me. I wish I could keep hiding it from her so that that doesn't happen, but I just *can't* anymore.

I knew that day was her birthday and I knew that she had been counting on me – it was her birthday after all – but I just couldn't make myself care. I was too stressed out about her putting all of the pieces together and figuring out what's been going on with me. When she tried to make me feel guilty for ignoring her all day, I actually hadn't cared one little bit. I actually kind of wanted to hurt her. It was such a miniscule thing compared to what I'm going through right now. There is something fucked up going on inside of me and I just couldn't pretend to care about anything else, let alone a *birthday*.

Kara

My birthday was a big letdown. It had hurt. I could barely admit it to myself, but it's almost exactly what I had expected. I'd expected him to forget or to not take the time to do anything. He's going through a lot and it can be hard to focus on other people when your life is crumbling around you. I just hadn't expected him to not care. I'd set him up for failure though. I mean, I'm at least *partially* to blame. I hadn't told him that I wanted him to do something for my birthday. I'd told him that I didn't expect much from him because I knew his finances were a mess and that he was in emotional turmoil. But, I'd still expected to be doted on for my birthday. Even though he had a lot going on emotionally, I still expected him to make me feel special for this one day. I knew that his life was crashing down around him. I knew that he wouldn't have been in the frame of mind to focus on me. It was only my birthday. I don't normally even care about birthdays. But, because I hadn't felt like I was holding much of Liam's focus lately, I'd created a fantasy that I knew, deep down, would fail. And then I felt almost justified in my anger at him. He's in a bad place though. Looking back, I knew that it wasn't the time to start fights over something as insignificant, in the grand scheme of things, as a birthday. It's been a couple of days since it happened so I've gotten a little space, and now I feel a little bit guilty. I'm still angry that he didn't care, and I feel entitled to that anger, but I feel guilty for setting him up to fail. I don't think I was fair to do that. That's not who I want to be, and that's not the kind of partner he needs or deserves. I realize that now, especially after what happened tonight.

Tonight, we went to an Alcoholics Anonymous meeting. It's a mandatory part of Liam's punishment for getting dropped from the SEAL training program for an alcohol-related episode. He has to go to eight sessions and get a piece of paper signed each time by the group leader, and it was strongly recommended that he speak. Tonight was his first meeting and I could see that he was really nervous, so I went with him in support. He seemed immensely grateful when I'd offered. The meeting was long and emotional. We heard story after story of intense alcohol addictions that had lead to ruined families, ruined relationships, loss of careers, serious health issues, and countless poor decisions that often put both the person's life, and the lives of others, in danger. Liam whispered to me that he didn't feel like he belonged there. He'd said he felt like his story would be making a mockery of their very serious problems. But, I'd held his hand and he'd shared. The group was warm and receptive. Then the meeting finished, Liam got his piece of paper signed, and we started walking to our car. A gentleman who looked far older than his years had walked after us. In the group, he'd said that he was in his early 40s, but I would've guessed late 50s to early 60s from just looking at him.

"Excuse me!" he called out. "Liam?"

We stopped and turned to look at him. "Hey, I'm Roy. You did great today by sharing. It's the first step, so I just wanted to congratulate you."

Liam gave him a quick and awkward smile. "Thanks. It was… tough. I'm glad that I had my girl with me." And then, with his arm around me, he squeezed my shoulders.

Roy looked at me. "It was really nice of you to come. A lot of us ended up here after we didn't have anyone to support us anymore and that is really hard. I wish I had gotten help sooner, but I had to hit absolute rock bottom before I could. And when I did, I had no one to help me anymore. I had no choice but to help myself, which only made it more difficult to realize that I deserved to get better."

Then Roy turned to look at Liam. "The people who come to this meeting are really supportive. It's a great group. After every meeting, a group of us go to either a coffee shop or my apartment and we chat. It can be nice to spend time with people who understand what you're going through outside of meetings. I hope you'll think about coming with us sometime," he said.

Liam smiled awkwardly again. "Thanks, I will. That's really nice of you."

Roy smiled. "Before you go, I wanted to give you this. It's mine from when I started. I got it from someone else in the program who got it from someone before them. We've all made notes in the margins. I think it will really help you. It's brought peace to me, and to many people before me. I hope it brings it to you too." Then he handed Liam a well-loved bible.

Liam tried to refuse the gift politely, but Roy had insisted. Finally, Liam took it. We thanked Roy and then we continued walking to Liam's truck.

"That was nice of him," I said, motioning to the bible.

"Ya, it was." He paused for a moment.

"What is it?" I asked.

"It's just… this isn't me, Kara. I don't have problems like those guys do. It's different. I messed up once. I had one bad night. And then I have to go in there for eight sessions and pretend that I'm on their level? I feel like that's offensive to them, and it's not going to help me at all. An addiction to alcohol isn't my problem."

"I understand," I told him. "A lot of those people have had some really rough lives and have been fighting alcoholism for a long time. But…" I paused because I didn't know how to continue. "But, you did have that one night and, while people get drunk, that wasn't a normal drunk. Maybe you got drugged and maybe you didn't, but you were using it to cope with something and isn't that often how alcoholism starts? Maybe it's good that you're here and talking to these people."

Liam's face looked pained. I'd stung him. "Kara, I'm not an alcoholic. I'm going through something really big right now and, yes, maybe I do drink too much and I have made some bad choices, but I'm not an alcoholic. These meetings aren't going to solve the problems I have. It's something I need to deal with on my own, not with a series of steps and talking it out with people who really don't understand."

I didn't know what to say to that, so I just lifted my chin up and kissed him. Then, I got into the car and waited. Liam followed, pausing to look at the bible before carefully placing it in his glove box.

As we drove in silence, my hand on his, I swear I saw tears in his eyes at one point. I wish I knew what exactly is going on in his head. Then, just maybe, I could help.

Twelve

Amidst the lights, music, and shouts from the thousands of tailgate parties that lined the parking lot of the Charger's stadium, Kara and Liam held hands quietly while sitting in the bed of his Chevy. With his newly shaved head, his arm muscles pumped from a few tablets of testosterone, and a long morning at the gym, Liam's smile was big and easy from the shots of Jack Daniels he'd already had, and his kisses were sweet and genuine. As she traced his calloused hands mindlessly, they watched as rows upon rows of college co-eds played beer pong and corn hole, laughed, and enjoyed themselves.

"Do you want to take a walk and see who else is here?" Liam asked, leaning back and eying her somewhat mischievously. In his good moods, he loved to meet new people. He could always make fast friends with anyone, winning himself a free beer or hamburger. People always seemed to want to talk about sports or the military with him, and often shared their life stories. The way that he looked at Kara as he tugged gently at her jean skirt suggested he had something different in mind.

"Come on, baby, let's go," he said.

She'd had a few too many drinks, but Kara reveled in how sexy he was making her feel. The sun, the beer, and him tugging at the corners of her clothing had her ready for anything. She wanted to feel his hands all over her, rushed and heated, in some semi-quiet corner where they could steal a few personal minutes amongst the crowd where their focus was entirely on each other.

"Okay." Kara grinned at him as she hopped off the tailgate in her flip-flops.

"Where are you two kids off to?" called Michael, a knowing grin on his face.

Liam just winked at him and took her hand, pulling her close to his side. Leaning down, he whispered something that only the two of them could hear. As he pulled his lips away from her, she squeezed his hand and looked up at him. It was obvious to anyone watching that, at that moment, he was her entire world. She giggled as she pulled her lips up towards his face and mumbled something back.

"What about over there?" she said. She motioned to a cement pillar towards the edge of the stadium. "Seems like those tailgaters have all left to watch the game."

He grinned at her and grabbed her ass. "Better get movin' then, girl. Otherwise we ain't gonna make it there."

Her heart fluttered. In that moment, she felt like the sexiest, and luckiest, girl in the stadium. When they'd first met, she'd felt that way every day and she missed it. She giggled playfully and swatted at his hand as she led him towards the pillar.

A little while later, the two of them emerged laughing and tugging at their clothing, pulling it back into place. A security guard strolled along about a half-minute behind them, seemingly oblivious to their presence. He was humming enthusiastically along to an unrecognizable tune in his head, giving the fully enthralled couple a very clear heads up to his incoming presence.

Still giggling by the time they returned to Liam's tailgate site, Michael cocked his eyebrow at them. "Meet some funny new friends, did ya?" he asked with his eyebrow raised.

Liam roughly pulled Kara against him by the waist in a way that left no question as to where they had been. He grinned. "Who needs new friends when you've got this girl," he said, looking down at her with a mixture of pride and lust.

Kara's cheeks were flushed. She basked in his appraising eyes for a moment before turning to smile shyly at Michael. She just shrugged her shoulders and shook her head in explanation.

Michael chuckled deeply. "Glad you kids seem to be in a good place, finally," he said.

Kara often texted him whenever she and Liam were fighting, especially since Liam had gotten dropped from the program. It helped her to know that someone nearby still cared for her. He'd brought her a cupcake with "Happy Birthday" written in icing when he returned from his conference and, subsequently, held her in a warm and comforting embrace while she cried when she was reminded of how Liam had treated her on her birthday.

"Who wants a beer?" Liam asked, letting go of Kara to reach into the cooler.

"I'll take one," chimed a series of nearby voices. Kara and Michael also nodded. Liam tossed everyone a beer before cracking his open to take a long swig. He leaned against the tailgate, his hand on Kara's seated leg until he finished a few more Budweisers.

Kara shifted her legs over the bed of the truck and she let herself relax. She could see girls eyeing him as they passed by, and she felt proud to be the one he was holding onto. As their friends ate, danced to the music blaring from someone's nearby truck, and played round after round of corn hole, she felt truly content. She sighed.

"You getting bored, babe? Want to go watch the game?" he asked.

Kara laughed and looked at him with one eyebrow raised. "You know me so well," she said, jokingly. She knew very little about football and preferred tailgates to the actual game. "But, sure. We can go if you want to."

Liam looked at her and felt his heart sink. He didn't want to watch the game either, but he needed a distraction. He felt the beer and whiskey mixing in his system, waking up feelings he had hoped to drown for the day. Suddenly, standing next to her with his hand on her thigh, his chest tightened. He felt like much less of a man than he had about an hour earlier behind the cement pillar. Now, he felt like a fraud hiding behind Kara's sun-tanned legs and was positive that every person who walked by could see into his mind.

"Maybe in a few minutes. It's looking like there is still a pretty long line to get in," he said, trying to calm his mind.

"Sounds good to me," said Kara.

They let about 10 minutes go by. Liam's hand never left Kara's thigh. He tried tracing designs with his finger from her knee to well past the hem of her skirt, attempting to refocus some of the testosterone he had fueling him earlier. It didn't work. His mind kept reeling. "Babe, you wait here… I'm tired of standing here so I'm going to take a walk. I'll come back and get you to go to the game." He smiled in what he hoped was a reassuring way. His plan was to walk around until he could find someone to buy a little cocaine off of. A bump always helped his mood. Kara knew what he was going to find. She knew that he couldn't have drunk as much as he had without wanting to take something else as well. But she tried not to let it affect her mood.

As he walked away from Kara, a small blonde girl from the party next to theirs walked up to him. She was petite and only came up to a little above his elbow. She was clearly very confident in her looks given her tailgate attire – a tight miniskirt with a tank top that emphasized her oversized breasts. Liam had seen her eyeing him while he was standing with Kara and she hadn't looked away embarrassed when he caught her, like most girls did. Instead, she'd just smiled and mouthed "Hi" to him. Looking at her now, she wasn't his type at all. However, she oozed sex and her flirtatious attitude towards him made him feel more masculine. Seeing that she was interested in him, and knowing that his girlfriend was within eyesight, he felt like a stud. So, he abandoned his plan to find cocaine and settled in to chat with this girl who introduced herself as Mandy.

"How are you enjoying your day?" he asked her, casually flexing his chest.

"It's a lot better now," she replied, dragging her fingers lightly along his forearm.

"Is that so?" he asked.

"Ya," she said. "I thought you were never going to leave that girl's side. I thought you saw me trying to get your attention, but it took you so long to come over."

Liam didn't tell her that he hadn't been heading her way. Instead, he just said, "Well, she is my girlfriend, so I had to stay with her for a little while or else she would have been suspicious." Liam held Mandy's eyes. He wasn't about to cheat on Kara. He wasn't even attracted to this girl. But, he didn't want her to know that. It made him feel like a man's man to pretend that he could be a player. During BUD/S, when he felt his most masculine, people always expected him to flirt with girls and cheat on his girlfriend. That's part of what made them feel like *men* and part of what led them to be seen as *men* by the public. Even though he was out of the program and he didn't want to live up to that stereotype, he liked the attention Mandy was giving him. His eyes stayed on Mandy's, slightly hoping that Kara was watching, and he grinned his easy smile.

Kara was still sitting on the tailgate, empty beer in hand, and watching as Liam wandered over to the other girl. Michael sat down beside her and followed her gaze to the tiny blonde.

"Looks like he's back to being Liam again," Michael stated, handing her a fresh beer.

Kara shook her head at the beer. "Looks like I'm going to have to drive, again," she said.

"You should go over there," he said.

"No, it's fine. They're just talking," she said, trying to keep her voice casual and nonchalant.

"Kara, you must know that whatever he's saying to her isn't entirely innocent. Just look at what she's wearing and how she's looking at him," he said quietly so that only she could hear him. "He loves you and he isn't going to cheat, but it doesn't mean that he should be doing that."

She looked at Liam. His right hand held a beer while his left was hooked casually into the pocket of his jeans. His broad body was turned towards the girl as they both looked over their shoulders, laughing, to look directly at her. The girl had her hand on his forearm, where Kara liked to rest hers, and Liam had given a fleeting, daring look at Kara.

"Go over there," Michael told her, seeing Liam look at Kara. "You have to now."

Kara knew he was right. She knew by the way Liam had looked at her that he was testing her, daring her, to do something. She gathered her courage, put down her beer can, and walked over.

"Hi!" she said with a big smile. "I'm Kara, Liam's girlfriend." She extended her hand to the girl and looked down. Her five-foot-eight frame towered over the other girl, and Kara guessed she couldn't have been more than five feet tall.

"Hey, I'm Mandy," the girl said in her high-pitched, squeaky voice. "Liam's a real charmer, isn't he?" She glanced at Liam with a giggle before staring her piercing blue eyes directly at Kara's soft, grey-green ones.

"Yeah, I'm a really lucky girl," she said, fighting hard to not roll her eyes at Liam.

He grinned at her. "You sure are. Do you want to make me a really lucky guy? Mandy and I have come up with a pretty good plan."

"Have you?" she asked, a note of caution in her tone. She recognized the look in Liam's eye.

Liam and Mandy exchanged a smiling, secretive look. It was the look of conspirators. Kara already didn't like their idea.

"How about… a threesome with Mandy, here?" Liam asked, a joking grin on his face but a hint of defiance in his eyes. Kara was speechless. Liam looped his arm around Mandy's shoulders and continued. "She's pretty hot, isn't she?"

Mandy's eyes had the evil glint of someone who thought that they'd won something they shouldn't have.

"What the hell? No fucking way!" Kara responded, shocked. Liam just grinned at her and squeezed Mandy's shoulders. "No way, and quit being such an ass," she said.

Liam looked from Mandy to Kara. "Well, how about I just sleep with her then?" he suggested with one eyebrow slightly raised.

Kara noticed that his arm was still around Mandy's shoulders.

"Are you serious, Liam?" Kara asked as icily as she could. There were hot tears welling behind her eyes, but she refused to let them fall before she was out of sight of this other girl.

Liam laughed heartily but his eyes were cold as stone. "See, I told you she wouldn't go for it." Mandy laughed with him and Kara watched him wink at her. "Well, I guess I'm in trouble now, so I better go." Liam let go of Mandy's shoulders and started walking back towards his truck.

As soon as Kara's back was to Mandy, the tears started to flow from her eyes, heated and angry, and her chest so tight that she felt like she'd forgotten how to breath. She refrained from wiping them away so that Mandy wouldn't see her lifting her hands to her face and feel like she had won whatever competition that had been happening between them. By the time Kara got into Liam's truck, her face was stained with tears, mascara, and a little bit of snot. She had never felt less attractive or less wanted. Michael grabbed her hand before she could shut the door.

"What happened?" he asked her.

"L-Liam wants to have sex with that girl." Kara sniffed. "He asked us to have a threesome a-and then w-when I said 'n-no' he said he wanted to have sex with j-just her then," she cried, refusing to look Michael in the eye because she felt too embarrassed.

"Oh, Kara. That's really terrible," he said. He hugged her, squeezing his tall frame into the low-riding truck. He buried his face in her hair, breathing in deeply. She was so vulnerable, but she smelled so good that he couldn't help it. "I'm sorry. Liam can be an idiot when he drinks."

"I-I know. I wish he w-wouldn't drink so much. He makes me cry so much now. Why does he w-want to hurt me n-now? Doesn't he l-love me still?" she asked, sobbing still.

Michael hugged her tighter. "He does. He... Well, he's just a dumbass. He loves you though. He just makes stupid decisions." Michael felt bad sticking up for Liam, but he was his friend too. Michael didn't like how often he'd had Kara crying on his shoulder over something Liam had said or done, but he also knew how Liam talked about her when she wasn't around. While he *did* make some very stupid decisions and wasn't always nice to her, he did love her more than he loved himself – that much was clear to Michael.

"Thanks, Michael. I just wish it could be like it used to be, you know?" Kara sniffed into his chest.

He stroked her hair and just nodded. "I know. One day. Maybe one day it will be like that again," he said.

Franceen interrupted them. "What's going on?" she asked accusingly as she took in Michael's arms around Kara. "Liam says Kara's crying and he can't handle it."

Michael filled her in quickly and let go of Kara. Kara turned to look at Franceen.

"I'm so sorry. That's not nice at all." She paused. "But, I do feel like it has been coming. I mean, I've had to tell you something for a long time now."

Kara's heart squeezed even tighter in her chest as her heart prepared itself to take more offense. Franceen had convinced herself recently that Liam was in love with her. Many of their conversations now revolved around the various things Liam had said to her or that they had in common. Kara knew he hardly even liked her as a person, so she found it difficult to believe that he might have any sort of feelings for her, but she was also growing tired of defending their relationship and wasn't quite sure what to believe anymore.

"What?" Kara asked.

"Well, Liam has been waiting for me naked a few times over the last couple of weeks. You know how you gave me a spare key to your apartment? Well, sometimes I let myself in to wait for you after class or something and… well, I found him naked on your bed with a suggestively placed laptop."

Michael spoke first. "What? That doesn't seem likely. You're sure he's not just looking at porn?"

Franceen looked offended. "Excuse me? You don't think Liam could be interested in me? I'm just saying, given the circumstances today, it's important for Kara to know that she's not… satisfying… him properly," said Franceen.

Kara wiped her eyes. "Look, he really just likes being naked when he's home alone. He was probably watching porn, like Michael suggested," she said with a forced roll of her eyes. She didn't believe that Liam was interested in Franceen, but something about his being home, alone, and naked when she wasn't there made her feel uneasy.

"Where's Liam? I want to go home now and I'm his ride." Kara pushed past Franceen to go find him.

As she'd expected, he was beside the cooler with an angry look on his face. "Let's go. I'm driving us home right now," she said coldly.

"No, you're not. I'm not done here. Plus, that's my truck and I'm the only one that drives it," he replied as he cracked open another beer.

"I think you've had enough," she said, pointing to his beer. "And you owe me, now, for being such an asshole with that girl."

"Me?" he looked at her with hate in his eyes. "You were fucking embarrassing over there. Crying like a baby because I asked you to do something for me? Come on."

"That hurt me, Liam!" she exclaimed, surprised at his outburst. "How did you expect me to react?"

"I don't know, maybe with a little bit of class? I'm embarrassed to be dating you right now." He took a swig of his beer. "That other girl took it so well. What do you think she's saying about you right now?" He paused and looked at her evenly. "Honestly, it's no wonder I would rather sleep with her than you tonight."

Kara couldn't form any words because her eyes had welled so full with tears that any spoken words would surely unleash them down her face. Luckily for her, Michael came to her rescue.

"Hey guys, we're going to head out now. Franceen is going to drive some other people home first, so I'm going to catch a ride with you two, if that's okay?" He posed it as a question, but Kara knew he was going to come either way. She could smell his musky cologne and its presence made her feel protected.

Liam looked at him and seemed to assess whether he was being genuine or not. In the end, he gave in and agreed to leave. However, he refused to give his keys to either Michael or Kara and declared adamantly that he was fit to drive. Michael was extremely sensitive to drinking and driving and would rarely drive with more than one beer in his system, but both he and Kara were powerless against Liam when he set his inebriated mind to doing something. He was far stronger than the both of them combined, and significantly more dangerous on the road if he was in a rage. Rather than causing him to become angrier, they appeased him by getting into the car after each saying a quick and silent prayer. Kara sat in the front seat next to Liam while Michael sat in the back.

Liam refused to speak the entire way home. His body was tense – the muscles under his jaw clenched and quivered. Kara cried silently, the tears falling from her eyes as she looked out of the window. Michael slipped his hand between her body and the car door, hidden from Liam, and patted her arm comfortingly while chatting happily at Liam in an attempt to continue calming him.

Kara was grateful for having Michael in her life, someone who could help her through some of the more difficult parts of her and Liam's relationship. He was unfailingly kind to her and always understood how to handle Liam when he fell into a rage. *He's always got my back*, she thought comfortingly to herself as she felt the warmth of his hand on her shaking arm, *and he's always got Liam's too. He gets him. He knows he's not bad. He knows he's got problems.* Michael's constant support made her feel foolish for crying so hard and so often. She wasn't as alone as she felt. While Liam hadn't been the most considerate boyfriend lately, she didn't feel like she was being the best girlfriend she could be either. Lately, she'd cried and yelled more than she had tried to support Liam, and Michael never judged her for that either. With the comfort of Michael in the car, Kara tried to think objectively about the situation, remembering her and Liam's plans to go to Nashville and the things they had talked about creating in their future.

Liam doesn't deserve the image of him I've painted with all of these tears, Kara thought to herself. *If it hadn't been for his one fantasy, I would have written everything off as some pent-up testosterone from getting dropped from BUD/S, and that would have been easier to understand.*

Liam

These days, it's all about feeling like a man. I just wish I could tell her that. It isn't about her, it isn't about us, it isn't about other girls – it's about me. I wore things under my uniform to work the other day, for fuck's sake, and I loved every minute of it. I loved feeling *naughty* and I loved having a secret from the other guys. At the same time, I hated myself. I still do. I hate what I have to do to get turned on now. I hate that I *want* to be turned on with men around me all the time. I hate that I've got all these secrets now from my brothers, the men who I was ready to die for just a few weeks ago. I just want to get turned on by my girlfriend, the girl I still plan to marry. Everyone else gets to live like that, so why can't I?

In all honestly, I didn't want to have a threesome with that girl. I didn't even want to see her naked... I would have walked right by her if she hadn't been so forward, but sometimes it's nice to talk to other girls. It's easy. It's calming. It feels like what reality *should* be and it helps me feel grounded. Then, when she made it so blatantly clear that she wanted me, it made me feel like a man. I know what they say about SEALs. A real SEAL wouldn't turn down an offer from a girl dressed like that. I know none of my friends would have. At the same time, I also know that my friends were never in love with the girls they were dating. I'm not even sure that any of them have ever actually been in love with anyone but themselves. It's different for me that way. I *love* Kara. I love her so much that a part of me breaks every time I hurt her, and that's been a lot of broken pieces lately. She's the one person that I trust more than myself, and that is terrifying because I don't know what will happen to me when she finds out the kind of lie I've been living.

I can't hurt her again. Being in a committed relationship doesn't make me less of a man, even though it's not necessarily what people expect of me, and I know that. I mean, I have a *hot* girlfriend, a lot of my old military buddies told me over and over again how lucky I was, but, for some reason, I just don't *feel* so lucky all the time anymore. I embarrassed her again, probably offended her, and definitely hurt her. I know she doesn't feel like enough for me, especially with what I've revealed to her lately, but I can't help it. I don't know how to fix it because it's a little bit true. She isn't enough but, at the same time, she's more than I could ever want. The pain I'm causing her is written all over her face. She isn't nearly as confident as she used to be, around me or anyone else, but I don't know how to change that. She isn't enough for me anymore, but that has nothing to do with her. It's me. It's all fucking me. I wish she *was* enough. God, I know she *should* be enough. If a teenaged me had just thought about her smooth, tanned body and her long brown hair, her long lashes and her amazingly kissable lips, he would've had a hard on for days. The teenage version of me could only daydream about girls like her. Now that I have her, every fiber in my body wishes that she were enough for me because, now that she's not, I'm fucked. If she can't get me there, no girl can. I should probably just stop the charade. Fuck that little blonde bimbo. Fuck those porn magazines I bought. Fuck them all. None of it will ever be enough.

    I've clearly been struggling. I'm so mad at myself that I can't even think straight anymore. Kara's really noticed and, in spite of how badly I've made her feel lately, she has still been trying to help me. She's been sweet and warm and supportive. She's been my friend as well as my girlfriend. One night, all of her support finally got through to me and I'd opened up to her. I broke down, actually cried on her shoulder, and told her that I wanted to have long hair like hers. Between that and our big fight over the bimbo at the football game, Kara'd had enough reasons to suggest that I see a shrink. She'd said that she thought some therapy might help me sort out my feelings. I mean, what else was she supposed to do? I didn't really give her much of a choice with everything I'd said and done over the last little while. When I'd told her about my desire for long hair like hers, she could've just run away. She could've slapped me. She could've been openly disgusted. But she hadn't been. Instead, she'd hugged me close to her and didn't let go until I felt safe enough to let go. I love her so much for that. She hadn't judged me, she hadn't run away, she'd hugged me and proved that she loved me. For the first time ever, I didn't feel 100 percent alone. And the least I can do for her is to see this shrink. I'm just terrified of what she'll say. These psychologists, they don't know what it's like to be in BUD/S. They don't know how homophobic the program is. They don't know what the people will be like wherever I get sent to next. They don't know what my military friends say about transgender people. Honestly, I think I know of a few guys from base who would actually beat up the latter for kicks. It's not a normal culture. For them, it's all about being the big, burly, masculine, heterosexual man. These psychologists are so disconnected from my world, how could they possibly help me "find myself"? With what's going on in my mind, I'm not even sure I want to know who I am. I can guarantee that my Navy buddies won't want to know who I am outside of uniform. Whatever I find out, they won't want to hear about it and then I'll be right back where I started – in hiding.

Kara

Lately, I'm never the priority in Liam's life. It's been so long since I've felt like number one with him. Generally, it feels like he gives priority to every other girl on the planet. The casual grin that drew me in that night at Blake's Tavern is almost always directed at some new girl – the girl at the football game, the waitress at the Kava bar we frequent, his buddies' girlfriends' friends, my friends… anyone. He charms them the way he charmed me. I watch him slide his rough fingers along their soft skin, locking his eyes on theirs, listening to their stories and sharing seemingly personal tidbits with "only them." I watch how their faces change as they begin to feel like they're the center of the universe. He's got skills; I'll give him that. Somehow, he manages to win over these girls and it still works with me sitting next to him, his hand in mine. I'm embarrassed to admit how many girls have actually come up to me and said, "Your boyfriend is really into me. I just thought you should know."

"Sister," I want to say, "he ain't into anyone these days." But I never do. Usually, I just smile and giggle awkwardly because I don't know what else to do. He might actually be into them. He really does enjoy the attention and I'm not so sure how well I even know him anymore.

One time, a couple weeks ago, the waitress at our local Kava bar had come up to me and said that same familiar line.

"Kara? Liam is really into me. He hasn't stopped flirting with me." She'd grinned at me with a cocky and almost evil look in her eye. I'd felt so challenged and so inadequate at the same time. "I just thought you should know," she'd continued.

That time was different. That time, I'd wanted to stand up for myself. "Ya?" I'd said. "Well, he's coming home with me, so he can't be *that* into you." I'd shrugged my shoulders, trying to appear unbothered.

"He might be going home with you, but he'll be thinking about me," she'd replied. With that, she'd walked to the edge of the counter nearest the bathroom, wrote something on a napkin, and handed it to Liam as he came out. He'd looked at it, grinned at her, and shoved it in his pocket.

I wish he had thrown it back in her face, or at least left it on the counter when we left. I'd asked him why he hadn't and all he said was that I was being "immature" and that leaving it behind would have been "rude." He'd said, "Girl, I'm not going to hurt an innocent girl's feelings because you're insecure."

That was the end of the discussion. But what about my feelings? He makes me feel like I'm not enough for him. I've tried everything. I try to do what he says he needs. I try to be the person

I think he needs. I listen. I care. I try to show him how much I love him. But he still goes after every other girl we meet. Yes, he comes home with me, but I'm not even sure he's really *with me* anymore. I don't turn him on anymore. I mean, maybe he's into my outfits sometimes. And sometimes he seems to get excited by me. But, I'm starting to think that it's only the clothes I can wear that turn him on and all that does is leave me feeling ashamed and alone. But I don't know what else to do to get him back.

Since he told me about his dreams of having long hair like a woman, I've been doing a lot of thinking about what that means. If he's been having those thoughts this whole time... well, I get why he hasn't been himself. But what does it mean?

He asked me out one night. All he'd said was that he needed to tell me something and we needed to be alone. My mind was reeling – was he going to break up with me? Had he cheated on me? Did he want to cheat on me? There were endless possibilities, all of which ended with me being alone. I was so scared. He'd brought me to the corner of a small dive bar and we sat down right beside a live band. I waited for him to say something. As the words started falling off of his lips, the darkness of the black walls had encroached on us. The music had faded into the background. All I was able to focus on was what he had been saying. At that moment, his words had taken over my world. When he was finished, I hugged him. I hugged him until he let me go. Then, he'd just bowed his head and rested it on my lap right there in the bar. His well-muscled arms and back seemed smaller to me then. For someone whose appearance was generally more than intimidating, it saddened me how small he'd felt. All I'd wanted to do was protect him and I'd racked my brain for how to do that. Looking back on everything, I wonder why I wasn't more surprised. I don't remember even being shocked by what he'd told me that night. All that I was able to think about at the time was love and fear and the urge to protect him. I'd had this feeling that things weren't going to be the same for us ever again, but I hadn't been surprised. I wonder what that means.

Since then I'd spent a lot of time on the internet trying to find out how to help him. According to several online forums, it's not an uncommon thought, especially for those in careers that celebrated masculinity. Since they live so many of their days in such rough, male-centric roles and rough clothing, they crave softness. Long hair and lacey panties are the yin to their yang. This had eased my mind a little bit, but I didn't feel comfortable with that as the sole explanation. So, I'd suggested that Liam see a therapist and I promised to take him there myself. I'd searched long and hard, but I finally found one that seemed suitable. Her specialty was listed as "sexuality in the military." She seemed perfect and worked out of her home office, which was only a 10-minute walk away.

Liam was so nervous that he asked me to go with him to his appointment. As we walked to her house hand in hand, he'd made me promise that I would wait for him in the office until it was over. He told me it would comfort him to know that I was there for him. *He'd needed me.* I hadn't felt needed in a long time. Since his big revelation at the bar, all he'd wanted to do was lay with me on the couch and watch movies. I hadn't even been to class since he told me. We were both so behind in our lives, but neither of us could think about anything else. I'd hoped, with every fiber of my being, that this psychologist would help him and that we could go back to the way things were when we'd first met. I missed how we were in those days – fun, free, and so in love that the rest of the world barely mattered.

When we arrived at her office, we had been greeted by a tall, slender, very well-muscled woman in her late 50s who, judging by the photos framed on her wall, had an affinity for whiskey, guns, and men in uniform. I felt Liam relax next to me. This was as close to "at home" as he could feel in a psychologist's office. He'd gone into the private therapy room with her and, with a glimmer of his easy smile, he told me I didn't have to wait if I didn't want to. I'd smiled because I was hopeful that she really *would* be the one to fix us. He'd seemed ready to open up and I thought that was a good sign. But I'd decided to wait for him anyway.

As it turned out, she'd said exactly the things I'd hoped she'd say… "You're fine, Liam. That's natural. You're straight. You're a man. You'll be able to serve your country well and do your family proud."

As badly as I wanted those to be true, I was pretty sure they were exactly the wrong things for her to have said. On our walk home, Liam said that they hadn't even chatted about his sexuality or identity until the very end of their meeting. Instead, they'd discussed their mutual love of whiskey, guns, and the military. He never once brought up his childhood, he'd said. She'd told him that it wasn't relevant to his current issues, regardless of what had happened. Then, as the hour drew to a close, he finally asked her about how to get back to who he used to be.

In response, she'd led him back to the waiting room where I sat and simply said, "Well, you have a pretty sweet girlfriend out there. Do you love her?"

He answered, "Of course. I'm crazy about her."

"Do you want to marry her?" she'd asked.

"With all of my heart," he replied.

"Look at her objectively and tell me if you think she's attractive?" she'd asked.

"Fuck, yes," he replied. "I think she's gorgeous."

"Well then, there you go. You've got nothing to worry about. Give her a kiss right now and fuck her every chance you get. You're as straight as they come – don't let her forget it."

With that, she'd opened the door for us to leave. And he did just as she'd told him. He picked me up, kissed me, and carried me out of the house looking back at her just long enough to wink.

Now, I'm not a psychologist – I almost failed my Psych 100 class in undergrad – but I don't think her advice was accurate. I have less than no experience in this area, but it all seemed very unprofessional and far too easy. Liam seems so much happier since her assessment though, so what else can I do but believe her too?

Thirteen

Coming home from a long day of class, Kara walked in the door flanked by Michael and Franceen at around 10pm. Distracted, they were laughing about one of Kara's attempts to answer a question about one of Mark Antony's speeches. She hadn't done the readings for the day, so her answer wasn't even an educated guess.

"Man, it's dark in here!" Michael remarked. "Is Liam out?" After getting dropped from the SEALs, it was unusual for Liam to not be home by dinner.

"I guess?" said Kara. She dropped her bags and went to start making margaritas for the three of them while Franceen and Michael sat down on the couch and turned the TV on.

Franceen gasped. Kara turned to look. Liam sat in front of Franceen in the reading chair they had bought from IKEA. He was completely naked with a bottle of Jack Daniels in his lap and a shot glass in his hand. The bottle looked to be about two-thirds of the way empty and she knew he had just bought it yesterday. He was not even registering their presence.

"Liam?" Kara asked softly, not wanting to startle him. Something about his sitting exposed made him seem almost childlike. Though he was obviously quite drunk, there was something innocent and broken about him. Franceen and Michael just looked at Kara for guidance on what to do.

Liam didn't move or show any indication that he had heard her.

"Liam, baby?" she tried again.

He blinked, as if coming out of a trance. He'd heard her speak to him, but he hadn't really realized that she was there. His head was filled with voices yelling at him, cursing him, laughing at him – hers, his parents', his commanding officers', his friends', even his own. He felt that he deserved every harsh word that he heard flashing through his mind. The shouts weren't the most painful, though. There were whispers coming from an unidentified voice that he recognized as himself but its tone was different. It sounded happy, clear, and softer. And it congratulated him. It congratulated him on losing the battle against himself that he'd been struggling with for so long. It reminded him that he was now free to act on all of his repressed feelings.

"What's going on?" Kara's voice pierced through the fusion of voices, a little louder this time.

He blinked harder to clear his mind and looked at her. She was kneeling in front of him and had one hand on his thigh, giving it a comforting squeeze. In her eyes, there was concern mixed with something else – fear. He paused before answering.

"I'm... I found out what they're going to do with me today since I can't be in BUD/S anymore," he said, reverting his eyes back to his bottle but refraining from taking another swig.

Kara's stomach sank and a cold sweat erupted over every inch of her skin. "Oh. And...?" she asked, unable to help from clenching his thigh slightly.

"They're sending me to a ship in Virginia," he said, keeping his voice as emotionless as possible. He was trying hard not to feel his failure. "I leave in one week." He shifted his eyes to meet hers. "Baby, I'm not meant to be on a ship," he said, his tone suddenly broken and slightly shaky. "This isn't how my life, our life, was supposed to go," he said.

Kara felt her heart break for him, but also for her and for their relationship. Kara hugged him, gently at first but then she pulled him into her arms harder as he buried his face in her hair.

"This isn't how it's supposed to be…" Liam said, over and over again. Kara didn't think she had ever seen him this vulnerable. It broke her heart and petrified her at the same time. She hadn't had to be the rock in their relationship yet, and she wasn't feeling quite up to the task. Sure, he'd had his problems and she'd had to step up and take care of certain situations, but he was always the man in their relationship. Somehow, he could always fix everything. She'd trusted in that. This time, it didn't look like he could fix this problem and it scared her. She just patted his lightly freckled back and sat on his lap, hiding him from the room to give him some modesty until Michael and Franceen decided to quietly leave, but not before Michael gave Liam a sympathetic pat on the back and shot Kara an understanding look.

"It'll work out, baby. You can re-apply to the SEALs in a year and next time you're going to make it all the way through graduation," she murmured. "And you and me? We'll be fine. We have all the time in the world to be together later," she said assuredly, though there were tears in her eyes as she said it.

Liam

    I wasn't going to fail this time. All through Hell Week, all through BUD/S and SQT, I never let myself fail. Sure, I'd wanted to quit a bunch of times. The exhaustion, the cold, the sand, it all fucking got to me. But, I never actually quit. I never *really* wanted to quit and I sure as hell did not want to fuck up. I was going to be a badass. I was going to make a difference. I was going to go after the bad guys. One night, one stupid night, where I just let myself get too stuck in my head and tried to make it go away. That fucking voice in my head, that incessant female voice, made my dreams go away. I tried to drown her out but she came back too strong and made me mess everything up. I would have made a kick-ass SEAL. I would have died for my country. I would have taken bullets for my brothers. I would have fought until the day I died or until the day came that I couldn't fight anymore. In the end, though, I guess they're making the right choice. Sure, they probably invested a ton of money in my training and I really can fight and shoot with the best of them. But, if I can't even win the war in my own head, what kind of soldier could I actually have been?

    What scares me the most now is that I won't have training to keep *her* at bay. Those feelings, they're going to come to me now every day. When I'm bored as fuck on a ship, sweeping up or some shit like that, there's going to be nothing keeping that voice out of my mind. It's going be the end, really. I don't know what it'll lead to, but it's going to be something. I don't know exactly what *I* want, but I know that *she* wants to come out and now I have no way of keeping her in anymore. The SEALs, and the masculine badassery that comes with being on a team, is gone. Kara's going to be on the other side of the country and I won't be able to hide in my love for her anymore. It's just going to be me, alone, with more time to think about what my brain is telling me without any kind of decent distraction. That thought alone is more daunting than anything I encountered in SEAL training. There's nothing I want to do less.

There is always the option of going back to Hell Week again in a year. Kara told me that she'd stay with me and support me if I re-applied. That's huge – she's never wanted to be a military wife. She hates this life. But she said she'd do it for me because she loves me. And that's what she thought would make me happy. Really, it just made things stressful. I would love to re-apply, and I tell everyone that I will, but I know in my heart that I never will. I may want to be a SEAL, but I also know that it's probably not going to happen anymore. There's something fucked up in my head that's messing with me too much now. Whatever it is that that the voice wants me to do – to wear women's clothes, to have boobs, and sometimes to even fuck men – it ain't right. It isn't what I want. I want what Kara wants – a life together with her. I want a family. I want to hold her at night. I want to watch our kids grow up and be there when they learn to walk, talk, and throw a football around. But, I can't silence it. So when she acts all supportive and says that she'll stay with me no matter what... well, it fucking scares me. It's too much pressure. It's what I want, but still, it scares me and I can't help but feel like it isn't right. I was raised with the expectation that I'd have a wife and kids and a house with a yard and fence. And I want that. I want kids. But a part of me also wants to fuck men, even if I don't love them. A part of me doesn't want the responsibility of a family but wants to be able to explore what's going on inside of me without the obligation. How twisted is that? I just... I just need space from Kara so that I process all of this, but the second I get that space I know that those urges I have are going to be overwhelming so I'm terrified to leave her side. I don't want to face all of the urges I have alone. I'm afraid that if there is distance between Kara and I that she'll realize what a mess I am and she won't love me anymore.

Kara

Some part of me feels like this is the end of our relationship. It isn't logical, it isn't what I want to believe, but something in the deepest pit of my stomach says that this is the end. This is the last time that it's going to be like this – him and I. For better or for worse, I've never felt like this before. Prior to today, I've always believed that he would be by my side forever. It feels like we're on borrowed time now and that makes me panic. When he leaves, I feel like I'm going to lose him for good because I won't be able to physically hold onto him anymore.

Since he found out that he was leaving, our ability to have normal conversations has gone seriously downhill. We've never had difficulty talking. Since the day we met, we've always been able to get lost in each other's words and ideas. We've always had something to say to each other. Granted, sometimes this looks like a screaming fight down the middle of 5th Avenue with traffic honking at us from both sides. But, we always make up. Usually, we're really good at communicating. We talk, we debate, we share. We talk about our futures and our pasts. We could talk about absolutely nothing for hours. Or, we could sit comfortably in silence for hours. Now, with him going, we can't talk because we're both lost in our own sadness and fears, and we always end up sitting in awkward silence. Our few spoken sentences are abrupt and broken. He doesn't want to address the fact that he's leaving, but it's all that I can think about. All I want to talk about is him leaving and what that means for us. I need him to assure me that we'll be fine. I need him to tell me that he loves me enough that we'll stay together despite the distance. For some reason, the distance isn't even my biggest fear. I have a pit in the bottom of my stomach that tells me he is going to cheat on me. All of those days with him being distant, all of those times I've watched him flirt with other girls, all of those times I've seen girls' names who I don't know pop up on his phone… they've resulted in my heart being too pessimistic to believe that we can make it. I'm terrified that he is excited to have some space from me so that he can do whatever he wants. Between that fear and my idiotic heart, I did something stupid – I asked him for an open relationship.

Who does that? I don't want that. I don't want to sleep with or kiss or even see other people. I want him, and only him. I want to walk down the aisle with him and dance all my dances with him. But we were sitting silently in a booth at Denny's and it just popped out. For a brief moment, I'd felt in control again. Since then, though, it's been nothing but panic for me. I may not want to be with anyone else but he's made it pretty clear over the last few months that he may not be so against the idea. When I asked him, he looked mildly shocked but he'd just shrugged and said, "If that's what you want, babe."

Is that good or bad? Does his answer mean he trusts me well enough to not act on my request? Does it mean he knows me well enough to know *why* I said it? Or does it mean he can't wait to meet the girls he'll be living and working with, day in and day out, while exploring new parts of the world?

I don't know, but thinking about it makes me feel sick. I don't know why, but I can't tell him that I've changed my mind – not yet. It makes me feel weak. Instead, I tried to fight it a different way. I wanted to surprise him one day after he got back from the gym in such a way that he wouldn't have been able to stop thinking about me, no matter what the girls on the ship said or did. I decided to wear something sexy – his favorite lingerie – I wanted to paint my nails bright red, put on some lipstick, and give him a night that would make him realize he didn't need any other girl.

The only problem was that I couldn't find my lingerie. It wasn't anywhere in the apartment. I checked under the bed and in every drawer. It wasn't anywhere. I had no idea where it had gone, but I spent way too long looking for it. I wasn't sure why, it was just clothing, but nothing turned him on more than that specific outfit. Sometimes, without it, he couldn't even get turned on. I'd needed it. But, eventually, I'd given up and decided to paint my nails. All I had been wearing was a robe. My hair was done, but I had no makeup, no sexy outfit, nothing. That's when he'd walked in – sweaty, shirtless, and with his muscles pumped so big that his veins were popping out. He'd never looked sexier. My heart fell. I'd missed my chance to surprise him and remind him of how sexy I was.

"Hey babe," I called out.

He stood in the doorway and grinned at me. "What are ya doin', girl? Goin' out somewhere?"

"I just wanted to look good for you," I responded shyly. For some reason, it made me feel embarrassed to admit it out loud.

His grin widened. "Want some help? Looks like you're havin' trouble painting with your left hand."

Then, he helped me paint my nails. Strangely, it was the most connected we had been in months. He was his old self, my best friend, for the entire night. We talked and laughed together until the sun came up. Nothing physical happened, but it didn't need to. It was soothing and real. Somehow, I trust him more now. I'd mentioned this to Franceen and a few other friends and they all seemed to judge us. Apparently, it's weird for your boyfriend to paint your nails and then not have sex with you. Well, I don't know. Maybe that's true for others but not for us. For us, it just worked.

Fourteen

Liam

I'm holed up in some cheap trucker motel parking lot, trying to catch a little shuteye before a guard taps on my window and motions for me to move along. I'm not thinking about my failure to become a real SEAL. I'm not thinking about the regret that eats away at me at every hour of every day for letting alcohol ruin my career. I'm not even thinking about what it means that I still want long hair and that I still love wearing Kara's panties. Right now, alone in my truck, I'm thinking about love. My mother always taught me that love conquers all, but I don't believe her anymore. The love I have with Kara, it's more real than anything I've ever had in my life. It's more real than I am. But our situation, my past and present, is conquering us. She'll never leave me and I could never leave her, but neither of us is the same as when we fell in love. We're shadows of our previous selves – scared, angry, distrusting versions of the old us – and it's my fault. I know that and she knows that, but neither of us has ever said it out loud.

When she suggested an open relationship it felt like a kick in the nuts. It made me realize that she might actually move on. More than that, that she *should* move on. Thank God she took it all back. She'd called me a few days after I left and sheepishly asked if I could forget that she'd said anything about an open relationship. She'd asked to just be us again. "Of course," I'd told her. She couldn't possibly have known how terrified I was for those two days. I know she couldn't even have guessed. I know how terrified she must have been though, so I told her that I'd never considered it anyway. I love her too much to put her through all of this with me, but I can't let her go either. I'm too fucking selfish, I guess. My dreams of being a SEAL and kicking ass around the world are being replaced by my worst nightmare of being trapped on a ship and doing nothing of any real value. My gun is going to be replaced by a mop, my abs by a beer gut, and my beautiful live-in girlfriend with a bunch of camo-clad dudes and butch chicks that would rather play video games than workout. I'll always have my military watch though. Its thick black strap and wide face with more features than the top-of-the-line civilian digital watch is my last reminder of the kind of man I could have become. It's never going to leave my wrist. It's a part of me now. It's a constant reminder of all that I've accomplished and all that I've endured while also reminding me that it all can go away with one fuck up.

Love doesn't conquer all. Love is powerful, sure, and love can inspire change. Sometimes, though, there are darker things that squeeze out any light in their path. That dark stuff, that's me right now. My urges are too dark to let anything good stay alive near me. My love for her, her love for me, my love for my country, it doesn't mean shit. Kara's going to be across the country, and I'm too fucking hard to love these days in the best of situations, let alone with almost 3,000 miles between us. I've let her down and I've let my country down. Still, I feel a strange sort of serenity that I've only ever felt after completing Hell Week. This is the last thing that I want but, for some reason, a tiny little part of me thinks it's exactly what I need to get sorted out. I feel like I might achieve something, finally. What the hell that could be, I'm scared to know.

Kara

I watched him drive his pick up away. I hate that low-riding, metallic-rimmed Chevy that is always filled with bottles upon bottles of dip spit – I'm usually embarrassed to be seen driving in it because I don't want to be mistaken for a drug dealer's wife – but I'm going to miss it. There are a lot of memories, some that I wouldn't mind forgetting, but so many good ones are etched into my brain that I'm actually sad that I won't be able to ride in it every day. I'm a little afraid that this is the end of our time to make memories in it. From him teaching me to drive a stick shift, to cruising the Pacific Coast Highway with some country tunes blaring through the radio, to sweaty sex after a long run in Balboa Park, there are too many memories that now bring tears to my eyes and cloud my vision of him driving away. We've had our low moments, and that truck has definitely seen those too, but that just makes it a part of us. Without it parked outside my bedroom window every morning with those god-awful rims shining in the morning sunlight, and that unforgiving suspension waiting to bruise my tailbone, it's going to be a constant reminder that somebody else could be learning to hate that truck just as much as I do. Or, worse yet, learning to love it just as much as he does.

I feel terrible for him, I really do. I've hated having to watch his dreams get crushed over the actions of just one night. But I also really feel bad for myself and for us because *our* dreams could be permanently crushed over the actions of one night. Since getting dropped from the program, he's been different. His alcohol and drug use has skyrocketed. I mean, when was the last time we actually went for a drive while he was completely sober? It's clear that something has been happening in his head that makes him dream of having long hair like a woman, and that is what has probably contributed to the drug use. Honestly, I don't think that we've had sex with him being entirely sober since he was dropped from BUD/S. So, I feel for us too. Those dreams of a place in the country with a white picket fence, a stable for my horses, and plenty of acres for him to hunt on, those are fading away. He's not going to become the man I fell in love with until he's a SEAL again. Often, ships deploy for over a year at a time – that isn't the life I signed up for. I don't want to be alone in our future home. He swore to me that nothing was going to change between us and when I looked up into his clear, sober green eyes before he left, I really wanted to believe him. But, for some reason, I just couldn't.

Fifteen

Liam

Kara's face lit up my screen five times in two minutes last night. It's been two weeks since I left her in San Diego, and I don't think either of us is handling the distance very well. She calls me a lot just to talk or to tell me that she misses me, but I just don't feel like picking up a lot of the time. At first, I felt guilty for ignoring her calls, but I did it again last night and I didn't feel so bad. I was sitting outside with my buddy and I just wanted to drink and smoke with him. I didn't want to think about anything, or anyone, else. After call number five, though, my buddy and I just sat there and watched her face light up my screen every few seconds. He made a drinking game of it. What had started as a game that called for a shot every time she called quickly became a game where we took a shot every three calls so we didn't end up in the emergency room. We got wasted. It was actually kind of funny, but it also made me really angry. After about 20 calls, I started to wonder, *why can't she just let go for a little bit.* She keeps trying to control me, to pull me back to her. She says that she feels like I'm drifting away and I think that she thinks talking to her will help fix that. I tell her that it won't, I tell her I'm just going through a rough patch with work, but she doesn't believe me. And she's right. I did tell her some confusing information before I left San Diego that probably suggested that my problems are not entirely work-related. I wish she would just take my word for it though. I need the space and freedom to think through all these thoughts and feelings for myself. I can't deal with her being needy and I can't comfort her fears right now. Talking to her just makes the weight on my chest heavier and heavier – and I'm starting to resent her for that.

It's not that I'm mad at her, or that I don't miss her, there's just something that flares up in me whenever I see her face flash onto my cellphone's screen. I get stressed out. Really stressed out. I already know the conversation that we're going to have when I finally do pick up and I don't want to have it. It'll go something like this:

"Hey babe, how's it going," I'll say.

"Why haven't you been answering my calls?" she'll say, with a slight waver in her voice.

"I've just been busy."

"With going out?"

"Well, yah. There isn't much else to do around here," I'll tell her.

"With other girls?"

"Kara, come on. You know it's not like that."

"So there were girls! Were they prettier than me?" she'll ask nervously.

"I'm not going out to meet other girls. I love you. I just like to go out and have some fun. You sound like you need to do the same."

Then she'll get upset and offended.

"Kara. I love you. We are in a committed relationship," I'll tell her. I'll want to add, *Get that through your thick skull.* But, I won't.

She never fully believes that I'm not cheating on her, but once we have that conversation she'll drop the issue and we'll talk about something else for a while before we hang up. I could probably pick up her calls more often so that she doesn't feel threatened, but I actually don't mind that she thinks that I could be cheating on her with another girl. It makes me feel normal. That's terrible, I know, but it's a hell of a lot easier than explaining to her why I'm actually avoiding her. I can't imagine telling her the truth. How can I say, *Yes, I do think about being with other people – men.* How can I tell her that sometimes I look at the way that girls flirt with my buddies at the bar and think about what it would be like to copy them and flirt with my own guy. This life on a ship has me going fucking crazy. I just need some space to figure this shit out.

I do miss her, though. I miss the way she would lay her head on my chest and how it would make me feel like her protector. I miss the way she would wait for me in the stairwell to throw her arms around me when I came home from work. I even miss the way she would pop the pimples on my back without asking – I always thought I'd hated that. It will be great to see her in person in a few days and show her off to all my friends and family. It will be easier to feel okay about us when I have her by my side. All of this space is probably good for me, but it's also what makes me struggle. When she's beside me, I think I'll be able to forget about all of these worries, at least for a little while. Seeing her look at me like a man, her man, will make me feel more masculine than I have in a long time. Even if this can only distract my mind for a little while, I can use that time to be the man that she deserves. I can be the partner that she deserves. And I can set all of her worries at ease. It may make me feel good sometimes to have her worry about me cheating like she would for other guys, but I don't want to be responsible for her sadness or stress. That's not what a real man does either. And so, to try to make things better for us, I have the best date planned for our anniversary. It's going to make her forget about all of her fears and have her falling in love with me all over again. I'll be back in my hometown with my family, friends, and my girl who will all look at me like I'm the man I wish I was. If that doesn't make me forget all this shit about other men and dresses and Kara's lingerie, then I don't know what will.

UNSEALED

<u>Kara</u>

I got the sweetest surprise today in the mail. Liam sent me a card from his port in Norfolk, Virginia that said:

I love you because...
You're sweet, kind, and honest.
You're so easy to love and you believe in me.
You make me laugh all the time, but you listen to me too.
And, most of all, you love us.

Inside, he wrote:

To my baby,

I picked this card for you because of the cover. Everything it says is you to a "T." You are amazing. You have never once doubted my abilities, have always believed in me, and have never failed to make me smile. The way you listen to me amazes me too – always wanting a new story from my day and then hanging on to every word. You never fail to make me feel special.

God Kara, I miss you so much. I can't wait until the time that we can be with each other all the time and for forever, wherever that time spent together takes place. There is so much I want to say on here but there isn't even close to enough space. Just know that I love you and I can't wait to hold you and kiss those lips. Love you!

Inside, he tucked a photo of us looking as happy as ever in front of the water complex at the horse show that we had gone to a few months earlier, along with his ticket stub from the event.

He really is special. He's one of a kind. After reading this card, I wonder why I get so nervous when I hear the voices of other girls in the background of his phone calls and why I get so manic and distrusting when he doesn't pick up. This is the Liam I fell in love with. This is who he really is – a romantic, amazing man who loves me and who sends surprise love notes to his long distance girlfriend. He loves talking to me, he loves being with me, and he can't wait to be with me in the future. I need to just trust in that. Sure, we've had our issues, but what couple doesn't? I don't know why I can't let all of that go. I'm lucky to have him. And I know that he knows he's lucky to have me. So why can't I just trust him again? Maybe I'm just worn out and insecure from too much fighting and not enough communication. I haven't been a priority of his in too long. I just don't feel wanted anymore.

    I guess all of these insecurities must have been building on each other because I snapped the other night. I'd called him 30 times. I can't even believe that I called him 30 times... in a row. I'd dreaded hearing that automated woman's voice start to recite his Tennessee area code, and yet I kept calling back. When he didn't pick up after the first call, I should have just let it go, like a normal person. I'd known that, but I couldn't stop. At first, I thought that I'd just wanted to hear that he was excited to see me. I'd wanted to hear him say that he not only remembered our anniversary, but that he was excited to celebrate it. I'd wanted to hear that he felt the same way I did – that two more nights apart was unbearable knowing that we'd see each other so soon. Then, after he'd ignored a few of my calls, I was offended that it was so easy for him to ignore me all the time and I'd become determined to tell him so. That isn't an excuse, though. I'm so embarrassed and angry at myself for acting the way I did. He could have been sleeping. He could have been out in a loud bar and just didn't hear his phone ring. He could have left his phone at home to charge. I wouldn't even let myself consider those possibilities though, which shows what kind of crazy girlfriend I've become. I was absolutely confident that he was ignoring me and that he had been avoiding me since he'd left San Diego. This isn't me. I don't know what's happened to me over the last few weeks and I don't know how to go back. I can feel myself spiraling out of control. Normally, I'd talk to Michael about my fears so that he could calm me down, but I'm too embarrassed of how I acted to talk to anyone. Even patient Michael, who knows how crazy Liam and I can drive each other, wouldn't understand why I'd called 30-fucking-times. That has to be my secret.

I need this trip to Nashville with Liam and his family. There is this dark fear burning a hole in my gut that says we'll never be who we used to be. I should take solace in the sweet and heartfelt words he wrote in the card, and I'm trying to do just that. I just can't shut out all of my fears though. I'm sure all of these doubts will fall away when he picks me up at the airport in DC and I can hold his hand and look into his eyes and see the old him. Once I can do that, I'll be fine.

Sixteen

Stepping onto the sidewalk outside of Dulles International Airport, Kara searched the curbside pick up area for Liam's truck. She couldn't see him, so she went to pull out her cell phone to call. As she did so, she saw Liam's truck rounding the bend, rims glinting in the sun. Stepping closer to the curb, she stood on her toes and waved. She hadn't needed to though because Liam had seen her the moment he'd rounded the corner. He stuck his hand out the window and pointed at her. "There's my baby," he yelled, though she couldn't hear him.

She flattened her form-fitting black, strapless dress before picking up her bags. More nervous than she cared to admit, she had tried to look her best. Since she'd last seen him in person, she'd become a regular at a yoga studio in Ocean Beach, which showed in her physique. She was the leanest and most flexible that she had ever been. She'd also spent many hours running on the beach, which had resulted in a perfected Californian tan and naturally highlighted hair. She'd waxed, threaded, and painted everything she could have before she'd left San Diego. There was nothing she hadn't done to look and feel her absolute best. While she had missed Liam more than anything, she hadn't missed his low-riding Chevy at all. *Distance doesn't always make the heart grow fonder,* she thought to herself with a little smile as she watched him drive up to the curb in front of her. When he stepped out of the truck and picked her up – bags and all – to kiss her while spinning her around, she forgot all about the bruised tailbone she'd have as soon as they drove over the first pothole.

Standing wrapped up in his arms, she buried her face in his neck and breathed in deeply. He smelled different than he used to – more musty than salty – though it comforted her to realize that he still used the same shower soap and cologne. Squeezing her tightly against him, he smelled the familiar scent of coconut in her hair as it billowed around his face in the hot breeze. He kissed her, holding her face in his big, rough hands. They had been standing together long enough that a security guard came over to tap their shoulders and hurry them along.

Kara giggled as she got into the car. "Just like old times, eh?"

Liam grinned at her as he tossed her luggage into the bed of his truck. "Remember when you missed your flight back home because we were making out for too long?" he asked.

Kara laughed. "Of course. We slept on the ground all night, eating takeout pizza and drinking the last of my beer. And then we got too wrapped up in our goodbyes at the airport and I missed my check-in time. It worked out well though, right? We got to do it all over again the next day," she said, squeezing his tattooed forearm.

"That was the best extended goodbye that a guy could ask for," he said. Holding her eyes for a moment, he gave her another kiss before putting his truck into gear.

Kara wrapped her arms around his right arm while he let his hand rest on her knee. She put her head on his shoulder and sighed contentedly.

"It's good to have you here, baby. I've really been looking forward to spending some time with you," he said softly, "and I can't wait for my family to meet you."

"I can't wait to meet them," she replied, smiling up at him.

After stopping for a quick dinner, they started on their long drive. Liam had finished his last shift early that afternoon, which had started in the first hours of the morning. There had been no time for him to take a nap and he had packed up and left immediately to meet Kara at the airport. Once at Dulles, he'd had to circle for an hour because her flight had been delayed. Before the drive to Nashville had even started, Liam was exhausted.

"Do you want me to drive part of the way? If you coach me for a few minutes, I might be able to manage it," Kara offered.

Liam just laughed and shook his head. "It's okay, babe. Remember what happened last time you drove this truck? We don't need to repeat that. It was in better condition then too. It hasn't had any maintenance done on it in a while, so who knows what will happen to it with you behind the wheel?" he said, winking at her.

Kara shrugged her shoulders. "Alright. Don't say I didn't offer," she said, though she was clearly relieved.

The sun set behind the Appalachian Mountains long before they were even halfway to their destination. Kara had stayed up all night the night before to try on different outfits that she could wear to impress both him and his family, so she was far more tired than she had hoped to be. She had little skill in warding off drowsiness, so she was worried about her ability to keep Liam alert and engaged throughout the drive. She had always chosen sleep over the extra one or two percent that another hour or two of studying might have earned her on an exam. Liam, on the other hand, was far more conditioned for sleepless nights with his military training, and was used to being alert when every fiber of his body wanted to rest. However, despite her inexperience, Kara tried hard to stay awake to keep Liam entertained throughout their drive. She updated him on how all of their friends in San Diego were doing, she talked about the progress she was making on her thesis, shared her new-found addiction to yoga, and bragged about all the time she'd spent at the Muay Thai gym practicing for their next mock fight. He laughed, enjoying her company and reminiscing on the life he had enjoyed before being relegated to the ship.

As the night grew darker, their conversation slowed until they were driving in silence, each focusing solely on keeping their eyelids open. Kara's head fell to her chest more than once, at which point she would always jerk awake with a guilty look and frantic apology. Liam would just smile at her and tell her to close her eyes and rest. She adamantly refused.

"Babe, if you're awake, I'm awake. I know you want to get home to see your folks and you don't want to spend any of your vacation in some crappy motel, and I don't blame you," she murmured. Before she knew it, though, she felt the warm sun on her eyelids and heard a soft, deep voice singing close to her ear. She opened her eyes.

When he heard her stirring, Liam sang, "Good morning, beautiful…" along with the rest of the chorus from the romantic Steve Holy tune in his soft, gravely twang. As she opened her eyes, he looked at her with a loving grin, his eyes slightly amused.

"Oh my god! Did I fall asleep on you? I'm so sorry, babe. I really wanted to stay awake with you!" she said groggily, trying to straighten herself in her seat. She felt guilty that she had slept on his shoulder while he'd driven.

He chuckled. "It's no problem, sweetie. You looked exhausted and were snoring so peacefully. I just couldn't bring myself wake you. You only slept for about an hour, anyway," he said, reassuringly.

Kara looked at the clock. It said 6:07am. She knew that she'd slept longer than an hour. The last time she remembered looking at the clock was not much later than 3am. Since the stereo was turned off, she also realized that he had turned it off to let her sleep peacefully. Her heart swelled at his consideration.

She looked up at him and smiled. "Thank you, sweetie. Could you keep singing though, please? That was the best way to wake up. I could listen to you sing all day."

His cheeks flushed, which was a rare occurrence. "Uh, babe, I don't know. I was just goofing around. I can't sing."

"Didn't you used to sing in bars when you were younger?" Kara asked. "Trust me, you can sing. I want to hear the rest of the song, anyway," she said, smiling at him.

Liam's cheeks only grew redder. "Just a few times. And I told you that in passing when we first started going out. How did you even remember that, girl?" He looked at her in surprise, but she just looked back at him, pleading with her eyes. Exasperated, Liam sighed. "Fine. I'll keep singing, but just for you, though. And can we have the song playing in the background?" he asked, his voice betraying his insecurity.

Kara smiled. For someone so naturally confident and outgoing, it was rare for her to see this raw, shy side of him.

She connected her iPhone to the car stereo and played Steve Holy's "Good Morning, Beautiful." She kept it quiet, though, so she could hear Liam's voice clearly as he serenaded her for three minutes and 30 seconds – the entire length of the song – as they drove into the sunrise over the Tennessee state line. Both had forgotten the tension and uncertainties of the past few weeks and were focused on simply enjoying each other's presence. With traffic, accidents, and pit stops, the trip had taken them almost 15 hours instead of the estimated 10, but Kara and Liam enjoyed every minute of it.

Seventeen

Kara

Within minutes of being in Liam's house, I'd felt at home. Both of his parents had greeted us, hugging their son tightly before taking me in their arms in a similar fashion. Stepping into their home, I was nervous. They hadn't seen their son in over a year and I was worried that they'd see me as intruding on their family time. They hadn't, though. Instead, they'd made me feel as welcome in their home as a family member.

After a quick breakfast, his parents had gone off to work while we'd crawled up the stairs to his bedroom to sleep. I curled up in Liam's arms and felt myself relax. It felt right to be there. He seems like he's in a good place, especially after his family clamored to hug him and hold him. I'd watched him grow taller and puff his chest out. He was so proud to receive all of that affection. They all looked up to him. It made me think about the way I interact with my own family. We're very close, so I know what pride looks like and I know what love looks like, but I've never seen something like this. He looks older when he's around his family. He doesn't act like a child of his parents. He acts like a man. He hugged his mother like he wanted to take care of her. He shook his father's hand more gently than he does with the guys his age. He's like a parent himself. Being here, surrounded by admiration and duty, he is back to the man that met my eyes at the bar a year ago. He is the man I craved when he fell into dismal moods. He is the man I know would have made a great SEAL. Maybe the psychologist was right, maybe it was just the program getting to him. Maybe he was just going through a rough patch in Norfolk because he'd had to adjust to life as a lowly Seaman after being a top SEAL candidate. Maybe, we will be okay.

Liam

I love how they look at me. I feel like a man. I also hate it. I feel like a fraud. It confuses me, but at the same time it liberates me. I can't be anyone else. They love this version of me. What about that voice in my head? *She* gets muffled here. Her protests get drowned out by all of their questions about the Navy, about BUD/S, about Kara and our future. It feels liberating to escape her voice for a while. But then she screams at night. Having Kara curled up against me helps. Her soft, rhythmic breathing, the way that she lets her hand rest on my chest, her head laying on my bicep, it's soothing. The way that she always has her leg intertwined with mine makes me feel like, subconsciously, she's decided to never let me go. That voice in my head just doesn't have the same kind of power that she did on the ship. For now, Kara can beat her. For now, my family can help mute her. Maybe, with some time spent at home, I can silence her completely. Maybe all I needed to do was to reset because, right now, this is all I want for forever. All that stuff her voice talks about, all those things she says I should be, I don't want them. I don't want to live that way. I want this. I want love and I want family. I don't want *her*.

Eighteen

The following few days were filled with sleeping in, Southern food, bonfires, and two-stepping in every live music venue on Broadway. Kara and Liam bought cowboy boots at a touristy shop on Broadway Street that had a two-for-one deal, and they didn't take them off for the entire week. Meals were spent either with family or alone. In the evening, they often partied with his friends from home or explored various musical venues on their own. It was relaxing, fun, and exactly the kind of vacation that reminded couples of why they had fallen in love in the first place.

Halfway through the week, Liam's cousin Billy woke them up at 9am, which was early considering they were on vacation, by throwing two towels at them.

"We're goin' cabrewin', y'all! Git up!" Billy yelled excitedly. "It's all kinds of sunny out. I'll get the cooler packed. Y'all just need to get your lazy asses out of bed!" Billy called as he tried to wake them up. After Billy ran downstairs, Kara and Liam could hear the clanking of beers going into a cooler. The clanking was hard and fast, so Kara made a mental note to not be the first to open one.

"What's cabrewin', babe?" she asked Liam, rolling onto her side to look at him. She could tell he was fighting exhaustion too – they had only gotten home a handful of hours ago from a night out on Broadway Street.

Liam yawned. "It's the best part of the South, darlin'. Usually, the water is too high at this time to go, but it's low this year. I can't wait for you to experience it and see why I love this place so much." His tiredness appeared to be dissipating because a new look of fresh excitement, not unlike a child on Christmas Day, started to awaken in his eyes. "There ain't nothin' better on a hot Tennessee day. You'll see," said Liam with a grin, in an exaggerated Southern drawl. Kara noticed that his drawl became just a little bit thicker with every day they spent in the South.

"What do you do? Is it a lot of movement? That last bar really did me in last night," she groaned, burying her face in his armpit. "I don't think I'll be drinking anymore shots of Fireball on this trip."

Liam rubbed her back. His eyes were shining with laughter and he had a big grin spread across his face. "My poor baby. You gave the bar your all, that's for sure. Damn near drank 'em dry, I'd say!"

Liam rolled her back over and lifted her chin so that he could kiss her. "You won't have to move much on the river. Billy and I will do the paddling. Basically, cabrewin' is canoeing with a cooler of beer. It's beautiful. I'll get you some Advil and then you can just sit back and enjoy the scenery."

Liam explained to Kara that, winding through over 100 miles of hills and vast expanses of farmland in the Middle of Tennessee, the Harpeth River is often populated with canoes and kayakers during spring and summer months, many of which carry coolers of canned beer and snacks with them. Rope swings are a popular sight and many stop their boats nearby to drink, swim, and play for an hour or two before moving on, often completely disregarding the "Trespassers Will Be Shot" signs plastering nearby trees.

Bouncing out of bed, Liam shook off his drowsiness and rummaged through his dresser for a bottle of Advil before starting to pack his backpack. He rarely moved this quickly in the mornings, and Kara found his excitement contagious. Once he found everything he was looking for in the dresser, he chucked the bottle of Advil onto the bed before hopping over Kara to the other side. He pulled on the first pair of swim trunks he found. Faded blue and very short, they were probably an old, shrunken pair from his skinny teen years. Kara giggled.

"Showing some thigh, there, aren't you?" she asked mockingly.

"Huh, what?" Liam sounded confused. He was busy searching for something in his closet now and Kara could tell he wasn't really listening to her.

"Don't want any tan lines, I guess?" Kara motioned to his bare, and glaringly white, thighs with a teasing smile when he finally looked back at her.

"Oh," Liam looked down and seemed to see his choice of swim trunks for the first time. "Well, whatever. We're going to be late! I don't have time to find anything else. Plus, don't you like my sexy legs?" he struck a model pose, flexing his legs as he did so.

Kara burst out laughing. "Okay, okay. You look great, babe," she told him. "You rock those short shorts."

He grinned playfully at her as he stood up. He'd found what he was looking for in the closet. He held up the sleeveless blue shirt against himself. "Guess I've gotten a little bigger since high school," he said, as the shirt barely stretched across his body and hung above his midriff. "Here, you wear it." He tossed the shirt to her on the bed while he picked another shirt off the top of the pile for himself. "And hurry! We've got to go before it gets too busy." He picked up his backpack and turned to the door. "Don't forget to wear running shoes!" he yelled back to her as he thudded down the stairs.

Kara fell back against the pillow and took two extra-strength Advil because the hot sun and more alcohol did not seem like the best way to cure a hangover. She'd had her hopes set on a Mexican feast on the patio of a local restaurant that was run by an older couple who could not speak a word of English, followed by drinking a gallon of water and taking a long nap. The local restaurant was quiet, delicious, and shaded, and seemed to be much more conducive to hangovers than her new plans. But, she couldn't help but be energized by Liam's excitement. He was acting like a kid, and she loved seeing it.

Liam called for her again, so she rolled out of bed, pulled on her cut-off jean shorts and Liam's high school football tank over her tie-dye string bikini, and jammed her feet in her running shoes while pulling her hair back into a ponytail. She ran down the stairs quickly after Billy and Liam.

They were already in Billy's truck – a big and lifted red Ford. Blake Shelton was blaring through the stereo and the cousins were singing along, oblivious to the rest of the world. Kara climbed into the back seat and put on her sunglasses.

"You boys ready?" she asked.

Her question was met with nothing but yells and hoots. She smiled to herself. Liam turned around to look at her from the front seat, "That shirt looks good on you, babe. It suits you."

Kara glowed inside. Regardless of how juvenile it may have seemed, she imagined what it would have been like to meet him in high school and to have fallen in love with him in between football games and Sonic slushies, instead of falling in love in between Navy SEAL workouts and over craft beer at beach parties. She would have worn his football clothing instead of his military branded sweats, and they would both have had the innocence of young teens in love. She smiled to herself at the thought.

First they stopped to rent a canoe from a man living in a fish bait store who, Kara was certain, had never left the city limits nor read anything other than *Field & Stream* or *Guns & Ammo*, if he was even able to read those. Toothless, rude, and entirely opposed to her "Yankee" accent, Kara got her first taste of the unromantic side of the South – the uneducated, ignorant, and closed-minded side.

From there, they had only one more stop to make before they got to the river – breakfast. They stopped at Sonic, which had become Kara's favorite American fast food chain, and each ordered a full breakfast. Liam and Kara needed to soak up the alcohol from the previous night before drinking anything else, and Billy just loved to eat.

Suddenly, a man – a very chiseled and attractive man with piercing blue eyes and light brown hair – popped his head into Liam's window.

"Hey man! Long time no see, brotha…" his voice was slow and accented with a thick drawl. He became distracted once he saw Kara in the back seat. "Hey there, you hot little thing, what are ya doin' with this guy? Why don't you come over with me and my friend and I'll show you how to have some real fun," he continued, ignoring Billy and Liam entirely, seemingly forgetting that he'd actually approached the vehicle to speak to them. He licked his lips and looked at her just a little too long for comfort. There was something hungry in his eyes, Kara noticed. Liam bristled and spoke up.

"What you been up to lately, Mick? Is that your new girl over there?" he asked, motioning to the truck a few parking spaces over. He was trying to stay polite for a reason Kara couldn't quite understand. Normally, when a man made rude advances in her direction, or any advance at all, it was all Kara could do to keep him from using every ounce of his combat training to shut the guy up.

The girl standing outside of his big, black pick up looked like a retired Hooters girl who'd lived a little too hard and a little too long in a trailer park. Her butt sagged out of her shorts and her boobs were almost popping out of her white crop top as she was puffing away on a cigarette with ruby red lips. Her hair was heavily bleached and Kara thought it looked like she had been mildly electrocuted. She was also wearing five-inch heels. With the canoe in the bed of the truck, there was little possibility that they were heading anywhere else but the same place as Kara, Liam, and Billy.

True to form, when Mick asked Kara, Liam, and Billy to join him on the river for a few drinks, Liam accepted. Neither Kara nor Billy had ever known Liam to decline an invitation to drink or catch up with someone, no matter how distant an acquaintance he or she might be.

"Why'd you say 'yes,' dude? Isn't he the guy that…" Billy asked.

Liam cut him off. "Yep, that's him. I haven't seen him in a while, so it might be good to hear what everyone is up to, right?"

Billy didn't look convinced.

"Babe, I don't want to talk to that girl. Please don't leave me alone with her," pleaded Kara.

"You can't judge a book by its cover, sweetie. She could be a nice girl," Liam replied.

"No, I can judge this one. I know I will have nothing in common with her… or him, for that matter," said Kara. Her innocent, white-collar upbringing flashed across her mind.

Liam paused. "Well, that may be true. But that isn't someone you want to say 'no' to, darlin'. He's best kept as a friendly acquaintance. We'll have a couple beers with them at the first beach we see and then we'll paddle hard and get ahead of them."

Luckily, the unwanted couple didn't even make it past the first beach. After about a half hour of floating with the current, the boys had finally caught up on which of their friends from high school were doing what drugs, who was in prison and who was recently released, who was onto their third marriage, and who had three kids with three different women before 25. Kara was surprised at how many people fell into the latter category. She felt like she was listening to gossip about a different world. The group stopped the canoes on a small beach where the boys could take a bathroom break in the bushes while the girls stayed with the boats. Kara didn't even try to make conversation with the girl. Instead, she just let her smoke in silence while trying not to stare at the pockmarks all over her skin. After another 20 minutes of chatter, Kara had learned that Mick had been accused of multiple counts of spousal abuse and had recently bought a gun to defend himself against his ex-wife's new boyfriend (who also happened to be Mick's old drug dealer, to whom Mick had neglected to pay a large sum of money). He'd also brought the gun with him in the canoe.

In explanation, Mick told them, "This dealer has a ton of friends who are all looking for me too. I'm totally fucked."

It was only at this point that Kara noticed the subtle twitch of his muscles at every sound and the way his eyes darted nervously towards the nearby highway, as though he were afraid any passer-by might take a shot at him. Kara slid closer to Liam so that he'd put his arm around her shoulders like a protective blanket. She was entirely out of her element and she did not like it.

Kara let a few more minutes go by so that Liam could finish his beer and then whispered in his ear, "Shouldn't we get going, babe? I want to go as far down the river as possible today. It's so beautiful… I want to see it all!"

Liam kissed her on the head. "Sure, babe," he said to her with a smile. "Y'all ready to get goin'?" he asked the rest of the group.

Billy looked equally as excited as Kara at the prospect of getting back into their own canoe, away from their current company.

Liam, Kara, and Billy weren't far from the beach before they heard screams – a man's and a woman's.

"Bet they fell in!" laughed Billy.

"You don't think it's more serious? What if it's the snakes?" Kara had a fear of accidentally coming across a family of swimming copperheads – a deadly poisonous snake commonly found in Tennessee at the edges of water or marshes.

Both Liam and Billy laughed this time. "Nah. They must have fallen in. They both looked a little too tipsy and they had way too much stuff in their canoe," said Liam.

The two boys yelled back to Mick. "Mick! Y'all okay? Do you need some help?"

Mick yelled back. "Our fuckin' canoe is gittin away!"

Billy and Liam laughed. Kara tried to stifle her smirk, but struggled as she conjured an image of the girl trying to swim after the canoe in five-inch heels while trying to keep her cigarette dry. The boys paddled hard against the current to try to help. When they couldn't gain much momentum against the rushing water, Liam yelled at Mick again, "We can't get up the river to help y'all. You guys going to be okay?"

Mick responded with a string of cuss words. "It's my gun! The river took my gun. It's sunk to the bottom and it's fucking deep here. I can't get it back!"

Just then, the canoe came into sight. It was flipped upside down and moving at a good pace and Billy mentioned that this was one of the fastest parts of the river. Since there wasn't much else that they could do, the boys paddled towards the renegade canoe and veered it into the shore so that rocks and trees blocked its movement.

Liam yelled back to Mick, "We got your canoe parked up here on the left! Just swim this way and you'll see it." The water wasn't too deep and the river was narrow at this point, so the boys knew that the two swimmers would be fine. Evidently, Kara learned, people flipped their canoes fairly often.

Mick didn't respond, but they could hear his yells floating on the wind so they decided to keep going. There wasn't much else that they could do and, by now, all three of them were looking forward to escaping the couple's company.

They paddled hard for a few minutes to widen the gap before relaxing and letting the river pull their boat along as they cracked open a few Bud Lights. For the next few hours they soaked in the hot sun. They played off of rope swings and they went exploring off the beaten path into the wilderness surrounding the river. The boys showed Kara popular hang outs for high school kids trying to escape authority and Kara imagined what it would have been like to grow up like this – wild and free, without a passion or competition or responsibility. She felt like she was finally getting to know Liam at his core. He was born and bred in the South – a true Southern boy. Finally, they reached the guys' favorite spot on the river – a place they called their Southern waterfall. Leaving their boat behind, the three hiked up a cliff to reach a hole under the freeway that let water trickle from the sewers into the river. They crouched down and made their way to the other side where, at the bottom of another cliff, was a quiet pool of water fed by a metal culvert. Surrounded by thick trees and tall rocks, the area felt quite secluded. The rushing water from the culvert drowned out the sound of highway traffic. In this area, Kara noticed, you really could feel alone.

Liam grinned at her. "We used to come here to skinny dip," he said. "Pretty, isn't it?"

Kara looked around her. It wasn't the blue water and sandy beaches that she so often thought to be the epitome of beauty. The water was brown and muddy looking, she was surrounded by sandstone rock, and the idea of a sewer-fed swim wasn't the most appealing, but he was right. It was beautiful. In its own way, it was serene.

She smiled at him. "Sure is, babe," she said. "It's beautiful here."

He smiled happily at her response. She could tell this place meant a lot to him. He wanted her to fall in love with the South and to love that part of him. At that moment, Liam ran off with the happiness of a child and jumped into the pool of water. Watching him swim, Billy stepped closer to her.

"So, when y'all gonna get married?" he asked her.

Kara was shocked at the sudden question and she wasn't sure how to answer. They had talked about marriage often, but she didn't want his family to think that they were moving too fast, especially because of all the problems they'd had recently. "I-I don't know. I don't know if that's what he wants. I mean, I can drive him crazy, you know? We have our ups and downs and I don't know what he wants now, with the SEALs not working out. Who knows what will happen," she said.

Billy just laughed and smiled at her. "Of course you do. He's going to marry you. He's crazy about you. We've never seen him look at anyone the way that he looks at you or talk about anyone the way he talks about you. We're gonna be family. I just hope it's soon – I'm ready for a big party!" Billy grinned.

Kara giggled at Billy's comment as she watched Liam swim, entirely unaware of their conversation. Her heart warmed and tears started to fill her eyes. She wiped them away quickly when she thought Billy wasn't looking. All of her worries started to melt away as she let Billy's words repeat in her head. She so badly wanted to believe him, and a large part of her did. She couldn't imagine spending her life with anyone else, and she couldn't imagine him loving anyone else more than her, but there was a small part of her that still couldn't get past the little seed of doubt in her stomach that said, *This isn't as perfect as it seems. You might not make it.* She pushed the doubt down, forcing its silence, and ran to join Liam in the water.

Nineteen

Kara

After a day like today, it's tough to remember why I've felt so paranoid and distrustful these last few months. Floating down the river with Liam and Billy was so peaceful. We laughed, we tanned, we drank, and we talked about the future. Billy expects us to get married. I know that Liam and I talk about that fairly often, but until his cousin told me that he believed that we'd be family one day, it meant something different. It's sunk in and feels like a real possibility now, except for that tiny part of me that doesn't believe it. I don't know what that is or what that means. I want it and he wants it, so why can't I fully believe that it will happen?

As the sun set below the rolling Tennessee hills, we'd dropped Billy off at home and switched trucks. Liam told me he had something he wanted to show me. Very secretively, he drove us through the back roads near his house. We drove up and down hills, around deep bends, through wooded areas and farmland. At first, I wanted to know where we were going, but he wouldn't give me any hints. I assumed it had something to do with our anniversary but, as far as I knew, all that we were going to do for that was go out to dinner the next day. He'd told me that he was going to take me to hear the best live music in Nashville after eating the most delicious barbecue I'd ever have.

This surprise wasn't a gift – it was better than that. It wiped out anything negative from my mind and left visions of wedding gowns and rings and forever-shared beds. We drove down a dead end road hidden amongst hills and trees and beyond gravel roads that were rarely used. He pulled over to the shoulder and we looked out over some land. It was green, lush, and had a river running through it. About a half-mile down the road, there was a little red brick house at the end of a winding drive, but there was nothing and no one else in sight.

"What are we doing here?" I asked. I truly had no idea as I climbed out and looked around.

He pulled out a blanket and put it over the bed of his truck.

"Well, babe. I just wanted to show you something. I thought I could show you where we could live if you moved to Tennessee with me after we get married."

He patted the spot next to him on the tailgate, so I sat down and leaned against him. He wrapped one arm around my shoulders while he handed me a cold bottle of water from the cooler.

"I know the guy that lives over there," he told me, motioning towards the red house. "He's getting older and doesn't need that much land anymore. He just wants to keep an acre for himself to retire on. He said that he'd sell me the rest when I get out of the Navy. He and I go way back. I used to do some fencing work for him when I was in high school. He doesn't have any sons or family, and he said I'm the next closest thing he has to a kid. He won't sell it to anyone else but me."

I just looked at him, more surprised than anything. It took a moment for his words to make sense.

"What?" I asked, looking up at him. I searched for something, I don't know what, in his face.

He just grinned at me. He liked how surprised I was.

"I thought we could put the barn over on those hills, so there would be a good cross breeze for the horses," he continued as he pointed towards a small hill.

"Horses?" I asked.

"Well, obviously you would bring your retired horse down. He'd need a buddy too, and I would need something to ride when we go on trail rides together. You know there are hundreds of miles of trails around here, right?" he said, squeezing my shoulder. "I'd need something big and solid, though," he laughed. "I'm a lot bigger than the riders you know. I was a bit of a cowboy when I was a teen, but I was about 40 pounds lighter then."

I giggled, still looking at him. His eyes stared unblinkingly into mine, like he didn't want to miss one second of my reaction.

"You know what else?" he asked. "It's in a great school district, so this place will be great for our kids too."

He was so happy there, in that moment, with me. It was real. That moment, that was the real us. Everything else – the drinking, the drugs, the anger – it all seemed like a dream. It felt so far in the past. This was the present. This was our future.

Liam

I want her for forever. She doubts me, and maybe she has reason to, but I do. I want her and no one else. No one. I don't want other girls, I don't want other guys, I don't want that damn voice inside my head. I don't want any of it.

I don't even want the SEALs anymore. All I want… no, all I need… is Kara.

That voice in my head takes everything good from me. She doesn't let me keep anything good. *It's a lie*, she says. *You're a fraud*, she says. *You don't deserve any of it*, she tells me. I'd fought with her for so long and so hard, but she won. She was right. I didn't deserve to be in the SEALs. I didn't deserve a girl like Kara. I was so fucked up that I didn't deserve any of it, and that only made her scream louder. But not anymore. Today, this trip, I'm shutting her down. Kara fits me. She makes me happy. I want to make her happy. That's what this day was about. I wanted to show her why I loved the South and watch her fall in love with it too. Being on the ship makes me weak. Being apart from Kara makes me weak. Being at home with my cowboy boots on and my family and friends around me, I'm strong. I can conquer her. This is the first time I've ever felt that I can do that. I haven't smoked weed or done any cocaine since I've been home. I haven't wanted to. Having Kara in my arms, looking at me the way she looked at me when we first met – that's enough. That's all I need to drown *her* out.

* * *

In the truck as we drove back to my parents' house, her arms wrapped around mine while I drove, I felt her sigh. She was so trusting again, so comfortable. It felt perfect. I felt myself relax. As much as I am confident in what I want, and as much as I meant everything I said and showed her today, there's still that little part of me that is trying hard to scream through my contentedness now that I am alone with my thoughts. I'm sitting here in bed, listening to her rhythmic breathing beside me, and I know that I need Kara in my life for forever because I cannot imagine living without her, but I don't think this voice is going anywhere either. I can feel the stress of those thoughts encroaching on me in the darkness even now, after a day like today. *She might be drowned out now, but I know she'll be back once I'm back on the ship. That image in my mind of Kara overlooking the land – our future land – and planning the kind of life we could have together... it's too perfect. And she never lets me hold on to anything that good.*

Twenty

Kara

"Hey, baby girl. I like your jeans. They make your ass look real good..." some guy murmured to me. I think his name was Ivan. Liam was in the back of the house snorting cocaine with someone he claims is his friend, though I'd never heard of him before tonight and, judging by the company he kept, I really hoped he wasn't actually a friend.

I'd looked up into Ivan's eyes as he spoke. There wasn't anything there but lust and greed. I'd felt small and weak and I rarely feel that way. I wasn't left with much choice in the situation though. After Liam had left me in the family room alone with this man, all I could do was watch the clock as the second hand ticked along. I'd waited. I'd watched. I'd looked for someone besides Ivan to talk to, someone who could help take the focus off of me. From the moment I'd walked in the door, I could feel Ivan's eyes on me and, the longer Liam had left us alone, the more naked I'd felt. But, there was no one there to help me. The other girls were different than me. I could see by the scabs on their arms and their thinning, matted hair that they had seen better days. With my hair curled, makeup on, and clear, healthy skin, I'd stood out and I could tell that they'd resented me for it. Their dull eyes just glared at me. They weren't going to help. The other guys were equally useless. One had his hand fully up the skirt of the girl next to him with the other on a beer. The rest were either ignoring me or eyeing me up and down, enough to make me feel a little safer with Ivan, who was, he'd told me, an ex-inmate.

"So you know, darlin', I've been inside for six long years," he'd told me.

Naively, I had to ask, "Inside? Inside where?"

He'd laughed, then, seemingly pleased by my innocence. "The big house? The slammer? I don't know what y'all call it up in Canada, but I was in prison on a drug charge. I just got out a few days ago."

My eyes had widened but I tried to play it cool. I hadn't wanted to start a scene and Liam had made it very clear that I was not supposed to embarrass him. So, I'd replied, "Wow, you must be happy to be out, then. Are you enjoying your freedom?"

He'd laughed. It wasn't a kind laugh, but rather a dark laugh. A sinister laugh. It was the kind of laugh that had made me feel like he was already touching me in ways I really didn't want him to. I'd hugged my arms tightly around me and watched the second-hand on the clock tick away. "Oh, it's been great. I haven't had any girls yet, though, and that's what I've been waiting for the most." Ivan had inched closer to me then. "Six years is a very long time," he'd whispered.

I'd stepped back from him, subtly trying to increase the distance he was trying hard to decrease. I'd looked at the girls on the couch with a mental plea to be included into their circle. However, their dull eyes remained focused in the direction of the television.

Stepping back seemed to only invite him to step closer. "You know, when I got out, I couldn't have dreamed of a hotter girl to welcome me back to life as a free man. You're a beautiful girl," he'd purred, stepping closer and wrapping his arm around my back, preventing me from taking another step away.

"I think Liam would agree," I'd said, more loudly than needed. I'd wanted Liam to hear. He either hadn't heard or he hadn't cared though because he didn't come out.

Ivan inched closer and closer, letting his hand wander over my back and down my ass. When he'd finally let his hands drop away to take a sip from his beer, my exhale was so enthusiastic that I'd feared it would offend him. I don't think anything could offend him. He didn't seem to react like a normal human. He'd just kept at it. He'd in turn flatter me and then share some shocking and sordid detail about what he'd like to do with me be if I let him take me out. Each time his tattooed fingers left the safety of his beer, I'd closed my eyes and hoped, prayed, that Liam would come out and catch him. I'd hoped he would be jealous and use his SEAL training to knock this guy on his ass. I'd wanted him to prove to everyone that I was his and that no one else was allowed to want me. The longer that Liam left me alone there, the more I'd considered yelling for him. I knew that he'd be furious at me if I made a scene, but I really hadn't liked the way this guy's breath was getting shorter and louder with every passing minute. I'd tried stepping back, but he'd just followed me. I hadn't wanted to offend him, but I'd thought maybe he would take the hint. He hadn't even noticed.

When Liam had finally finished, he came out and put his hand on my shoulder, not saying a word about how closely Ivan was standing, and asked, "Ready to go, baby? We're going to miss our reservations." He was playing the good boyfriend. Our reservations were long gone. As he'd said bye, we'd walked out, and he'd had the nerve to say to me, "See babe? It was fast, and more fun than going downtown would have been. Let's hit a drive-through."

What a romantic one-year anniversary. When he'd said he didn't want to sit through dinner without being high, he'd really just meant he didn't want to sit through dinner. Part of me wanted to yell at him, but the other part just couldn't be bothered. I am so tired. In the drugs vs. girlfriend battle, the score is now 1,000 - none. What would yelling change? So much for all of this shit being in our past. I knew the happily-ever-after picture he had painted for us while we'd sat in the back of his pick up was too good to be true. It was so perfect that it had seemed like a fantasy. And, in fact, it was nothing more than a fantasy.

Liam

I really do love her. I mean it. I still want her as my future. Having her here this week, with my family, has been great. She fits right in. We planned our future last night. I'm gonna marry this girl, there's no doubt about it in my mind, only, the fact that she's my future can apparently cause me to spiral out of control just as easily as it can soothe the toughest moments.

We had a romantic night last night. Kara wanted one. Before she'd come to Tennessee, she told me that she felt like we needed one. Doesn't she understand what those do to me? We've been through this so many times. Sometimes I just can't have a romantic one-on-one night. And last night was one of those nights. *She* came back last night once we'd gotten home, stronger than ever. Romance must feed her. When I think I might be happy, that voice just starts getting louder and louder in my head. It drives me crazy. I've told Kara that sometimes I just need space. I will always come back. It will always work out. But, sometimes, I just need space. She takes it so personally though. I would hope that by now she'd understand, but how could she? I don't understand either. But still, an anniversary is just another day. I had planned something for us because I knew it meant something to her, but I was just too tired and too stressed to follow through. I tried to back out. I tried to tell her that I was too broke now to take her out, but she just said that I could take her anywhere – Sonic included – as long as it was just the two of us. She was trying to help but it only stressed me out more. I just couldn't do it that day. I had too much shit happening in my head and it was scaring me.

    I could see the disappointment in her eyes when I told her I couldn't do anything for our anniversary though, so I agreed to take her to dinner anyway. I told her that I just needed to make one stop and then I would be all hers. I'd meant that wholeheartedly. It just… well, it didn't work out. I fucked up again, like I always do, and it led to another fight, like it always does. Only, this one was bad. This one was dark. And I really messed up. I should never have left her alone and I should never have expected her to make friends with those people. I knew that they weren't good people. I don't even like talking to them and we speak the same language. Kara's different. She's innocent and she was brought up to be a good girl. She's got nothing in common with those people and I left her alone. She pleaded with me not to. She told me she wouldn't know what to say and that she didn't want to be left alone with those kinds of people. It stung me to hear her describe them as "those kinds of people." I'm one of those people now. Maybe not on the outside, but I'm messed up too. I need the release just as much as they do. Does that make me a bad person? Does that make me one of "those people" in her eyes? I really hope not because I'm still me. I'm a good guy who loves her. I'm just going through something right now, something she couldn't possibly understand.

It's like the couple that we were last night vanished. No matter how perfect we are, I can't escape the stress. Sometimes, I need nights filled with drugs and blowing off steam or else Kara won't have a man to come home to in the future. I actually think I'll go crazy or I'll just be better off gone. I don't think I mean that, I like being here, but that's how fucking messed up I am right now. It only gets worse when Kara gets upset with me. When that happens, the voice in my head, *her* voice, gets louder very quickly. When I stop feeling like the man that Kara wants me to be, that she *deserves*, I start wondering what it would be like to be the woman that that voice wants me to be. I thought that being at home would drown it out. I thought that showing Kara our future together would drown her out. I really thought that I'd gotten rid of her. But I think that was just her plan because it seems like she was resting for this. She was waiting for me to think I could be happy without her, and then she just came back stronger to try and prove me wrong.

Leading up to this visit, Kara sent me so many photos of herself. She said she wanted to get me excited to see her, so she'd showed me the new outfit she bought for dinner and the lingerie she'd wanted to surprise me with after. She asked if I would want to show her off to my friends. It stung that she needed to ask that. Of course I do. I guess I can't blame her for doubting that sometimes, especially given how I acted tonight, and that hurts me. I hid her away tonight, and I abandoned her, and she knew it. But, sometimes, I don't want to take her to the busiest, or most popular, places because when we walk down the street, I see how men look at her but never at me. So I compare my butt to hers, imagine her boobs on my chest, her hair blowing behind me in the wind. I wonder, *If I had all that, would guys look at me the same way?* Now, how fucked up is that? I'm not fucking gay. But I'm jealous of her. She thinks that I don't want to spend time with her and would rather use the money on drugs because I like drugs more than her. Not at all. I love her. I showed her that yesterday. I did my best to show her where I want to be and where I want us to go... I'm just not there yet. I have so much shit going on in my head that I mess up sometimes.

I can't always take her out like she wants, or deserves. And sometimes, I just can't be sober. It doesn't mean that I don't want all of the good things that I told her to be true. It doesn't mean that everything we felt and said last night isn't true. Those dreams and goals are as true as I can make them. They're just only a part of our reality right now. I'm trying to make those moments count for everything, to outweigh all the stress, but I just don't know what to do anymore. I'm trying, though. And I am so full of regret for all the pain that I've caused her, and all the pain I will cause her if I can't sort these feelings out, that I don't know how to keep it all hidden inside anymore. It's so constant for me, I don't even feel it anymore. I just wish she'd see that and that she'd believe me.

Sometimes, I feel like I've gone way past crazy and should just stop everything. The last few days seem like a distant memory now, almost like a dream. This constant duality is our reality now, my reality. It's inescapable. And it's fucked up.

Twenty-One

After the anniversary incident, as Kara called it from there on out, some of the fairy-tale qualities of the trip were erased. Upon returning to San Diego, she still trusted that Liam loved her but the feeling of dread was stronger than ever. She was no longer worried about other girls grabbing his attention, but she couldn't put her finger on what she *was* worried about. All she knew was that he was keeping something from her and that ate away at her trust, regardless of how happy they had been together for the majority of their vacation.

The morning after she got back to San Diego, she knocked on Michael's door bright and early in the morning, long before he usually cared to be awake on his days off from being a busy T.A.

"Want to go to the beach?" she asked, shining a bright and persuasive smile at him.

Still groggy, he rubbed his eyes and adjusted his t-shirt. "Uh, sure. Give me a few minutes to shower and change," he said, opening the door for her to come in. "Franceen is here too, just so you know," he added.

Kara rolled her eyes, only half-jokingly. "Of course. I guess she can come too," she replied, with a short laugh. She didn't relish talking about the highs and lows of her trip with Franceen there to listen, but she wanted to talk to someone about it so she couldn't turn back now.

Michael chuckled and pulled her in for a hug. "We've missed you here. Can't wait to hear all about Liam's antics while you were away. Is he surviving life on a ship? That man was not meant to be confined to a ship. And he most certainly wasn't made to sweep decks."

Kara thought it felt like he knew she needed a hug and that made her feel good. She felt like he'd always *understood* her, better than anyone else she had known in the city besides Liam, and that made her feel less alone when Liam was away. She breathed in his slightly musty scent and let herself relax into his embrace. "Oh, we made some stories." She laughed lightly. "I'll tell you all about them when we're on the beach."

Kara sat down on Michael's couch to watch television while he went to shower and wake up Franceen. It wasn't long before she heard her loud voice say, "Hey girl, heyyyyy," over the sound of a *Friends* rerun. Kara cringed. It was Franceen's favorite way to greet her girlfriends, but Kara always thought it sounded like she was trying too hard to be "cool" as though they were still in high school, and it was off-putting.

"How was Liam? Did he miss me? I bet he did. There can't be any fun girls on those ships," she said, sitting down next to Kara and putting her arm around her.

"Ha – sure, Franceen. I think he does miss everyone here. He doesn't seem happy being on a ship," said Kara, trying to deflect the focus from Franceen.

"Well, of course. He and I are the same. We ride on the same wavelength. He's not going to find anyone to replace me out there," she said, smiling happily at the thought.

Kara just forced a smile and nodded, willing Michael to get dressed faster.

"What did you guys do?" she asked.

"Well, I was going to tell you and Michael the story when we got to the beach. It was kind of a crazy week," Kara said.

"Oh, don't worry about Michael. He doesn't care. He hates gossip. Tell me *everything*," Franceen said, letting her arm rest on the couch behind Kara, focusing her eyes on hers.

"Michael will get a kick out of some of it," Kara responded, "but I guess I can tell you a little bit."

Rather than share the story of their anniversary, the confusing story that Kara had wanted to talk to Michael about, Kara proceeded to tell Franceen about Liam's search for the perfect place to build their first house together. She told her how he had planned an evening around his big unveil, how they had watched over the land and created their dream property as the sun set behind the hills. She told her, too, how Billy had said that he expected them to get married. She may have elaborated a little on how excited he and Liam's parents were to have Kara as part of the family, but she wanted to ensure that it was clear to Franceen that both Liam and his family wanted *her*, not Franceen, to be a part of their family. *She* was his special person, not Franceen.

As usual, Franceen missed the social cues and said, "That sounds perfect. I'll have to teach you how to be Southern before the next time you go! Southern girls like me are always the preferred type of girl to families like his. They were probably just being polite to you. I'll help you be the kind of girl they'll *really* like for your next visit."

"Weren't you born and raised in Los Angeles?" Kara's voice was dry with annoyance.

"Well, yes, but I spent a couple summers with my aunt and uncle in Arkansas where I picked up this drawl and learned how to be a proper Southern girl," she said in a voice that was instantly laden with prolonged vowels and spoken with a loose jaw.

"Okay, so that makes you Southern, then," Kara said sarcastically.

Franceen didn't pick up on the sarcasm and simply agreed. "Yep. Let me know when you want to talk. There's a reason Liam likes me so much, and this is it," she said. Whether she was trying to be helpful or snide, Kara wasn't sure.

Michael finished his shower a few moments later and Kara was saved from more one-on-one time with Franceen.

On the beach, Kara noticed that Franceen had bought the same American flag printed bikini that she had before she left for Nashville, so now they matched as they lay on the beach. Michael lay down between them on his stomach, letting his back face the sun, and turned his head towards Kara.

"So, how was your trip?" he said to her.

Kara looked towards Franceen's pale white legs stretched out in front of her and resented her infringing on the time she had with the only person she could talk to about her fears. More importantly, she felt too embarrassed of their relationships imperfections to share them with Franceen, who so clearly thought that any problems between Kara and Liam were a result of Liam's secret love for her. Luckily, she seemed to be involved in reading a textbook. Kara paused for a moment, wondering whether or not she should be getting caught up on the readings she had missed while in Nashville, but decided to leave that for later in the evening and looked towards Michael to tell her story.

"Well, in a nutshell, it was everything amazing and perfect and sweet that I could have hoped for, while also a reminder of everything that's wrong with us." Kara paused. "I don't even know how to describe it. It was perfect. Liam was perfect. We were perfect. That is, we were perfect until we weren't. Everything was great until the last day and then something snapped. It was like he couldn't take the perfection anymore and, well, he took me to a crack house for our anniversary."

Michael's eyebrows shot up and an amused grin toyed at the corners of his mouth at the bluntness of her last statement, but he listened as she told him everything – from the canoe trip with Liam and Billy, to Billy talking about marriage, to Liam finding their land and having their future planned out, to meeting his parents and grandparents and high school friends and how in love and how solid that all had made her feel. Then, she finished with their anniversary trip where Liam was supposed to take her out to dinner but instead took her to a crack house, leaving her alone in the living room with convicted felons while he did drugs in the back.

When she was finished the story, she felt tired. Exhausted. Yet, she felt calm. Michael had that effect on her. He never judged Liam for acting the way he did, he never judged her for how she handled it, he just listened, and that was all she needed.

"Hah! Wow. That's quite a story." Michael chuckled to himself for a moment before continuing. "Liam will always be Liam, though. Good or bad, he will always be who he is. He does what he wants. But, because of that, you really should trust in his love for you. He loves you. He completely adores you. You know he does because he wouldn't do any of those romantic things for someone he didn't feel that way about. He's got some demons though. Honestly, I think anyone who does what he does for a living has demons. You need them to even make it through training, I'd think. Even if you don't have them at the start, you have them after a few years of service. How can you not? So, accept that part of him and focus on the good parts. No one's perfect, but you know what you're getting with him. He's open and he's honest. You know where I live, too. Whenever it's bad, just come by and I'll pour you a drink. We'll talk all night if we have to, but I'll get you through it." Michael smiled at her. "It'll all be okay in the end.

Twenty-Two

While Kara was still processing the highs and lows of her visit to Nashville, Liam had started to feel more changes burning inside of him and, rather than fighting them, he gave into them, little by little.

Before Liam had left Kara at Dulles International at the security checkpoint, she had cried. She had cried a lot – her face hot and wet from the tears streaming down it and her chest heaving with sobs. She bent her head into his shoulder and couldn't stop herself from shaking. She tried hard at first to keep it in, but once Liam's voice sounded choked as well she couldn't help but cry. Neither knew why they were crying. They'd left each other before so this feeling wasn't new. Kara had forgiven Liam for their anniversary evening when he had apologized with clear regret in his eyes and, though it still played in her memory, there weren't any hard feelings that were causing them to cry. But something about this departure felt different to each of them, though they didn't verbalize any of these fears to each other.

Liam

Life on a ship is dull to say the least. I hate it. I feel like all my skills are being wasted. I could do so much more than they let me here. I sweep, I clean, I do what little training they offer me just to try to get ahead. They finally let me into the armory to assist with cleaning the guns. The guys I report to in there are so much less trained than I am. It seems like they've barely even shot a gun. Yet, they tell me what to do and I have to do it. And because they don't like that I was so close to becoming a SEAL, they won't let me touch anything. They just make me sit in the corner and watch them do things or, more often, do nothing. The most I can hope for is to be a rescue swimmer one day. Even that would be a lucky achievement – the training takes a long time and would only be available when there is a space open for a rescue swimmer. That's the closest thing to the physical fitness and importance of being a SEAL on this godforsaken ship and, unfortunately, our ship has filled its quota.

When I first got back here, I missed Kara every day. I thought about her during rounds, during chores, and during training. I bragged about her at meals and I dreamt about her at night. I'm not sure why, but that feeling started to fade. And then, that voice, that woman in my head, started to take over my thoughts again and I couldn't stop it. There's too much time on a ship to daydream. It's like she knew that because she wouldn't let me rest. *She* pushed Kara out of my mind and made herself the center of my thoughts. Soon, instead of daydreaming about Kara rocking a baby on our white front porch while I mended fences and tended the horses, I daydreamed about what it would be like to *be* her. I started to catch myself thinking about what she could be like – if she would have a high voice or a smoker's husk? Would she be girly or would she be a strong country girl? How would the boys like her? Would she be flirty or maybe a bit of a slut? I don't know what this means, but I hate thinking about it. It's wrong. I know in my head it's wrong, but my heart won't let me stop. It feels good. I've stopped talking to the guys on my ship as much. I almost never join them when they go out at night anymore. I talk to the girls, but I don't want to date them. I still only want to date Kara. She's the only one for me. But I can't relate to the guys as well anymore.

It makes Kara wildly jealous to hear that I'm hanging out with a bunch of girls. She always wants me to admit that she's prettier than them, and I think that's because it makes her feel more secure. I'm sure it's true. For me, there is no one prettier than her. But I can't tell her that. Something about telling her that feels wrong to me. I don't want to make these girls feel like less than they are. They're all pretty in their own way. They can't help the way they look. I just... I don't know. It sounds silly, but I feel for them. They deserve to feel pretty and secretly, I want to feel pretty like them. No one ever tells me I'm prettier than anyone else and I kind of crave that too. The difference is, I don't know if anyone will ever say that about me. So I try to stand up for these girls. I talk to them and it feels good. It feels real. I like their attention. I don't really like when they flirt with me; it makes me feel embarrassed. I want them to talk to me like they talk to each other – as a friend. I don't want anything else with them. Sometimes, it gets a little awkward because they clearly don't see the version of me that I wish they did, but how can they? I don't even know what that version is or what she would look like. I just know that when we talk – just talk – I feel whole when I'm with them.

We have a mock deployment coming up. I haven't told Kara, but I think it's going to be good for me. I won't have to deal with her jealousy and I won't have to deal with he guys wanting to go out and hit on girls. *Her* voice will be louder, sure, but she never seems as insistent when I'm with the girls on the ship. When I'm hanging out with them she leaves me alone. And on the mock deployment it'll just be my new friends, my work, and me. There's peace in that, somehow.

Kara

I don't know why, but I'm so insanely jealous of the girls that Liam's hangs out with. It's nonsense, I know. But I just can't help it! I know he has something going on, something deep down. He's got a secret. That much is clear, but I don't think he's cheating. Does it have to do with his wanting long hair? I don't think so. He hasn't mentioned that in a long time and we've had some really good points in our relationship since then. The psychologist thought it had to do with the stress of the SEAL program and that's gone now, so it must be something else. People can have secrets, though, right? If he needed my help, he'd ask. He asked before and he would do it again. He loves me and he trusts me. I trust that he loves me but I really want to be able to *trust* him again, whole-heartedly. So maybe I should just let him be? Obviously he needs to deal with whatever this is on his own. I just can't let go for some reason. I'm afraid that if I let go, if I get over being jealous, if I let him live like he wants, that he won't come back to me. I'm so scared that we won't make it. He assures me that we will. He sounds so confident, too. I don't know why I don't believe him.

"I have a plan for us, baby," he says. "We're going to grow old together."

That's what we both want, so why am I nervous? We don't argue as much as we used to. And I guess he still doesn't always pick up my calls, but I know he hates talking on the phone. That's what I keep telling myself to calm myself down. Liam has been sweet and kind, and more like the guy he used to be. We've been at our worst with each other but never once have we talked about *not* being together for forever. So I don't know why I'm having such a hard time believing that we'll last.

Liam

She asks if I look at the girls the same way that I look at her. Frankly, I kinda do. But that doesn't mean I look at them the way that I used to look at her. No, it's a new way of looking at girls. I look at them almost like I imagine younger sisters look at their older sisters. I admire them. I *envy* them. I don't want to sleep with them. I want them to hang out with me, to like me, to understand me, and I feel like they do. So when Kara accuses me of looking at them like I should be looking at her, it hurts me but it also makes me angry. I'm not mad because it feels like she doesn't trust me. I feel like I deserve that. It hurts because she doesn't believe me when I tell her that I love her more than I could ever love anyone else. It's like she suspects that something is really different this time. On the other hand, it makes me mad because she can't believe the most honest thing about me right now – my devotion to her. It makes me angry and scared because I don't know what to say about my feelings. It *is* different now. I am looking at the girls on the ship the way I look at her – with envy. I still love her though. Kara is still my girl.

Throughout our deployment, I've really liked listening to the girls talk about their boyfriends or the various guys they've met recently at the bar. I've had a lot of time to think about my relationships with them. I think about how I like going shopping with them when we're at port. I might grumble sometimes because that's what a guy like me is supposed to do, but going shopping with them makes me the happiest I've been in a long time. It feels *right*, somehow. The best part about these girls is that they don't care how I act, so I can just be me. If I forget to be annoyed by how many dresses they're trying on, they don't seem to question me. They just invite me to go shopping more often. If I don't check out every attractive girl that walks by, they don't comment. They just assume that they're the prettiest girls out there. The problem is, whenever I'm with them doing those things, it's harder for me to pick up Kara's calls and I don't know what that means. I think I'm embarrassed by what I'm doing. I want to be a real man for her and, when I'm with them, I'm not. I think that voice in my head is really starting to win.

I met this one girl on the ship. She's an open lesbian. Sometimes people give her a hard time for it, but I admire her. She is who she is, and it looks like she feels so free because of it. She's a pretty happy person. She goes out when she wants, where she wants, with whoever she wants. I want to feel that free. I don't really know who or what it is that I want to be, but it's not the guy that Kara fell in love with anymore, at least not right now. I think that I want to be someone more like who I am when I'm with those girls. I want to be softer, warmer, prettier. You know what's funny? I haven't used any drugs since I figured this out. I mean, I have been on a ship but, if I really wanted some, there are always ways to get the drugs I'd want. The guys on the ship think I've just gone straight because of the constant threat of drug testing, but really I just found another way to cope with my thoughts – by giving in. Whenever that voice in my head gets too loud, I pull on this nice little red pair of panties that I "borrowed" from Kara and then *she* quiets right down. I hang out with the girls. I listen to their gossip. I do whatever she tells me to do and then she quiets down and I'm happy. Everything she wants to do feels right, so I might as well do it. I'm so tired of fighting and never feeling right.

I thought about it long and hard on the mock deployment and I think I need to tell Kara something. I need to tell her that I'm confused. I don't know what any of this means but it means something. Does it mean I'm gay? I mean, what else could it be? I'm going to tell her that I think I'm gay. I have to tell her something. I can't keep hiding from her. I need to be me and I need her to *know* the real me, whoever that turns out to be. I was hoping to know who that was before telling her anything, but I think that's going to take me a while longer to figure out and I feel too bad letting her think everything is the same between us.

<u>Kara</u>

Liam came back from his weeklong mock deployment and called me at the exact time he told me he would. I'd missed him. When his FaceTime call came in and I saw his smiling face looking back at me, my heart skipped a beat. It felt like the first time in so many ways. He looked so happy to see me. We chatted for a few minutes before his entire face changed. It became shadowed and pinched. He struggled to look me in the eye, so he seemed to focus on something off the screen to his right – maybe his hand. Sometimes, when he's nervous, he picks at his nails. I thought that's what he was doing.

Maybe I should have been nervous, but I wasn't. Despite all the times that I feared him breaking up with me for someone else, I wasn't scared of that this time. Finally, he looked me in the eyes.

"Kara, I need to tell you something," he said.

My stomach tightened. "Of course, baby, anything," I replied.

"I… I've done some thinking while on the ocean and…" his voice trailed off. He seemed to summon more courage before he said, "Well, I think I might be gay."

I felt a little bit nauseous and waited for the tears to come, but I wasn't as surprised as I think I should have been. Instead, I felt almost thankful that he hadn't stopped loving me. What does that kind of reaction possibly mean about me? How strange is it that I wasn't surprised when my boyfriend told me he might be gay?

"Oh…" I started. My stomach lurched and a wave of nausea rolled over me so I took a moment to just focus on breathing before I continued to respond. "I want to hug you so tightly right now. Are you okay?" I racked my brain for more words, but I was completely unsure about what else to say.

"I'm okay. I just… I just need to figure it out, you know what I mean? I need to test it out so…" he paused. "I love you so much, baby, but I need to know if this is who I am. I need to go out to a bar. Jas, the lesbian girl I told you about, told me about a place here in Norfolk. I want to go tonight so… So I think we should break up," he told me. He looked at me with such pain in his eyes that my heart went out to him.

"Baby, we don't need to break up for that. I'll give you a pass. You can do whatever you need to with whoever you want, as long as it's not a girl," I told him, half-joking with the last part. It was crazy, I knew. I should want to run. I should let him be who he wants to be, free of my expectations. I just *couldn't* give him up. I couldn't let him go entirely in case he didn't come back to me. And, looking back, a part of me really feared that, if I didn't give him a pass and didn't support him, that he wouldn't come back to me. And that was something I couldn't handle. "I'm here for you, whatever you need, I'm here. If you're scared, call me. I want you to figure this out."

"Really? You would do that for me?" he asked, so clearly relieved and more than a little bit shocked.

"Of course. We're a team and I love you. I want you to be happy," I told him. "I want you to find out who you are. I'm okay waiting for that."

He smiled at me – gratitude, love, comfort, and nervousness emanated from his face. I was happy with how I'd handled it. I didn't tell him, though, that it wasn't entirely selfless. The idea of breaking up with him terrified me, even if it was because he was gay. I couldn't bear to break up with him, not yet. Some part of me feels better about what he might be doing tonight if he is still in a relationship with me. This way, it will feel like I'm still the most important person in his life.

Twenty-Three

After sharing his most feared secret with Kara, Liam struggled through the rest of his day. While having her support eased his mind on some things, he still feared walking into that bar, alone, with the intention of finding a man to go home with. It was something that had never really crossed his mind before, at least seriously, and now that he was trying to figure out whether or not this was supposed to be his new reality, it was at once exciting and overwhelming. Liam's mind raced as he absent-mindedly did his chores, watching the time tick by on his watch the way a hawk watches its prey. At that moment, there was nothing else he could think about except what it would feel like to walk into that bar. He'd been to gay bars before with Kara – she loved to go to gay bars to dance – but he'd always kept her wrapped tightly around him. He'd always made sure everyone saw him as straight. Tonight would be different, and the thought of it engulfed him in fear.

Kara, across the country in San Diego, was also reeling. She wasn't that surprised, but her body was going through mild shock – she couldn't stop shivering in the hot San Diego sun. Whether that was because some deep part of her subconscious had suspected it and was now mourning her relationship with Liam, or because she hadn't let herself process the news yet, she wasn't sure. Instead, she was worried about whom it would be that he took home, about whether that someone could replace her, and about how Liam would handle coming out to the rest of his friends and family. So, like she always did when stressed, she ran. She ran along the beach and, when she couldn't run any more, she sat in the sand and watched the ocean. The waves calmed her – steady and unfaltering, they just kept coming. People laughed and chattered around her. A few people were playing beach volleyball not too far away while some surfer-types lit up a joint on her other side. She tried to take comfort in their presence. It just proved that life goes on. However, as they laughed with each other and she thought about what Liam was probably doing in that same moment, she felt so very alone.

Just then Kara's phone rang. Liam's smiling face looked back at her. She debated ignoring it, thinking that it must just have been an accidental dial from his pocket, but she couldn't. It was nearing dusk in San Diego and she knew that, if he wasn't already at the bar, he was likely on his way and was calling for support.

"Hey babe," she said, trying to keep her voice calm.

"Hey sweetie, I'm walking in. Please help me," he said, his voice laced with panic.

"Sure, Liam. What do you need?"

"I just need you to talk to me. Just stay on the phone with me until I get settled. I can't go in here alone, I just can't, baby." His voice was cracking from nerves.

"Of course, of course. Don't be so stressed. I'm here. I won't go anywhere until you want me to," said Kara, trying to make her voice as soothing as possible as her mind realized the absurdity of their current situation.

Kara and Liam talked on the phone until Liam was comfortably seated at the bar with a drink in his hand. At that point, a man in his early thirties, with the shaved head and muscles of a military man but without the demeanor, sat down next to him and asked to buy him a drink.

"I've gotta go. Talk to you later," he said quickly to Kara, hanging up before she could say anything in return.

Kara stayed sitting on the beach, watching the waves and soaking in the company of strangers until long after the sun had left the sky.

Liam

It didn't feel right. I mean, it didn't feel bad but it felt wrong. I mean, after it all ended, I just showed the guy pictures of Kara. All I wanted to do was see her face and show her off. It didn't matter that it probably wasn't an appropriate situation to do that, I had to see her. He said she was stunning and had a very kind smile. That made me miss her. He was also jealous, he told me, that she was willing to help me figure out who I am. Honestly, that was more comforting than the physical stuff, I think. She's my best friend. That girl will always support me, no matter what. I just want to do that for her. I'd do anything for her. That's real love, isn't it? If I can love her like that, how can I be gay? I mean, this was just sex and it wasn't even that good. It felt so awkward. Well, it felt good and weird at the same time. I'm so tired of feeling awkward and uncomfortable. I want to be happy and love makes people happy, right? So, then, I need to be with Kara, which is exactly what I told her the next morning.

I called her and said, "Baby, thank you for being so understanding. I just needed to try it so that I knew. I don't think I'm gay though. I mean, after... you know... everything... I couldn't stop myself from showing the guy photos of you. He said you were beautiful and I think so too. What you and I have is the real thing and that's what I want. I don't know how I could have thought that it wasn't for me."

I could just about hear her relieved smile through the phone.

Kara

In my mind, I know I should be more concerned than I am. My heart is just so relieved that he picked me. He loves *me*. I'm still his number one person and he doesn't want that to change. Maybe I should question *why* he felt he needed to explore this option. Maybe I should be a little more hesitant to take him back after he slept with a random man from a bar. But, I'm not. I adore Liam and, frankly, if this was the secret that's been causing him so much stress then I'm happy about it. All it took was one night and now, maybe, we can move forward from this mess of anger, confusion, and mistrust. One night is a small price to pay for a lifetime of happiness, I think.

Twenty-Four

As her last semester wrapped up, Kara finished off her thesis and prepared to defend it. Her mind had been at ease ever since Liam's night of experimentation had ended in her favor, so she let herself enjoy her last few weeks on the sunshine coast by attending beach parties, playing volleyball, doing yoga by the water, and soaking in as much of the San Diego lifestyle as she could.

Meanwhile, in Virginia, Liam felt an odd release after the night he went to the gay bar. He felt calm again, like his mind wasn't constantly at battle with itself anymore. That feeling didn't last long, though. About a week later, he felt the familiar pressure build in his chest, the urge to use drugs come back stronger, and the return of the whisper in his head, telling him that he hadn't actually figured out his problem yet.

However, he didn't let Kara know about his feelings and fears returning. Instead, he picked up every call from her and continued to promise that their futures would be forever intertwined. Whether it was to protect her feelings, wishful thinking, or both, he wasn't sure.

Another week went by and, as his frustrations grew, his level of experimentation followed. Once Kara had given him the go-ahead to figure out whether he was gay or not, and had been there for him when he had needed her, his thoughts came more freely. He let himself explore his feelings for a little bit longer than he did before. Finally, one night he went to visit Jas. She was going to a friend's house for a barbecue and, being his only confidant in Norfolk, she had invited him so that he could relax with a few beers and some people who would be understanding of his situation.

They lit a campfire in the backyard, cracked open a few cold beers, turned on some music, and sat down to talk. Couples cuddled together, many of the men with men and many of the women with women, and Liam noticed that no one thought anything of it. He settled further into his chair, a new air of ease around him, and let their conversation float over him. He heard snippets of conversation about costume parties, dates, clothes, football, and guns; all while his brain immersed himself in each story. He envisioned what it would be like to enjoy every event or subject freely, and it relaxed him.

Liam

It's like no one cared that the girls were dating girls, or that they used dip and wore baggy jeans. No one looked twice at the guys whose voices were higher than Kara's and who wore low cut V-necks or liked to kiss in public. Nobody judged anybody there. They talked about one friend who would go out once every month dressed as a woman. They talked about a girl they knew who refused to be called by male or female pronouns and would only be referred to by their name. They weren't talking about these people like freaks, but just as friends. Their desires and actions were briefly mentioned in passing, probably for my benefit since I was new to the group, and then they'd carry on with the story of some party or event they had gone to together. Nobody dwelled. Nobody cringed. They treated each other like people. They didn't care that I'd had a one-night stand with a guy I had met at a gay bar. I'd even told them, when they brought up their cross-dressing friend, that I sometimes thought about it. I'd never told that to anyone but Kara (and she'd had to work hard at understanding and getting past that drunken revelation) because I'd been so terrified of what people might say. But, I felt safe amongst the people tonight so I'd spoken up. They treated it as if it were an entirely normal confession. One guy even said, "I do that sometimes too! They're real soft against the skin. I love it."

They get it. I thought about all those times I'd put on Kara's clothes and sit in the bathroom, toying with her makeup and feeling so wonderful about myself, and then, as the realization would hit that she could easily wake up and need to use the restroom, the intense self-loathing would begin. When I'm alone, it's a constant tug-of-war between feeling *so* right and *so* wrong. When I was with them tonight, it just felt... like me. It felt real. It wasn't extreme. It wasn't shocking. It was... verging on normal. Maybe it seems drastic, or too fast, but tonight made me realize what it is that I want. I'm not ready to tell Kara yet, and I'm not sure that I'm ready to live that way either, but I'm ready to try something new. Maybe I don't actually want *everything* that I think about, but maybe I should consider it. I didn't meet anyone last night who seemed to want what I want, or think how I do, so I guess I'm still alone. I felt safe with them though. I felt like they might understand because they at least understand feeling different. It's just scary to think about wanting to be *that* different. Honestly, I don't know if one night a month with a guy would be okay with me. I don't know *who* it is that I want to have sitting on my lap. Maybe it's Kara and maybe it's not. I do want Kara to be in my life. I'm just not entirely convinced about the way that I want her there anymore. I mean, I love her more than anything in the world. I'm just not sure if it's romantic love anymore. At least, maybe it's not all the time. When I'm with her, I don't feel complete. Those couples from tonight looked *whole*. I want to feel whole.

Twenty-Five

Liam

I tried to will myself to just accept these feelings about who I might be inside, to try giving in to the urges to dress up in feminine clothing and to use feminine products. The few times Jas and I have gone to visit her friends they've given me a sort of sanctuary away from the ship to experiment with female clothing and stuff if I want to, but I can't. It isn't enough. Everything has changed. Everything is different now. Kara calls and I pick up, like a good boyfriend. I want to talk to her about everything. I just... I just don't feel the words I say in the same the way that I used to. We talk about the future – marriage, kids, pets... everything. I bounce ideas off of her and I ask for her advice on finding a career after the military. I want to mean all of it. And, honestly, a part of me does. But a part of me also doesn't. I want us to be happy. I just don't feel the same way about our relationship anymore. There is no future for me without her in it. That's a fact. There's just something that feels different when we talk about what our future will look like. I always feel like I'm lying to myself, and to Kara, when I talk to her. I feel like I'm lying even though it's what I want. Or, at least, it's what I *want* to want. In truth, I also can't see a future without giving into these desires. I want to be able to wear what I want to wear, talk to who I want to talk to, and to be with who I want to be with; and the latter isn't always Kara anymore. And I don't know if Kara will want to be with me anymore when I'm wearing the things that I want to wear. How could she? She loves me as "her *man.*" She likes being the pretty girlfriend. I don't think she'd be able to love me the same way if I told her that I wanted to be her pretty girlfriend. But, I still want her by my side. I want both lives and I really don't know how that can be possible. I need Kara to stay with me while I figure all of this out. I want to be the person that the voice in my head, that woman, has been telling me to be for too long now – I want to be the real me. I deserve that, I think. But, I'm also scared to let go of the person I am now. I've talked to a lot of people who live... well, "alternative lifestyles." I've read a lot on the internet. I even joined a dating service for people who are either transgender or are interested in transgender people. I probably shouldn't have because I'm still dating Kara, but the website isn't supposed to be for cheating on her. I would never do that. I just want to know if I'm attracted to anyone on there... or if they're attracted to me, the way I am now or even when I'm a big, bulky man dressed up in women's clothes. And... well, I think I'm into some of them. I don't know if I need to dress up to feel good, but I know I need someone else.

I've realized that I am interested in the transgender community. I think I always have been, subconsciously. I stumbled on some trans-porn when I was a teen and, well, it's always kind of been there in the back of my mind. I've always tried to ignore it, but I think they're beautiful. I've met some really interesting people on this site, and some really honest people, and they've opened my eyes to what I've been repressing.

I need a change. I just don't want to go through everything that they've all gone through. Stories of lost loves and families and friends spilled from their lips almost every time we talk on the phone. I couldn't bear to lose Kara. She is still my future, somehow. I can't imagine telling my family. They're so proud of the man I am. If I tell them that I want to be a woman, I can't even begin to imagine how disappointed they'll be in me. They won't understand. They won't believe it. Maybe I can just stifle this need for a little while longer. Maybe, if I can *be* with someone like who I want to be, that'll be enough.

The problem is, deep down, I don't think it will be. I have no idea how I'm going to do this, but I know I need to try it. And I need to do it soon, before I drive myself, and Kara, completely crazy.

Twenty-Six

Liam asked Kara to try to understand as he went in search of himself for one more week. He needed to explore some more to see whether or not living as a man who pursued transgender women could satisfy him romantically, even though he somewhat envied them for their appearance. Secretly, he wondered if he would rather be one of those transgender women that he'd been so curious about for so many years. He didn't tell Kara about the second possibility, though. *Not yet. Not until I know for sure*, he told himself.

Kara agreed, though it pained her so much that she hardly ate or slept the entire week. Liam spent every night with a different transgender woman that he'd met either at a bar or online but, this time, he never called Kara for support.

"This is just something I need to do by myself. I can't have my feelings for you clouding my judgment," he had told her.

And so he let himself be swept away by these women. Some nights, he'd be caught up in physical passion while with others he was fascinated by their knowledge and insight into what life as a transgender woman meant. By the end of the week, the same feelings of "wrongness" filled him again.

"How did you know what you wanted?" Liam asked one of the women over dinner. "How did you know that you wanted to be a woman?"

"I just *knew*," she told him. "I always felt like I was in the wrong body. I dreamed about myself as a woman and that always felt more real than my reality."

Liam paused, unsure about how her answer made him feel. "Did you ever doubt it?" he asked her.

"Yes and no. I had a lot of doubt, but it was never about what I wanted. It was about actually doing what I wanted. I repressed the feelings and thoughts about transitioning because, in my mind, it was wrong. I didn't *want* to transition. My family and friends aren't the most liberal and I was too scared to bring it up to them. I thought I would for sure lose them. I was right about a few, but I was also wrong about a few of them. I fought the urges hard, but, in the end, they ended up driving me crazy. Really, what it came down to was that I couldn't deny myself the kind of life that my family and friends seemed to be living – feeling 'right' with my body, and not constantly being at war with it."

The woman looked deep into Liam's eyes. It made him feel exposed, but comforted. He'd never let himself be seen the way that she was looking at him.

"Oh…" he said, unsure about what to say next. He wanted to reveal his feelings to her, but he wasn't sure that he was entirely ready.

"Not everyone reacts badly," she continued. "And, when I became who I really wanted to be, the people I really needed in my life loved me even more," she said. "I became a better version of myself."

Liam smiled in appreciation, his mind reeling about the conversation he'd have to have with Kara when he returned home. Her words hit home – Liam wanted peace with himself.

Liam

I think it's what I want. She was right. I can't live through the people I date. I can't just give into these thoughts one day a week or month or year. If I'm going to do it, it's going to be every day. Day in, day out, at work, at home, out with friends, or alone with strangers – I'm going to have to be the person that, deep down, I want to be and have been fighting to ignore for too many years now. I don't think I've ever been so scared to do something in my whole life. I don't even know if I fully understand why I want to do this. I mean, I feel like a woman inside, I want to be a woman on the outside, and I want to feel free to date men, women – whoever I want – while letting them see the part of me that I think is sexiest. I think that these feelings mean that I'm transgender. The more I learn about being transgender, the more my mind feels at peace and the better I understand myself. I can take hormones to transition my body, I can train my voice to sound more feminine, and I can wear all the clothes that I envy other girls for wearing if I want to. Maybe, if I'm lucky, Kara will even give me a few of my favorites from her closet. I've had my eye on a few pieces of hers. I used to wear them a lot when I would dress up in our San Diego apartment while she slept, and I always felt so good in them. But, on the other hand, I really don't hate who I was before. I kind of like him, the hyper-masculine me. And I'm not completely sure that I'm ready to give him up. I'm sure most people feel that way though before they transition. It must be natural. Right?

Wow. I can't believe I'm going to go through with this. It's exciting, but scary and intimidating at the same time. I've been watching videos on YouTube that other people in my situation have posted about coming out and I've seen how difficult it can be. Most cry. These people are turning to an online community for support because their families, friends, and partners didn't understand. So many, too many, ended up going through the transition alone and were hoping that some stranger on YouTube might leave a supportive comment. I can't do that. I don't want to do that. I may not be happy with how things are with my life right now, and I may not really want everything I thought I once did with Kara, but I do want a future with her. I want a future with her, with my family, with my friends, and I want to have a good job. I'm worried that, if I go down this path of becoming who I am inside, I won't be able to have that kind of success in my life. It doesn't seem fair. How do I pick which life I want? Can I have both?

I decided that I was going to tell Kara in person. After my revelation last week, I called her and, at the time, I was too scared to really realize what I wanted. I was too scared of losing my life with her to tell her that some of what the women had said really struck me. So I told her that I wanted her again, and only her. She's coming to visit me in just two days for my pre-deployment leave from the Navy. I'll tell her the truth then. I need to sleep and get these YouTube monologues out of my mind for now. They depress me and make me afraid to tell her. It'll be easier to tell her in person, face-to-face, I think. She deserves that much from me, anyway. Part of me wonders whether I should tell her before she comes, though. Or at least warn her that something has changed. But, I'm selfish. What if I warn her and she chooses not to come? I want her to come. I need her to come. I just can't imagine what uttering those words to her will feel like, or what it will feel like for her to hear them. I need to see her, though. I really need a hug from her.

Kara

Liam called me tonight. I'm supposed to fly out tomorrow morning at 6am to see him in Nashville. But he called me tonight, the day of my graduation of all days, to tell me that he feels differently. I mean, just a few days ago he said that he didn't want to date transgender people. He said that isn't what this is about. But, what else am I supposed to think? It has to be about that. He came back after his experience at a gay bar and professed his love to me over and over again. Then, he asked for a week to explore whether he might want to date transgender people. He thought that doing that might have fulfilled whatever gap inside of him that he'd been trying to fill, so that he was ready to be with just me going forward. I don't think that these things work that way. I haven't told him, or anyone else, but he left his Facebook account open on my computer before he left for Virginia. I can't help but check it every once in a while and this time I found messages from a couple of the transgender women he'd gone out with. I didn't open the messages – I would have felt worse snooping like that – but I could read the first part of the messages from both of the women. One read, "It was so great to talk with you the other night..." The other read, "Ur sexy. I'm so glad we met on TGPersonals.com. Tell me a little bit..."

Weirdly, the messages didn't bother me that much. That surprised me a little. I'd been a little nervous about the content, but the fact that Liam had these secret messages didn't hurt me that badly. I didn't cry. I just felt proven right. I've felt like Liam has been drifting farther away from me, and I've been so stressed about holding onto him and keeping him close to me, but he never admitted to feeling the same way. I was right. He obviously has been preoccupied.

When he called me earlier tonight, I'd asked if he was excited to see me tomorrow. Regardless of whether he's been preoccupied or not, *I'm* still his girlfriend. I know that and he knows that. We've both been looking forward to this trip. He paused before answering, though. And in that moment I knew that something had happened on those dates he'd gone on.

"Hey babe," he started.

"Hey. Are you excited to see me?"

"That's what I wanted to talk to you about…"

My stomach clenched and I wanted to vomit, but I just waited for him to continue instead.

"I… I… I feel differently about you."

"What do you mean, 'differently?' Do you not love me anymore?"

"Of course I care about you. I just… I think we need to take a break for real this time. Like I said, I feel differently about you," he said, his voice gruff and distant.

"Well, should I still come tomorrow?" I asked as my mind swirled through memories of him, of us together, his secret fetishes, and our visit to the psychologist. I realized that he didn't say that he still loved me.

"Do whatever you want," he said.

I waited for something more to come but it didn't. Just when I was about to hang up, he added, "But it would be good to see you."

So, I still packed up my stuff and got on my 6am flight to Nashville, Tennessee to stay with my now ex-boyfriend and his family.

I didn't know what to expect when I got there, but it was far from what greeted me. What greeted me was Liam as his old happy, loving, touchy, doting-self. We went to my favorite pub – called the Street-side Bar – in a small town next to his where he ordered me my favorite, fried pickles and a draft of Yuengling, while he ate a burger and fries. As I ate, I felt his hand tracing my knee and I saw him laugh whole-heartedly as I told him stories from home. His eyes lit up as I spoke and I felt the same kind of flirty connection we had when we first started dating. It was so confusing. I'd wanted to look my best for him. I'd wanted to make him rethink breaking up with me. So I'd worn my little jean skirt with flip-flops and a white strapless top that really accentuated my chest. He couldn't stop looking at me. It felt good. Looking at him and watching him watch me, I knew that he still loved me and that he still wanted me. Finally, I interrupted him in the middle of a story about something, I'm not sure what, and said, "Look at you. You still love me, don't you?" I tried to grin light-heartedly, but I could feel a couple tears spring into my eyes.

He stopped talking immediately and I saw sadness overwhelm his face. "That's what you thought? Gosh... baby, no. It's not like that. I love you more than anything..." His voice drifted off. "That's really what you thought? I'm so sorry. I love you, I do. But I am not *in* love with you the way I should be anymore. I have... some things on my mind. I thought that telling you that I felt differently would make all of this easier on us but I guess I was wrong."

He dropped a couple $20 bills on the table and got up to leave.

"Let's take a drive."

And that's when he told me.

We drove through the back roads like we did when I had first visited, but this time he kept the windows up and the music off. He was wrapped up in his own thoughts, so I let him be. I just watched him. His face looked torn. Eventually, he pulled over on a dead end street and looked at me. He took a deep breath and said, "Baby, I'm going to become a woman."

My heart should have stopped with shock. I should have been surprised. But I wasn't. I should have felt all these things that I didn't. My stomach didn't clench up. I didn't cry. I didn't feel anything but a surge of worry in my heart. And, later, a heavy sadness for us and for what was to come. I hugged him close to me and he gripped me back hard. He buried his face into my neck and pulled at my clothes as though he was trying to pull me even closer but that wasn't possible. Looking back, I think he was trying not to cry because he whispered, "I'm so scared, Kara. This is just something I have to do." All I could do was stroke his back and promise to help him in any and every way that I could. I meant it, too, and still do. All that I wanted to do at the time, though, was to text someone, anyone, and ask them what to do. I needed guidance. For this situation though, there was no one who could understand. It was just us.

"You're not going to have to do it alone, baby," I told him. There is no way in hell I'm going to let him fight through this on his own.

Twenty-Seven

<u>Liam</u>

I did it. I told her. I looked in her eyes as I said it and watched her heart break into a million pieces. I felt like a huge sack of shit, worse than I ever had before, so I had to look away. It took her only a split second to react though. She couldn't have fully processed it but, as she always does, she just loved me. She wrapped her arms around me and, for the first time in a long time, I felt safe.

I feel badly asking her for her help with clothes and makeup but I also need it. She offered to help me learn how to do makeup and other "girly" things right there in my truck. I felt bad, but I couldn't decline her help. She offered and I have no one else to teach me these things. Plus, I really, really love her style. I want her to teach me how she looks the way she does – natural, yet irresistibly feminine. So far, she seems okay with it. I don't want to ask too many questions on the subject and push my luck because, well, I'm just so happy that she didn't freak out and leave when I told her that I am going to transition.

Today, we drove to a department store a few towns over, for privacy's sake, to pick out some new clothes for going out. She chose a pretty purple dress for me. It cut just above my knees and hugged my butt, but it also draped loosely across my chest so that my muscular figure looked somewhat feminine. I picked out a pair of gold heels while she searched through the lingerie section for something that could help boost the… femininity… of my appearance. When all of the items were in the basket, I can't even explain how excited I was. It felt so real and surreal at the same time. Then, Kara started leading me towards the fitting room and I just about had a heart attack. I couldn't do it. My feet were glued to the floor. Ironically, I was trained to move forward no matter what, no matter who was shooting at me, yelling at me, or trying to beat me down… but I just couldn't move my feet towards the fitting rooms. Kara looked at me with concern in her eyes but didn't say anything. She just took my hand and pulled me, surprisingly hard, towards the fitting room. She told the attendant that she was trying on some clothes and wanted her boyfriend's opinion, smiling sweetly at the older woman. When she smiles like that, she looks so innocent that it's hard for people to say "no" to her. In fact, they almost never do. She's used that look on me more times than I can count. I would have laughed to myself if I hadn't been so nervous. It worked, though. The attendant opened the handicap room for us and, with a slight air of judgment around her, left us alone. Kara sat down and turned her eyes away to let me change. I was happy she did. Even though nothing's changed yet, it didn't feel right for her to see my naked body anymore. I wasn't her boyfriend anymore and I didn't want to feel looked at like a man.

Once I was dressed, the feeling I had was indescribable. I felt beautiful, whole, sexy, and powerful. Everything felt *right*. I looked in the mirror and felt like a goddess. Realistically, I still looked like a man dressed in women's clothes. I knew that. But, when I looked at myself in the mirror, I didn't see that – I saw happiness. I felt warm all over. I could see glimmers of that woman I knew was deep inside of me and who had been screaming at me to let her out all of this time.

"Kara, what do you think?" I asked.

She looked at me up and down. Her eyes were pained, but I didn't dwell on that because of how good I felt. "You look beautiful," she said, smiling at me. "We could put some make up on you too, later. Maybe some eye shadow, some mascara, and a little bit of lipstick!" Her voice was getting higher, verging on squeaky. She seemed really excited for me. Looking back on it, she sounded more nervous than anything else, but, at the time, I didn't really notice. I was too excited at the prospect of looking even more feminine.

We went home and I got changed again into the clothes we had bought at the store. Kara did my makeup and then we just hung out, like two girlfriends would. I asked her to take photos of me and I practiced posing like a girl. I strutted and jutted my hip out with my hand on it. I smiled, I pursed my lips, I pretended to look coy and flirtatious. I tried all the facial expressions and poses I'd seen my girl friends on Facebook use. Sometimes it worked and sometimes it didn't, but it was fun. We couldn't leave my bedroom because I was too afraid that someone in my family might come home and catch me, but I at least felt free in one room in the house.

After all of that, I didn't wear the outfit to the bar that night. I just couldn't build up the courage. Instead, I put on jeans that were a little too small to show off my legs and butt and a black t-shirt with a deep V-neck. Sitting in the car in the bar's parking lot, Kara offered to put makeup on me. I agreed, hesitantly, and said, "Please don't do anything too extreme."

She replied with a small laugh. "Don't worry. I'm just going to do a little faint contouring of your face, put on a touch of mascara, and put some neutral gloss on your lips. You're going to look so natural that everyone will think you've been doing this your whole life." She smiled at me. It was a reassuring to have her with me, but I still couldn't believe that I was going to go into public looking like I did. I'm not sure that I would have even made it out of the car if she hadn't promised to stay by my side the entire night.

Kara led Liam into Sugar, the gay bar on Church St. that was advertised as having a laidback and inclusive atmosphere. Liam's eyes darted around, taking in everything he that could with an excited yet withdrawn air about him. Kara saw the bar and walked directly to it, sitting down on a stool directly in front of the bartender. Liam sat down next to her and eyed the bartender up and down with interest before remembering that he was wearing makeup. Then, he avoided eye contact.

UNSEALED

"What can I get you guys?" the bartender asked. Looking no older than 21, he could have been a close cousin of Harry Styles with how similar they looked. He was dressed immaculately with more flare than Liam had ever seen at the other bars he frequented when at home in Nashville. Normally, it was a big, burly, bearded man or a tiny, young blonde with large breasts behind the bar. He liked this change. It comforted him, albeit only slightly.

Kara

Tonight was surreal. I'm sitting here, mulling it over, while he sleeps soundly next to me. For what feels like the first time since we started dating, he fell asleep before me. He must have felt so peaceful. We climbed into bed. I was on his left, as always. What's weird is that it didn't even *feel* that different, though I knew in my mind that everything had changed. He climbed in next to me and gave me a kiss on the cheek. "Thank you," he whispered. "Thank you for tonight." Then, he rolled over and, within seconds, I could hear his breathing turn peaceful and rhythmic as sleep overtook him.

I, on the other hand, have taken his place as the insomniac. Now it's my mind that can't turn off. My thoughts oscillate between shock and sadness over the end of our relationship, the realization that the future, as we had planned it, is no more, and with concern for Liam's future.

We drove around for a while after we had finished shopping earlier today. At one point, we pulled over to the side of a quiet, dirt road and just sat in the bed of his truck. Instead of resting my head on his shoulder like I used to, I let him rest his head on mine. He seemed smaller to me, somehow. He still has bulging muscles that make his six-foot frame weigh in at 210lbs, but he seemed smaller and I wanted to wrap my arms around him to protect him from breaking. I've never felt that way about him before. I've always thought of him as unbreakable. The vulnerability that he's shown me today is hard to see. It scares me a little bit. It's very unlike the man I fell in love with and the pressure is on me now to rise to the challenge of being his rock.

After a couple hours, he stirred slightly. Still wide-awake, I asked him quietly, "When did you know?"

He rolled over towards me and replied with a shrug and a look of shame on his face. "I think I've always known on some level. I just never really understood it." He paused and I just waited. "I used to dress up when I was a kid. It started when I was really young – five years old, maybe? I remember putting on my mom's shoes and getting into her makeup bag so that I could wear lipstick and blush too. I got caught a few times. My parents didn't like it. So, as I got older and was allowed to stay home alone, I started doing it in secret when I couldn't get in trouble. But then I started hearing the kids make fun of the boys who liked to play with dolls or hung out with girls too often. I heard their parents tell them to "man up" and "act properly." Some other kids' parents even said it to me if I took too much of an interest in one of my friend's sister's toys or put on a woman's hat when we played dress up games. So after getting caught or reprimanded by all these different people, I always felt like dressing up was wrong so I didn't do it very much after that. There was often that urge, though."

I looked at him for a little while longer as I tried to work out my thoughts and then squeezed his shoulders comfortingly because I didn't know what else to do. It was then that he told me about being molested as a child at the hands of his best friend's older brother. He'd never told anyone about it before. It's, what, 10, 15 years later now? That's a big secret to bury inside for so long and from such a young age. To be honest, I wasn't too surprised, though. That's a difficult topic to talk about. That's a tough secret for anyone to reveal, as well as keep buried inside. After hearing about how adults in his life reacted to him dressing up, along with having grown up next to some rigidly religious neighbors who I knew hadn't had a compassionate word for anyone who didn't live by their views, I can understand that it was probably very hard to know where to turn and who to trust with that secret. And that made me sad. I can understand why Liam has felt such a strong need to repress his feelings and his memories. I wish he had understood that it wasn't his fault though. I wish he'd had, or felt like he'd had, a support network for those thoughts and memories.

I can't blame his parents, neighbors, or any one set of adult influences for Liam feeling like he had nowhere to turn. It's something about this whole town, maybe even this whole state. Or, it's at least a response to this feeling of deserved alienation for being "different" that is perpetuated by a very loud and close-minded portion of the population. I love this place. I was going to make this place my home, but I'm seeing it differently now. It's great when you fit the "acceptable" mold – the South is filled with kind and generous people. But, it's a completely different world when you're different. It's more than just not being liberal. I knew that coming down here. The South isn't known for its democratic views. What was more shocking to me was the reality of the lack of cultural open-mindedness some of its citizens have. It's pervasive. Even when I thought we'd be safe from it and find a supportive network for Liam at the bar, there was the same kind of pushing of un-solicited and ungrounded opinions. Maybe it's like this everywhere and I'm only now in a position to see it, but I don't know. I was shocked, and honestly quite offended, by the lack of support Liam found at the gay bar earlier tonight. Granted, it was just a few men and I can't use their opinions to judge the entire community, but it was a tough way for Liam to enter his new life. Each of these men had their own traumatic coming out story – conservative parents, a military job, homophobic teammates – all of which Liam could identify with. Yet, when it came time for him to share his coming out story, he received no support. Instead, they mocked him. They told him that his decision was wrong. They candidly told Liam all the reasons that he shouldn't be transgender – as if it were a choice.

"Dude, you're too good-looking to be trans," said one.

"You're a hot man, but you'll be one ugly girl," laughed another.

"Stay a man. You'll do better as a man," they chorused, each looking at him with hunger in their eyes.

What made me angry was that they never asked him to explain his feelings. They didn't care. They just projected their own views onto him and I hated them for it. It was Liam's first night out in his new life and he was only met with resistance. I would have thought they, of all people, would have understood that it *wasn't* a choice, given the fights they'd had with friends and family over their own coming out experiences, but I was wrong. Apparently, that sort of understanding hadn't yet expanded to encompass transgender individuals in their minds.

I will give them credit for admitting as much, though. One of them had said, "I just don't understand, man, why you'd want to be a woman. I just don't get it. If you like men, just fuck a man. Problem solved."

Maybe I'm the one whose mind needs broadening. Maybe I shouldn't have assumed that Liam could just walk into a gay bar and have all of its patrons be welcoming, or at least understanding. Each member of the community is different too, with their own battles, issues, and levels of open-mindedness. Just because the rest of society has grouped them together doesn't mean they necessarily understand every other group, does it? I'm not sure. Maybe we just met the wrong group of gay men. I don't know. I feel guilty about this experience though. This was the place we chose to go on his first night "out" as a transgender woman solely because, after I'd searched online, we thought that it would be the most accepting of him. He seemed so excited at the thought that someone might understand him, finally. Of all the places he could've gone to in Nashville, of all the people he could've met, he was certain that he'd find the people who understood him at that bar. Instead, I think he walked away feeling even more alone. On our way out, he said to me, "All I want to do is be me, Kara. But I'm not sure who that is anymore. Do you think I'm doing the right thing? What if I'm not?"

My heart broke because I didn't know what to say. I don't know how to make him feel better. Of course I thought that he was doing the right thing. I could see it in his eyes – he really wanted this. There was a raw vulnerability that I had never seen before and that was how I knew it was the right thing for him. But, I wish he were able to be confident without fearing prejudice at every turn. All I could say was, "Yes, sweetie. Of course you're doing the right thing. This is what you want." Meanwhile, my heart broke at my own loss and tears stung in my eyes as I realized how difficult it was going to be for him to actually transition. On one hand, I'm losing the man I love and thought I'd grow old with. We'd made it through so much. I did everything I could to hold us together and it wasn't enough. I had hoped with every fiber of my being that that would be it, all of that bad stuff would be in the past and we could just be happy. And now I just can't imagine moving on. Now, we're both so far from happy and we can't rely on each other anymore for happiness, no matter how much we love each other. We're on our own now. We have to be happy alone. I think Liam is ready for that, but I don't think I am. And I'm worried that, because of that, he's going to go on to be happy without me and I'm going to be left alone with this broken heart that I don't know how to heal. At the same time, though, I'm so worried for him. He's strong, accomplished, intelligent, and so incredibly loving. But when it comes to his coming out, he's got the innocence of a child. I'm scared, now, that this unwelcoming town is going to shatter that innocence all too soon. His childhood was fairly void of innocence so it isn't that he won't be able to handle it. It's just that, after everything that he's endured and feared, I want the world to reward him with the opportunity to grow into the person that he wants to be with the same innocence that I was awarded as a child – one that comes with the opportunity to be surrounded by unconditional love and acceptance.

Twenty-Eight

The next few days passed in a sort of fog for both Liam and Kara. Liam wasn't ready to tell his parents, siblings, or his friends. That meant that Kara still played the role of his girlfriend in most social situations, which wasn't hard at first because the realness of the situation hadn't completely sunk in. When Liam wasn't dressed up, their relationship still felt normal to her. Pretending to still be his girlfriend meant that she held his hand at every family meal, kissed him in front of all of his high school friends at parties, and giggled as he spun her into moments of two-step when on a double date with Billy and his girlfriend. Those moments still felt real, but only until they were alone. Without any eyes on him, Liam easily slipped back into daydreaming and brainstorming about his future as a woman. At that point, Kara would be jolted back into reality as Liam asked for makeup tips, was caught checking out the male bartender, or pleaded with her to revisit a gay bar. For Liam, the moments with Kara were real, only different than before. He loved her in both situations. Only, in his ideal new life, he wasn't *in love* with her anymore; instead he was starting to finally love himself. For Kara, everything felt real and dreamlike almost simultaneously.

Kara encouraged Liam to start telling his closest friends. Not only did she believe that it was the right thing to do because Liam would need support when he returned from deployment and she would be home in Canada, but she also was struggling with being alone with his secret and acting as his sole supporter. Liam listened and agreed to start by telling one friend – one he had known since he was a young child – Jacob. Liam had decided that before the week was up, he would tell Jacob; but after he'd seen him a few times first. Only a couple of days after Liam told Kara about his decision, Liam and Kara visited Jacob's new apartment. As they drove, Kara asked, "So, are you going to tell him?"

Liam paused. "Not tonight. I mean, I don't know how he'll respond, you know? I don't think I could handle someone not being supportive at this point. I just want to enjoy figuring it out with you."

Kara nodded. She'd met Jacob before and, while extremely warm and friendly, he was quite conservative. "He's known you since you were a kid, though. You don't think he'd understand, or that he would at least try to understand?"

Liam shot her a look. His mocking smirk was half-hearted and betrayed his deep insecurity. "Well, it's kind of a fucked up thing to hear, isn't it?"

Kara had to nod slightly in concession. She'd had her moments of difficulty over the past couple days with his revelation. She'd cried, she'd lashed out, and she had developed a migraine that just would not subside. She'd even slept through an entire party in Liam's truck, oblivious to a fight that had broken out outside her window. Liam had been angry that she'd missed the party and hadn't been at his side to act like his girlfriend, but her mind had needed a few hours to completely shut off in order to cope.

"Jacob loves you though. I'm sure he'll be supportive, just like I am," she offered, with more hope in her voice than conviction. She really wasn't sure how Jacob, or anyone else in Liam's life, would react to the news.

Liam chuckled darkly. "We'll see. Let's just eat some pizza and then we can go home and watch that DVD you bought."

After Liam had told her the news, Kara had been unable to sleep. She wanted to do something that showed her support better than the telltale tears that she felt were easily visible in her eyes any time she looked at Liam. As he slept, she had gone online and searched for DVDs and books about transgender people or stories about the experience of coming out as trans. There were more available than she had expected, but still quite a poor selection. She hadn't heard of any of the titles so she relied on reviews to point her towards her ultimate choice – *Transamerica*. With great reviews, it seemed to be one of the defining films available at that time so she purchased it and requested expedited shipping. Liam had been touched when the package arrived that morning and, after reading the reviews himself, he was eager to watch it. It was a whole new world for him and, still not having anyone who could truly understand the situation to talk to, it seemed to him that this film might be able to really speak to him. Kara, on the other hand, was more apprehensive about the film and feared that it might make the situation all the more real.

That night, Liam had put on his most masculine clothes – baggy, dirty jeans, work boots, a dark and plain t-shirt, and a hat he had gotten while in survival training while he was in BUD/S. Liam looked just like his old self when Jacob opened his door except for one small detail – he and Kara had gone to have his eyebrows shaped on the way over. Liam had really wanted to have it done. Keeping his hat on while inside to distract from that fairly visible change, Liam was pleased when Jacob didn't seem to notice. Kara concentrated on keeping her eyes averted.

As they drank beer and ate pizza, it was easy for Kara to forget Liam's recent changes as Jacob remarked, "Just like old times, isn't it, bud? Only difference now is that you've got this gem instead of Caligula."

Liam laughed. "Yep, this girl is a keeper. She's the best thing that's ever happened to me," he said, smiling warmly in Kara's direction.

Kara's heart panged with sadness as she realized that he actually meant it, but that they would never again be the couple Jacob thought they were. She grinned back, nonetheless. "Damn right, I am," she said as she winked at Liam.

Jacob watched them both with a smile. "So, when do I get to start my best man duties?" he asked. "And don't tell me Billy gets to do it. We can split it or something, but I already got some ideas brewin' for your bachelor party."

Instantly, Liam and Kara stiffened. Kara avoided Jacob's eyes and stared intently at the crusts left on her plate.

"What? What did I say?" Jacob asked, confused.

"Uh, well buddy... I've got some news," said Liam, hesitantly.

"What? Are you guys okay?" Jacob looked from Liam to Kara while Kara focused her eyes on Liam in support.

"We're fine," started Liam. "Well, maybe not fine. We actually broke up because... because I'm going to be a woman."

Liam's revelation was met with silence. Only then did Kara look up and see Jacob's face blank with shock. A smile twitched at his lips as his mind debated whether Liam was playing a joke or not. She rested her hand on Liam's forearm and squeezed.

"I mean that I'm transgender. I'm still me though buddy. I'm still exactly the same. I still love football and beer and chewing tobacco and shooting stuff. I still love my friends and I still love this girl here," he said, putting his arm around Kara's shoulders. "I'm just not necessarily *in love* with her anymore so we've ended things romantically and are going to just be friends. I'm still exactly who I used to be, man. I'm still going to be the old me. I'm just going to look different soon."

Jacob continued to stare, but comprehension was starting to dawn on his face. Kara could see him notice Liam's eyebrows as he continued to listen.

"I've felt this way for a while. Maybe ever since I was a kid. I didn't really understand what it was, but I do now. I was just born into the wrong body. Do you get it?"

Kara could tell that Liam was nervous because his words were coming out faster and faster the longer that Jacob stayed silent.

"Hey, man. Just do you," Jacob replied, finally. "It doesn't matter to me what you look like." He grinned at Liam and clapped him on the shoulder.

Liam laughed, relieved. "Good, 'cause I may be one badass chick, but I could also be one ugly-ass chick too."

Kara laughed along although she and Jacob shared a look that said neither were laughing on the inside. Instead, she saw her feelings reflected in his eyes – he too was overwhelmed and sad for Liam.

A few moments of silence followed, which Liam broke with an excited question. "Since you know now, would you want to watch a movie with Kara and I? She found it. It's about a transgender woman living in the U.S. It's supposed to be really great," he asked, hopefully.

Kara watched for Jacob's response. It felt good for her to not be alone with Liam's secret anymore.

"Sure," Jacob replied.

Liam got up to make popcorn and to grab the movie from his truck. As he worked to get the movie playing, Jacob asked him, "What's the Navy going to say about this? Do they know?"

Kara listened carefully. She had often thought about asking the same question, but never did because she didn't want to stress Liam out anymore than he already was.

"Dude, I don't even know. I think I'll just have to lie about it. I can cover up any changes pretty easily. I've just got to do my time and get out, ya know?" Liam replied with a heavy sigh.

Jacob nodded and Liam pressed play on the DVD player.

All three sat silently throughout the movie. Liam sat on the end of the couch beside the window. Jacob sat on the other end of the couch, next to the big, comfy chair that Kara had curled into. As the movie played, Jacob could see Kara wiping tears from her face. He noticed her cry during the parts where the main character discussed love and relationships, when she faced the kind of prejudice and hate that they all knew would likely be in Liam's future, and sometimes Kara just seemed to cry at the fact that the movie was playing. For a while, Jacob just let her cry.

Then, when Liam got up to use the restroom, he interrupted her. "It's pretty crazy, huh?"

"Yeah," she replied while wiping away her tears before Liam came back.

"It's pretty tough to think about, isn't it? I know it is for me and I wasn't even dating the guy."

"Yeah. It sucks, that's for sure. I mean, on the one hand, my brain quite literally cannot process it. You know, when people say, 'my mind is blown,' and it's considered a figure of speech? Well, I'm fairly certain that I'm experiencing the actual version of it. But, on the other hand, watching things like this bring me around to Liam's perspective and it scares me. That transgender woman got so little support from the people who should have been supporting her most and it'll break my heart if that happens to Liam."

"He's going to need us now more than ever." Jacob nodded in agreement.

"Mhmm." Kara smiled. "Seems like it. Thank you for supporting him. I appreciate it too. He was really nervous to tell you. You're the first person to know other than me."

"Like I said, I don't care what he looks like. He's like my brother and he's got to do what makes him happy." Jacob paused before adding, "It's going to be tough to see, though. I can't imagine him being or looking any different than he always has."

"Tell me about it. I really never thought it would end this way with him." Kara paused to giggle. "Well, obviously I didn't. But, I guess it's a blessing that it's all happening so fast because, to be honest, I haven't had much of a chance to really think about all the little changes he's already made until just now, sitting here watching this movie. The next few months are going to be the hardest though. This… this is all still a whirlwind and I haven't really grasped the entirety of the situation yet. I'm sure it'll settle in at some point and that's when it'll really suck." She smiled wryly at Jacob.

At that moment, Liam returned and, with a look of shared sadness, Kara and Jacob turned back to finish the movie.

Fortunately, Jacob's seemingly supportive reaction alleviated some of Liam and Kara's stress. Unfortunately, it didn't take long for Kara or Liam to see how much difficulty Jacob was actually having with processing the reality of Liam's transition. Like Kara, he started lashing out at Liam in anger over little, and sometimes imaginary, things. Unlike Kara, he became more angry than sad. In the end, several months later, Billy caught him keying Liam's truck, proving that while words of support can be meaningful, actions prove their legitimacy. Jacob simply could not handle watching his friend transition, nor did he want to try.

Liam

Now that both of my best friends know, I feel relieved. Jacob took it better than I thought. He said he didn't care. I told him that I wasn't going to change anything except for my appearance and he seemed to understand that. I mean, that's probably a bit of a lie because I'll obviously be doing some new things – like shopping – but I'm still going to be me and I want him to understand that. It felt good to have them both there, to both know, and for them to both watch that movie with me. I feel so supported. I really feel like I can do this. Kara has been hugely supportive over the last few days, but it never really felt like I was actually going to be okay until someone from here supported me too. I know that I'm going to have to do this without Kara by my side all of the time because she's going to have to go home eventually. To have someone that's going to be here and have my back when things start changing, that's going to make all the difference. That movie was inspiring but also pretty sad. I don't want to lose the people in my life because of what I'll look like.

What Jacob and Kara don't know is that I've been on YouTube searching for coming out stories of other transgender people. You know what almost all of them have in common? They all did it alone. They didn't have people that stayed by them. They lost loved ones, family members, and friends. They recreated their lives again afterward but almost always found that their relationships with people from before the transition were strained, at best. I don't want that. I love everyone in my life right now. I can't imagine it changing. I can't imagine having to go through all of this without them. Being with Kara and Jacob tonight made me feel like I won't have to be so alone.

Twenty-Nine

Nearing the end of Kara's two week visit, Liam asked her whether or not she would be willing to go to another gay bar on their final night together. She agreed. But before they could go, Billy and his girlfriend, Mary, had invited them to a party at a local bar that all of their old friends from high school planned to attend. Liam was all at once excited to go and angry at having to put off the gay bar until later. With girls who used to chase him, girls who wanted to chase him now, and almost every single player from his former football team in attendance, Liam felt pressured to represent himself as the man who, as far as they knew, was becoming a Navy SEAL. He felt guilty that he didn't want to be that person anymore. Well, at least not in his entirety. Liam still thought of himself as "one badass mother fucker." That part of him, the Navy SEAL confidence, would always be a part of him. However the social pressures he felt from his old peers led him to being foul-tempered and extremely flirtatious with the other girls while he left Kara to sit, embarrassed and alone, with Billy and Mary.

"Well, Liam's in fine form tonight," said Billy, watching as Liam circulated the room, doing shots with whoever asked.

"I wouldn't stand for it," said Mary. "I mean, you should stand up for yourself and yell at him. I'll do it for you, if you'd like, because even I'm angry with how he's behaving!"

Kara smiled, appreciatively. "No, no, it's okay. He's going through a lot right now. It's fine – I'm fine," she said, though she could tell by the look on Mary's face that Mary didn't believe her.

"He's lucky he's dating you because I'd be out that door and back home in my comfy bed by now, if I were you." Mary shot Billy a pointed look.

Kara laughed slightly and rolled her eyes, though her stomach turned at the word "dating."

It was difficult to keep Liam's secret to herself. She wanted to explain why he was acting so rude and she wanted to explain why she was tolerating it. She didn't want people to think that she was weak. She wanted to defend herself, and Liam, but the only way she knew how to do so was to share his story. Unfortunately, she knew that it wasn't hers to share.

Kara saw Jack, one of Liam's old friends with whom she'd gotten along with well at various other gatherings during her visit, coming into the bar. The warmest of Liam's friends, she'd often enjoyed Jack's company while Liam caught up with old friends. Tonight, she felt the need to be closer to him than she ever had. She craved a calm and relaxed male presence near her.

As Kara left the table to go greet Jack, she passed Liam as he was yelling whole-heartedly to the entire room that he, and everyone there, should leave and go to a house party. No one seemed to respond because, Kara later learned, the house belonged to a known and convicted drug dealer with whom no one wanted to associate. At the time, that fact didn't seem to bother Liam. Kara knew it was all for show – that Liam would never miss an opportunity to go to the gay bar with her, especially when it was her last night in town. So she ignored him.

"Hey, Jack," she said with a smile as she reached him. He was leaning casually against a wall with a couple of girls surrounding him.

When he saw her, he turned away from the other girls and grinned back. "Hey, Kara. How's it going? Liam seems to be in fine form tonight." He rolled his eyes.

Kara laughed. "You're not the first person to point that out," she said.

Jack was a mechanic who had a love of hunting and fishing. He was a little taller than Liam, leaner, but still very muscular with clearly defined arms and a rock-solid stomach. His hair was short and he had a chiseled face. With a singsong Southern drawl, Jack was, in Kara's opinion, very attractive and she wanted nothing more at that moment than to tell him the truth and to be comforted by his strong arms. The pair chatted for a few minutes and Kara noticed that his attention was entirely on her. He didn't look around for other girls or other friends. The girls he had been standing with when she arrived had left. He didn't even seem impatient to get another beer once he'd finished the one he'd been drinking. While a relatively normal interaction, it caused a rush of warmth to come over Kara. She enjoyed feeling like the focus of a man's attention, especially since she'd given all of her focus to Liam over the last few days. Greedy or not, she wanted some attention too. In that moment, she had been confident that the feeling was mutual, that she and Jack had a connection. Though, upon reflection, she realized it was likely all in her mind and a result of her desire to feel attractive and desired again.

Before too long, Liam strode over and, after a few more minutes of chatting to Jack and Kara, said, "Babe, ready to go?"

"Where are you guys off to?" interrupted Jack.

"Maybe the after party at Benny's place? Or, maybe we'll just head back home. It's her last night here," Liam replied with a suggestive wink. Only Kara knew that it was entirely for show and that they were going to a gay bar again, or maybe two or three judging by how rowdy Liam was acting. She was tired and didn't want to go. "Kara, wait here for a minute while I pay the tab and then we can leave."

Kara stayed standing in front of Jack.

"It looks like y'all are doin' well, then." Jack smiled warmly at Kara.

Kara struggled to find words to answer. "Well, you know…" she managed to say with a meek smile. She looked deep into his eyes, unblinkingly, with hope that he could read the truth there. She willed him to see everything she knew, really *see* it, but all he could see was a girl with pretty eyes and a sweet smile that he wished he had met first.

Liam returned and Kara turned to leave. "Hope to see you around again soon," said Jack, before giving her a hug.

Kara smiled into his neck. "Yeah. Soon," she said, breathing in his comforting smell as she enjoyed the security she felt in his strong arms. She used to feel that way with Liam, but those days felt like a distant memory after everything that had happened over this visit.

Liam waited, heart racing, as he thought about the eyeliner and lipstick that he had hidden in the glove compartment of his car. Tonight, he told himself, he was going to go out with confidence. It was his last chance because he wasn't sure if he'd be brave enough to go to any gay dance clubs alone, and, after tonight, Kara wouldn't be there to support him anymore.

Kara

I lost control. Something in me snapped. I was banging and banging on the door of this apartment belonging to a stranger we met at the bar, tears streaming down my face, my mind full of snapshots from the night… I kept seeing him making out with a man on the dance floor; I kept hearing a bitter trans girl tell us to come home with her so that I could hear what Liam sounded like when he was "truly pleasured"; and I remembered a mammoth sized woman bringing a weed-whacker into the bar to try to kill me with because she "don't want no foreigners like me in her bar."

As I hit the door again and again, the trans girl's words rang in my ears. *"Truly pleasured."* Even if it wasn't her on the other side of the door, it was still happening. I could hear him moaning, oblivious to (or unconcerned about) my shouting.

Telepathically, I pleaded with him. Pick me. Put me first. Make sure that guy knows that I'm still your number one. I guess I knew that I might not have been in his future, and that I wasn't on his mind anymore at that moment, but I pleaded anyway because I still felt like I should have been. After everything I had done to help him on this trip, didn't I deserve to be number one in his books? I have been trying so hard. I'm his girl. I'm his number one. I should always be his number one after everything we have been through and everything we have meant to each other. I just couldn't accept that Liam would pick a stranger over me just because that stranger had told him that he was hot while he was wearing makeup. I could understand wanting to feel accepted. I could understand that, maybe after finally figuring out what it is that you wanted, that it might have been easy to become a little… manic. What I didn't get was stomping all over the people – or, rather, the person – who already accepted you and supported you. So, I tried over and over again to interrupt them so that I could make Liam see exactly that. I couldn't stop myself. It didn't matter that I knew he wouldn't answer; I couldn't just sit back and let him enjoy his time with that asshole. Just two weeks ago, Liam and I were going to be married and stay together for the rest of our lives. Now, I'm locked outside of a stranger's apartment while he has sex with someone he's known for less than five hours and who has been nothing but mean to me. It's like Liam tossed all that love and respect for me out the window. Basically, he was telling me that I didn't matter anymore. I *needed* him to know that he was wrong. I matter. I should matter the most.

Each time I banged on the door, my knocks and sobbed pleas were met with silence. Each time, I returned to Danny's arms. (Danny was an acquaintance of the awful guy Liam was… spending time with… inside, but Danny was actually kind and sweet, and tried to comfort me.) Each time I came back to sit on the stairs that led into the apartment, Danny would open his arms and pull me in. He'd wipe the tears off my face and say, "Girl, I wish we'd both been lesbians. Guys are cruel and hurtful." Then he'd wink at me and, for a moment, I wouldn't feel so alone. He even tried to distract me by showing me his scars. He had so many – his whole body was covered. My mouth gaped open and, by way of explanation, he simply said, "They're from years of dealing with pain using razor blades." His wrists, forearms, thighs, and stomach were all striped like a tiger. I felt awful for him. But my mind was too blown to really take in the enormity of his pain at the time. Looking back, I wish I had reciprocated with more comfort. But, at the time, it just felt good to listen to someone try to distract me.

Danny continued to talk to me (I think to prevent me from trying to interrupt Liam and Nick anymore). He told me the stories of every one of his breakups that led to him making marks on his body. He told me about the embarrassment he still felt at having been woken up in the hospital with his ex looking at him with nothing but pity. He told me how he regretted cutting himself after a particularly difficult breakup and how, when his ex saw the results, that the stress of that embarrassment had actually pushed Danny to cut again. And to end up in the hospital again. "And you know who came to visit?" he asked. "My ex. Again. Nothing has ever hurt more."

With more experience in heartbreak than me, he tried hard to give me advice and to make me hear it. Looking back, I wasn't ready then. Danny told me, "Be mad at Liam in the morning. Forget about Nick, forget about this, and then move on with your life. Holding onto the anger you feel right now won't do you or Liam any good. It's poison and it's going to eat away at you and drive you crazy."

"But I just want him to *understand* how terribly he is treating me right now!" I cried as he wrapped his arm around my shoulders.

"Kara, he will one day. It may not be tonight, it may not be tomorrow or next week, or even next year, but it'll come. Until then, you're wasting your breath. You've got to find a way to get over it on your own."

I heard what he said but I didn't know if I could let it go. However, I wanted to listen to him and I wanted to try. "How do I do that?" I asked. "I really don't know how to get over it on my own. I don't know how to forgive him, especially because he really doesn't seem to think that he needs forgiveness. I think that makes me the angriest."

"Sweetheart, I have no idea. I'm not very good at it either, as you've seen." He half-grinned. "But that doesn't mean I'm wrong." He stroked my hair and chuckled. "If you figure it out, though, let me know?"

I tried to sit there with him and wait patiently, but I couldn't. After a few minutes, the urge to interrupt Liam and Nick again was too strong. Danny pleaded with me not to go, but I couldn't listen. I needed to have Liam choose to ignore me again. That's when I got stuck in a loop of knocking and yelling and knocking and waiting. I didn't really expect Liam to answer the door. If he were going to, he would have opened it the first time. I just wanted to dare him not to. Then, when he didn't, I just got angrier and angrier. It was like I was challenging him to let me down over and over again. Apparently, I was a glutton for punishment and needed to prove to myself that Liam, at that moment, did not care about me. I knew, somewhere deep in my mind, that he saw this as *his* night, *his* coming out night. I just didn't expect him to officially be able to end our relationship so easily and so quickly. But, I guess he'd basically been done for a while. What angered me the most was that Nick had pretended to be my friend at the bar. When the trans girl was bullying me, he had stepped in and offered words of condolences. When Liam was grinding with a random guy on the dance floor, he had suggested that we all go back to his place to have a casual hangout. But it was all a ploy to get to Liam and that made me angrier than Liam ignoring me. I was tired of other people making me feel sad and I had channeled that into an insatiable rage. And so I kept calling Liam's name over and over again, and he ignored me every time.

I'd lost count of how many times I had knocked, but eventually I heard a noise. The door slammed open and hit my face with enough force to throw me into the neighbor's door across the hall. I expected to see Liam on the other side but it was Nick. His eyes locked on me.

"Shut the fuck up, you stupid cunt. My neighbors are sleeping. Let him have some good sex for once and go away. Don't be such a selfish bitch." Nick was peering down on me, his breath hot on my face, his muscles flinching as his arms acted like prison bars and pinned me against the wall.

How dare he say that to me! How dare he threaten me like this, I thought.

Foolishly, I had expected Liam to be there, to pull him off and tell him to leave me alone. But he didn't. Indignant, I had met Nick's gaze. "What are you going to do about it?" I hissed at him. "He's still mine. He needs to take me home now."

Nick just smirked while Liam looked over his shoulder and said, "You need to settle down girl. You're embarrassing me. Don't get mad at me for having sex. Don't you want me to finally feel something good?"

So what about the last year and a half? Was there nothing good in that? I thought as fresh tears sprung to my eyes. His words hurt. The sun was coming up and the paperboy had turned onto the street. "I'm going now, Liam. My flight leaves today, I'm exhausted, and still need to pack. Take me home."

I ducked under the big, black, tattooed arms and headed for Liam's truck. I paused by my new friend, the stranger who had held me when my almost-fiancé shoved me away, and felt grateful that he'd been there. I looked up at him and he just wiped the tears off my face, smiled, and said, "Seriously, girl, become a lesbian. I know some really great girls for you." With that, he winked and let me go, and I couldn't help but smile a little as I got into Liam's truck while Liam followed slowly behind.

We drove back to Liam's family home in silence. I had turned away from him and looked out the window, silently shaking and trying to stifle the tears that were threatening to flow down my cheeks. He hadn't said one word, even though I knew that he'd seen me. By the time we had gotten to his house, it was almost

6am and we hadn't slept at all. So, we went right upstairs. I had hoped that we'd talk, but he had gone right into his bed and rolled over. I couldn't believe it. He wasn't going to say it. He wasn't going to say "sorry," or anything apologetic about the entire night. I couldn't take it.

"Really? You're not going to apologize?" I snapped at him.

He just yawned and said, "Apologize? That's on you. You acted like a jealous idiot today. It was embarrassing."

My stomach dropped and a wave of ice washed over me. I couldn't believe it. He had no idea that he was in the wrong. Danny was right.

"Really? It's on me? You selfish asshole. We broke up TWO WEEKS AGO and yet I've had to hang on our arm and pretend to be 'your girl' to all of you family and friends and now, tonight, you expected me to have no problem sitting back and watching you hook up with someone else. You made me listen to it, too. But not before you asked me to listen to you hook up with a trans girl, and not before a lady wanted to kill me with a weed-whacker while you were too busy flirting with other people to notice. You owe ME an apology."

I shouldn't have said that. I shouldn't have pushed him. I knew that he wasn't in a good place and that he wasn't the same Liam I had fallen in love with anymore, especially in that moment. In response, he had spun around and stood up, backing me against the wall while glaring down at me. "It isn't your business who I sleep with! It isn't anyone's business. Couldn't you just let me be happy for one goddamn night, Kara?! It was a fucking *guy* for God's sakes. You can't tell me you were jealous of *that*."

I watched as the same tattoo I that had lovingly traced with my fingers during countless morning cuddles and long drives pulsed with anger and frustration above a clenched fist.

"I'll forgive you this time. I know you're struggling with this. But you've really got to get it under control. I'm not hiding myself anymore. I'm going to do whatever the fuck I want. You say you love me. Well, now's the time to prove it."

With that, he just stared at me for a while, like he was challenging me to say something.

A part of me wondered where his family was and why they weren't coming to see what all the commotion was about. I knew that they were sleeping in their rooms only a few feet away and that, with the thin walls, they should have heard everything. A different part of me was listening to what he was saying too, and trying to think of a response. But, mostly, I was focused on his eyes. I couldn't look away. There wasn't any of "my Liam" in his eyes anymore. There was just vacant anger. His blank eyes were locked on mine, entirely glazed over with anger and what was left of the booze in his system. I didn't know what else to do; I silently begged him to see the tears in my eyes and to see *me* for once. I wanted him to see the pain, the sadness, the hurt, and all the exhausted effort that was pent up inside of me because of how his new reality was affecting me. But he really wasn't seeing me at all. He was just, kind of, gone.

Finally, the fury in his eyes was replaced by exhaustion and so he turned away and went back to bed. I stayed standing, both out of shock and anger that I hadn't said anything in response, as well as a little bit of fear, until I heard his breath even out and a soft snoring come from his body. He was curled into the fetal position. He looked so harmless, and so much like the old Liam that it was hard to believe that so much had changed during this visit. I had wanted to stroke his back to comfort him, to ease the pain he had to have been feeling to act like that, but I was hurt too. In the end, I didn't know what else to do so I crawled into the bed next to him, just as I'd always done, and wrapped my arm around his side. While asleep, he wrapped his fingers around mine and gently squeezed.

The earlier events of the night had made me realize that our relationship was actually over. Until tonight, he'd still been a little too nervous to really flirt or to entertain the idea of being with anyone else at those bars. Until tonight, I had still felt like he was *mine*. Tonight, he had made it abundantly clear, intentionally or not, that he wasn't mine anymore. It should have been fine. Well, I wanted it to be fine. That was what happened in breakups, right? I just wasn't sure how it could work. I don't think we know how to be friends yet. I still can't bear the thought of not being the most important person in his life. I can't bear to lose him.

Liam

This was *my* night. It was my first night out as *me*, the real me, and she ruined it. She wanted me to feel guilty and, honestly, I've done nothing but feel guilty for years. This was my time to *finally* do what I wanted and to not feel guilty about it. Instead, she got jealous even though I wasn't going out to meet other girls. I just wanted to *be* one of the other girls. She was the one who put my makeup on, the one who gave me a bra to help squeeze my pecks together to look like cleavage, and the one who sprayed me with her perfume. She was the one who covered the windows of my truck and stood guard while I changed out of my old, male clothes. She said she would be okay with it, and I needed her to be okay. I really, really needed her to be okay with me being *me*. It was scary as hell showing other people who I was for the first time, especially in

Nashville. Nashville's got a lot of great things, but tolerance is definitely not one of them. I didn't tell her this, of course. I knew she was already worried for me and she probably already knew that, and I didn't want to make her worry more. But I needed her to be okay and to help me through this night. I needed her to have fun with me while I was being *me*. But instead, she just cried, got mad, and eventually begged me to take her home after interrupting something good that I had going with someone who wanted me for me, the new me. It felt really good to be wanted while presenting how I truly felt inside.

Didn't she see the hot guy I was dancing with? I danced like a girl, a slutty girl, and he loved it. I'm not her boyfriend anymore. The guy from the club had taken me to the corner of the dance floor where we were mostly hidden by people and had grabbed a hold of me from behind. I could feel his hot breath on the back of my neck. He was thin and tall but had his head bent down to mine. Lady Gaga had come on the speakers singing "Born This Way," and there couldn't have been a better moment to start dancing close to him, just like Kara had done to me when we used to go out. I practiced thrusting my ass into him, and then rotated my hips to the beat of the music while letting his hands guide me. I didn't feel like Liam anymore. I felt like *me*. I felt like the girl I always dreamed about. It wasn't hard to let go of my masculine self at all. Once I was there and someone had accepted me, it was easy. I liked his hands telling me where to go. I liked being the girl. The man that Kara was dating, the boyfriend I was before, was finally gone. How could she still have been so jealous about someone who didn't exist anymore?

We danced and I liked it, at least until I saw Kara looking at me through the crowd. She was so still and she looked so alone. She had her arm through Danny's, but she was only looking at me. Danny was pulling her to go dance. I could see his efforts and I appreciated it, but Kara wouldn't budge. And that's when the night was ruined. I felt guilty. Again, I felt the pressure to be her *man*. Again, I felt like I had to take care of her. The look on her face brought me back to who I still was to the rest of the world, and to her. I didn't want to be that guy for her anymore, but I couldn't just ignore her either. So I went to her. She hugged me when I got there and buried her face in my chest. In that moment, I hated her. She had gotten so drunk that she puked as soon as we left the bar. I hated her for being another responsibility, for not being strong enough to let me go, and for not realizing how much this night meant to me. But, as angry as I was at her, I still love her more than anything else in the world so I took her hand in mine, just as I'd always done.

I wasn't ready to end my night so when Danny's friend Nick had suggested that we all go back to his place to hang out I was ecstatic. I thought that it would be the best solution. We could all hang out together as friends. She shouldn't have had a reason to be jealous then.

I really thought it was going be platonic. How was I supposed to know how things were going to unfold? I didn't think that Nick liked me. But when I found out that he did, it awakened something inside of me. He was *hot*. He said he liked my boobs. That felt really, really good. I thought that I was being thoughtful by leaving the bar. That's what I was trying to be, anyway. Instead, all she saw was me being selfish. I'm really trying to do right by myself right now. I wasn't trying to hurt her, but I still don't understand how she was so jealous when she knows that I'm going to be a woman. Plus, it's not like I was going for another girl.

I'm so tired. I drank way too much, stayed out way too late, and there were way too many emotions flying through the air. I don't want to have to deal with anything. Kara is so mad at me. She keeps demanding that I apologize for my actions and I just can't, and I won't. I'm not fucking apologizing for who I am anymore. Now is finally my time to be selfish. I've been living according to other peoples' rules for too long. This is my time. I need her to just let me figure myself out.

Thirty

Liam and Kara parted ways, both teary-eyed at having to leave each other despite their anger from the night before. Kara went home to Canada while Liam went back to the ship. He felt sick as he packed all of his men's clothing into a bag and left everything new he'd accumulated behind in a box hidden at the back of his closet. He couldn't bear to leave *everything*, so he slipped a few of the lacy panties he'd recently acquired into a zipped compartment of his duffle bag.

Before Kara left, she'd made him promise to tell his parents.

"You can't be alone in this secret when you're home. Sure, Jacob knows, but he's not around all of the time and who knows how he's going to react when he actually sees the changes? Tell your parents. You live there. You can't keep a secret like that confined to your bedroom. You'll drive yourself crazy," she said to him. "Plus, they're going to realize that we broke up eventually. Don't you want them to know why so that you can finally be able to be yourself?"

Liam smiled. "Okay," he said. "I promise."

He dreaded the moment he'd have to tell his parents, his father especially. But, he knew that Kara was right. He knew that he had to tell them and he preferred to do it when he could leave immediately after and let them deal with their emotions alone and away from him. While he knew that they loved him and would try to find a way to be supportive, he feared that the shock would be too great for their relationship to recover fully. He hoped to feel relieved after telling them like he had with Kara and Jacob, but the more he thought about it, the more he worried about their reaction. Even if they were going to try to be supportive and understanding, he realized that trusting in their support would be a risk in and of itself – and that their support could easily disappear. He worried that once they were able to see how he was physically changing that, even if they were trying to support him, they would have a hard time being as supportive as he would need them to be. He worried that they would be disapproving and that he would lose them. Kara tried to reassure him by telling him that the relationship he had with his parents now was very different than the one he had as a child. He didn't see it, but she did. She saw parents who trusted their child, relied on him at times, and looked up to him with pride. He fixed their dishwasher when it broke, repainted their home when it was needed, built their large back deck, installed their metallic fire bowl, and maintained their barbeque. He grocery shopped and he puppy sat, and he looked in on his aging grandparents whenever he was home. And they were proud of him. Kara knew that his parents hadn't had an easy life either, especially since Liam had left for the Navy, and she thought it had softened them. Liam didn't believe it. He feared that they lived in exactly the same black-and-white world in which he'd grown up. But, as he prepared to tell them, he started seeing the differences. They hadn't noticed his eyebrows yet, which he felt certain they would have in his youth. They hadn't said anything about the fight he'd had with Kara the night before, which they would have in his youth. They ignored all of the subtle changes. It was with this realization that his real worry set in. He'd been worried about breaking Kara's heart because, in his mind, that was the only heart he could really break. Otherwise, he feared rejection from others more than causing any pain. Only after talking to Kara did he realize that he might also break his parents' hearts. With the fear of rejection mingling with the pressure of possibly hurting and disappointing his parents, Liam knocked on their bedroom door to speak with his mother first, before his father got home from work.

Telling his mother was difficult because she cried. She cried and cried and cried. But, she didn't kick him out and she didn't disown him. She wasn't disgusted with him like so many mothers he'd read about online had been.

"When did you know?" she asked tearfully.

"I think it's been on my mind forever, Mom," Liam replied.

She nodded. "Is this what you really want?"

"Yes, it is. I need to do this."

She nodded again. "Does Kara know?"

"Yes. I told her as soon as she got here. She's been helping me explore it all week and I've been really happy."

"Are you two...?" Liam's mother started to ask.

"Together?" Liam interrupted. "No. But we're friends and she's going to stand by me. She's actually the reason I'm telling you about this right now. She's been great about all of it and has been so supportive. I really need the support, Mom. Do you understand? Do you think you can support me?"

Liam's mother thought quietly for a moment. "I love you, Liam. I love you no matter what. You're my son, my baby." She hugged him tightly and cried into the top of his head. Liam lay next to his mother and relished her warmth beside him. He felt comforted. It didn't bother him that she had still referred to him as her "son." It didn't bother him because she hadn't rejected him. She had said that she loved him no matter what and, in that moment, that was enough for Liam.

Telling his father was more difficult. He couldn't rely on a mothering instinct to make his father understand. He couldn't curl up beside him. That wasn't their relationship. They had always interacted like two men. They didn't talk about feelings very often, they hugged only to say hello and goodbye, and they preferred to focus their conversations on football, hunting, work, or food. After telling his mother, Liam knew that he needed to worry more about breaking his father's heart than being rejected. He knew that Kara had been right about his relationship with his parents being better; his mother had proven that to him. But that didn't ease his anxiety. He knew that it would crush his father to have his son, his son who was man enough to almost become a Navy SEAL, become a woman. What would they have in common anymore? What would they talk about? Liam knew he could tell him the same thing that he'd told Jacob – that he would still be the same person – but he knew it wouldn't be true for his father. As he struggled to find the right words, Liam tried to focus on the hope that there was some part of his father that longed for a daughter. His father looked at him after hearing the news, long and hard, and then started asking questions.

"Are you sure this is right for you?" he asked Liam.

"Yes. This is me. This is who I am," Liam replied, refusing to let his voice shake.

"Did we do something, your mother and I, to make you feel like this?"

"Not at all. This is just me. I was born like this."

"So, you've been feeling this way since you were a child?"

"Yes, I think so. At least on some level, and in different ways, but yes."

"Why didn't you ever come to us before? Maybe we could have helped you."

Liam tried to smile reassuringly. "I don't think you wanted to hear it back then, Dad."

Liam's father nodded, sadness and guilt in his eyes. "You still should have told us, told me. We're supposed to help you. Maybe you wouldn't feel this way if… if we had been there for you."

Liam sat silently and waited, unsure of how to alleviate his father's guilt in that moment.

"I'm here for you now. We are. I can't say I understand or feel entirely comfortable with this, but I love you and I need you to know that we are here for you now," Liam's father said, breaking the silence.

Liam breathed a sigh of relief and said, "Well, in that case, I've got something to tell you then." And then he told his father the whole truth about his childhood. He shared the secret he had never trusted anyone but Kara with – the truth about Christian and what he had done to Liam. Then, his father hugged him.

So far, it's not too bad. I think I've got some pretty great people in my life, Liam thought to himself. *I can handle this. I can do this. I've got people who love me.*

In his heart, Liam knew that it wouldn't end with those reactions. Things were going to be different when he came back from deployment and could finally start transitioning. People would react differently when the changes were actually visible. He'd heard it on nearly every YouTube confession that he'd watched: "The real test of love and friendship comes when the visible changes start to happen. They come as outfits change, as breasts grow, and muscles shrink (or vice versa); as voices are altered and hair is lost in some places and grown in others. That's when the real tests of friendship come. They come when you have to learn who still wants to be seen with you and who can act the same way with you when you start looking differently – when you're outside of society's norms." He knew this was true in his heart. With a yearlong deployment on his mind, where he would be stuck on a ship where no one knew his secret and no one *could* know his secret, Liam refused to dwell on what the future would hold. Instead, he focused on the positivity of the reactions he'd received so far.

Kara

It's been a couple of months since I've been home and, so far, it's been extremely dramatic. While Liam's been on deployment, his parents have been calling and texting me to check up on Liam because they don't want to talk to him themselves. Apparently, they "just aren't ready." What bullshit. They just don't *want* to be ready. They pretended to be okay when he came out to them and now they've decided that they cannot cope. *That's sad that you can't even be there for your son when he needs you the most,* I want to say to them. But I know that it's difficult information to process. What bothers me the most is that the stress of them being unsupportive must be breaking Liam's heart.

You're his parents. You can't just turn off your responsibilities to love and care for your child when it's uncomfortable or challenging. Quite honestly, that's when you need to step up the most, I wanted to say to them when they called me, but I didn't.

Liam wouldn't want me to fight with his parents. So instead, I've been listening to them, answering their questions and comments, and relaying any necessary or appropriate information to Liam. Any comments that could possibly be taken as unsupportive or would require Liam to defend himself have been buried in my memory. I refuse to play the intermediary in any situations that could add stress to Liam's life.

    With Liam, I oscillate between feeling like a burden to him and being a sympathetic and understanding ear. I often get jealous of the girls that he hangs out with and get angry that he lets them believe that he's single. Well, I guess he is single (technically) but I'm still his girl. He's only single in the sense that he doesn't want to date girls anymore and it bothers me that those girls think that they could have a chance with him. As far as his transition, I was, and still am, Liam's key supporter as he explores his femininity. When he emails me or calls me from the ship, we discuss clothes, makeup, haircuts, sexuality, ideas about who and what he'd like to do after his career in the military – everything that he's been thinking about in regards to becoming a woman. I have been here to talk about all of it. Sometimes, I even try to suggest certain ideas for him, like classes or certifications that may help him achieve his various goals. I send him outfits that help him look more feminine while he still has the muscles of an ex-Navy SEAL candidate. I send him make up samples and small items of jewelry. I send him ideas for female names as they come to me. All of these are sent with a coded message of course – "Warning: XXX – Love you!" That way, if anyone was reading over his shoulder, they would just assume that it was just something dirty from his girlfriend (or ex-girlfriend, I guess) and he'd be left alone to open it. I have tried to think of everything.

    I've been thinking about Liam and his situation so much lately that I haven't been able to focus on anything else. I spend my time either worried about Liam being with the other girls on the ship (ridiculous, I know), or I'm looking for ways to make my ex-boyfriend look like a woman. My brain is in a constant fog. It's like I have to battle through quicksand just to find the capacity to have a basic social interaction with someone who isn't connected to this situation. I need a distraction. I want to be able to focus on my own life again. I just feel guilty whenever I try to do that. I want to be the best support that I can be for Liam. I need to be or else I'm afraid that I'll regret not trying harder when this is all over.

Liam

Only four months into a 12-month deployment and it happened. They caught me. My ass was in the air and my heart was in my throat as I scrambled to pick up all the pieces of red, blue, purple, and zebra print lace underwear that I'd dropped all over the floor of the laundry room. It was midnight, so I didn't think that anyone would be doing laundry. It turns out that I was wrong. All I needed was for one insomniac to try to be productive during his sleepless night to ruin my secret and that's exactly what I'd gotten. If I'd known that he was coming, I wouldn't have gone down to the laundry room. Or, at the very least, I would have made sure to keep everything hidden. He'd surprised me though. I had my guard down and I got caught. He didn't even say much. He just dropped his bag of laundry and muttered "Dude..." with his eyes really wide. Then, he turned and walked quickly away.

It's terrifying, really, to have everyone know. But, at the same time, it's also liberating. The news spread throughout the ship really quickly, like all gossip does; even news much less shocking than this spreads quickly in such a confined place. I feel naked when I walk around the ship now. I can feel their eyes prying into me. Girls who once shamelessly flirted with me now avert their eyes as their mouths form a grimace of disgust. Girls either react in that way or see an opportunity for a gay best friend (even though I'm not gay) and try to use me like a "gal pal." Still, it is a bit of a relief to not have to keep this secret anymore. I won't admit it to anyone if they ask, but I am a little bit afraid around some of the guys. I can handle myself better than a lot of guys, but I can't defend myself against a big group, especially in the tight confines of the ship. A lot of the guys look at me with disgust. They don't understand me. They don't want to share quarters with me, but I'm not allowed to move into the girls' quarters. So I've been trying to wait until everyone is asleep before I go into the barracks and then I set my alarm to go off really early. I'm tired, *so* tired, but at least I've been able to work out a lot. Ever since I was a teenager, the gym has been my safe haven, so that's where I've been going in all of my spare time. Only now, instead of spending hours in the weights area, I'm running. I hate running. Ever since BUD/S, my body and brain have hated running. But, I was really slim at the peak of BUD/S and now that I'm going to transition I want to get back to that. Though, I don't want to slim down too much. I do love my muscles. Maybe I can be slim, but still have the look of a woman who body builds. I don't know. Or, maybe, I'll just be one badass chick and full-on body build once I slim down a little more and then I can start fresh. Regardless, the gym is my sanctuary on this ship.

It won't be this way for much longer though. I'm fairly certain that I'm going to get kicked out. Just a week after getting "outed," my bosses told me that my drug test from the earlier on in the deployment came back positive for marijuana. I think I smoked once, maybe twice, leading up to deployment, and I thought it would be long enough away from the test date that the drug wouldn't be in my system anymore. But I guess I was wrong. I know I shouldn't have smoked at all, but it was only once and I've had so much on my mind that I just needed to relax. I can't help but think that it's also possible that someone told my superiors to test me because they hate who I am becoming. It's no secret that I like to smoke weed and spice, but I'm not alone in that. At least, I didn't feel alone. But I guess when the mere sight of me makes a good chunk of the guys on the ship uncomfortable, I really can't expect anyone to keep my bad habits a secret for me anymore. Either way, I fucked up, but I don't know if I would change my decisions if I went back to do it all over again. This is a lot to bury inside.

    I feel ashamed of myself – really ashamed. I really had thought that I was going to make it until the end of deployment, but that's definitely not going to happen anymore. I also never dreamed that I'd get a dishonorable discharge, and that's what I'm probably looking at now. Or, at the very least, an "other than honorable" discharge if they take into consideration the stress that I've been under. Some people have said that I should fight it and take another test, or claim that I was under extreme stress because of my situation. I just know that the Navy won't care. Most people on this ship have made it very clear that they don't want me here anymore. They're too uncomfortable around me now. To be honest, though, I'm pretty thankful that I have a way out of here. As much as I don't want to be kicked out because I'll feel like I let myself down and like I failed, which I hate to do, I will be happy to have the opportunity to go home and to finally start living the rest of my life the way I want to.

Kara

Now that Liam has come out to a lot more people and is probably leaving the Navy, he's planning to go home and start living as a woman. So when does the transition actually happen? When do I actually see it? When will I really *believe* it? When am I supposed to start calling Liam a *her* instead of a *him*? I mean, I've been doing it to his face or when talking to him as often as I remember to, but when am I supposed to do it all the time? How do I start using feminine words to describe him in my own mind? I know this is the correct thing to do because he says he is a woman. It would be wrong of me to choose to not recognize that, but at the same time it's a real struggle because I met him as a man, all of our memories together contain him as a man, and I've always pictured him as a man in the future. It's a lot for my mind to unravel and to change and, honestly, I'm feeling so confused that I don't know when this will ever be easy for me. I mean, I'm getting fairly comfortable using the right pronouns while we are texting or even talking on the phone now, and he's made it clear to me that he likes it. But, when I'm by myself or talking to my friends and family, he's still a *him*. That's who he is in *my* mind. When does that change?

When we Skype while he's on the ship, Liam has asked me to make sure I stick to calling him by male pronouns in case anyone overhears our conversation, which has made things a little easier on me. It's allowing me to transition more slowly from the past to the present. But is that making it even harder? Between lying about being his girlfriend and being "just a friend," to calling him a woman sometimes and a man others, I'm not really sure that my brain is processing anything that's happening. It's a lot to keep straight. Looking at him, looking at the man who shared my bed and promised to wait for me at the end of the aisle in a tux, I only see those memories and I only see him as a man. He hasn't changed physically yet. He doesn't *look* like a woman yet. And calling him one feels a little like I'm betraying all of those happy memories that we shared. It would make them all feel like a lie. But, on the other hand, his personality *is* changing. He's becoming calmer. He's still the same strong-minded soul that he's always been, but the edge that has always been a part of his personality seems to be dissipating. He's less angry. Even when I cry and yell at him, or call him a billion times, he gets frustrated but he doesn't get angry anymore. He's also started to show some vulnerability – when going out in new clothes, meeting men for dates, testing out more feminine voices, he's nervous and he lets me see it. It's refreshing but it's also a little bit strange and sad for me. Seeing him vulnerable makes me uncomfortable because it's something I've never seen from him. I don't think any less of him. If anything, I admire him more. It's just nerve-wracking. It's also hard because he's so uncertain of himself now that I wish I could fully wrap my head around his transition and only think of him as a woman. I wish I could call him a "she" to his face *and* when he's not around. Honestly, I wish I didn't have to think about it at all and that the right pronouns just came naturally. I wish it wasn't so hard. Then, I'd be a real support. I feel like right now I'm supporting him because I want him to be happy but, on some level, I feel like I'm faking it because I still think of him as a man who wants to be living like a woman and I don't know how to change that.

I know that probably makes me an awful person. I want to think of him in the way he wants me to, the way he thinks I really do. I've let him think that I'm fine with his transition and that it's not that hard for me to deal with him becoming woman. I want that to be true, I know it makes him really happy. But I'm just not there yet.

Not fully, anyway. It still feels forced. But, maybe that's okay? I'm trying. I *really* am. That's all I can do, right?

I feel like I need to be okay, though. Especially since I'm the one who seems to be in control of his story outside of the ship. I have his family, his friends, and his old coworkers (who must have found out from someone on the ship) all emailing *me* and asking *me* about the validity of *his* decision. His family has asked me to help him decide not to transition because "This isn't him. He's a man." They're struggling, I know, but so am I. Their struggle isn't mine to deal with. It offends me on Liam's behalf that they don't want to at least try to understand him or to let him be who he wants to be, especially after they pretended to be supportive when he came out to them. They can easily get a hold of Liam when he's on the ship if they want to, and frankly, I feel like they haven't been trying, so I'm stuck fighting his battles and I just don't feel prepared to do that. I don't have the answers. All I can do is try to get them to just accept it, and I don't have much confidence that they want to hear what I have to say.

When Liam was in port, he called Kara often. He always told her ahead of time when he'd have the ability to call so she wouldn't be in the middle of doing something. This time, before being in port, he had told Kara via email that he would call her over the weekend. The problem was that, this time, he'd changed his mind and didn't want to call her anymore. Instead, he wanted to work out at the gym and watch movies alone on the ship while everyone else went to explore the city. He wanted take some much needed time to himself. However, after not hearing anything from him all day, Kara called him. She texted. She left voicemails. Her messages started off being calm, but they escalated quickly. By the end of the 45 calls placed that weekend, she had sounded furious and hurt. She yelled while crying into Liam's voicemail, "Why aren't you calling me back? Don't you care? I'm trying so hard to be there for you. You need to be there for me too! Don't be so fucking insensitive that you can't even pick up my phone calls to let me know that you're okay. I know what's happening on the ship. I'm so worried for you. Call me back."

Liam felt overwhelmed by guilt, which made him feel increasingly stressed. With everything going on and the constant worrying about where he should and shouldn't be on the ship, or who he should and shouldn't be talking to, he couldn't handle Kara's yelling. He felt guilty that he hadn't followed through on his promise to call, but he couldn't handle calling her back. So, unsure of what to do, Liam tucked the phone into his bag while he watched one of the DVDs that Kara had sent in a care package. As he sat and watched, he tried to determine whether he felt more stressed out or guilty, and whether or not he should call her back that day or leave it until he felt more able to cope.

Liam

I wonder who Kara has told by now. Has she told her friends? Has she told any strangers? I know that she told her parents as soon as she'd gotten home from visiting me because she told me that she had. I was pretty uneasy about them finding out. It was almost like I was telling my own parents all over again. I mean, I only met them the one time, but I'd been planning to marry their daughter since I'd met her and I was still training to be a SEAL when I'd met them. Well, until the day I met them I had been. I feel like I'm letting them down, too. When I met them, we'd gotten along really well. They'd known that Kara and I were serious about our future and they welcomed me in with open arms. I didn't want my transition to color their opinion of me. I didn't want them to think less of me and I didn't want them to hate me for how sad and stressed my transition was making their daughter. When I'd told her this, Kara said that I was being ridiculous.

"My parents are very liberal. They're not going to judge you for it, I promise," she'd tried to assure me. "They are going to sympathize with you and want to help in any way they can, just like me."

I hadn't really believed her. Her parents could so easily have seen me as a liar who deceived their daughter from the start. I didn't want them to think that I never really loved Kara at all. I didn't want them to think that I'd strung her along until I was ready to come out. I wasn't ever trying to hurt Kara. I knew that I wasn't *that guy*, but what if they had started to see me that way? What if Kara started to see me that way too? I didn't want that.

I know that Kara is struggling with everything. It's evident in her voice – it's almost always strained and she often sounds like she is on the verge of tears. Well, she is always on the verge of tears. If I forget to call her back or I spend too long hanging out with my new friends or I don't ask her how she's doing often enough, she cries. She cries and then she yells at me. When she calls, she tries to hold it together at first. She asks how I'm doing, how the transition is going, and how I'm feeling. She tries, because that's who she is, but then something snaps and she loses it. She'll call me over and over again until I pick up and then she'll just cry and yell at me for being a terrible friend to her because I don't act the same way that I used to when I was her boyfriend and when things were solid between us. She may seem strong on the outside, but she's a big gooey mess on the inside and I need her to be strong all the way through right now. I can't deal with her freaking out on top of everything else. I can't be her boyfriend anymore and I can't always be the kind of friend she wants me to be while also trying to figure out my life. It's too much. It's too confusing.

If she's this sensitive with me, I can only assume that she's just as sensitive with everyone at home in Canada too. If so, her parents must at least blame me for that. I wish she could hold it together better. Luckily, Kara told me that when she told her parents I was transitioning they were completely supportive. They've been completely supportive of her through her emotional outbreaks and have also been supportive of me. They frequently ask Kara how I'm doing and ask her if there is anything that they can do to help me, or to help her help me. Apparently, they told her that they were proud of me for having the courage to come out. Honestly, that felt pretty great. No one has said that they were proud of me in a long time, and no one has said it yet about coming out. No one.

I just hope Kara finds more support for herself because this is too much to do alone. Trust me, I know. It's also too much for me to cope with if she doesn't – I need her to let go of me enough that I can explore this new life freely. She needs to find support elsewhere. I can't emotionally support the both of us right now. I am just learning how to support myself.

Kara

I've already told my family and a few close friends, but I haven't really sought support from anyone else yet. My family took it in stride. While shocked, they focused their energy on being supportive, concerned, eager to help, and compassionate. My friends were shocked and concerned, but they all rose to the occasion and are also being supportive and understanding. That being said, I've been too busy obsessing about Liam to think about how I'm doing. I can't stop worrying about or caring about his safety and his mental wellbeing, so I haven't really worked that hard on fixing myself. Honestly, I haven't really worked at it at all. I don't know how. I don't know how to fix myself because I'm pretty sure it means letting go of some feelings that I'm not ready to let go of yet. I know how to worry about him, though, and I know what I can do for him to show my support. And that makes him happy. But even though I know how to make him happy, I don't know how to make myself happy anymore. I don't feel ready to help myself. When my focus is on me, I feel guilty and alone. Besides, my focus should be Liam right now. He needs me more than I need myself. I love him and I'm all he has. I can fix myself later.

However, Liam has been pushing me to reach out to people. The other day he pleaded with me to talk to my friends more because he said that he still feels like *my* support system and he doesn't feel capable of being that for me anymore. Mentally, that made sense to me. Emotionally, it felt like he was breaking up with me all over again.

Telling everyone else was extremely nerve wracking. It was a situation that I'd never really given thought to and I was worried that people might feel equally blindsided and that they would judge him since they didn't know him as well as I do. At the very least, I knew that they wouldn't understand why I was helping him through the transition. I really didn't want to defend my choices to anyone. I've been struggling enough with just accepting the changes for myself and trying to be supportive of Liam. I don't have the energy to defend *why* I'm doing it. I'm so tired of fighting. When people openly judged and questioned my decision, all I could say was, "I love him. Why wouldn't I help?" But, quite honestly, that isn't much of an explanation and, when they pressed me at all, I just ended up crying. That wasn't a strong argument for me being happy enough to help him, let alone for me being happy for him.

While some people I told were shocked and didn't understand, so many people were more accepting than I'd expected, and I am so grateful for that. Instead of judging us for how we were handling the situation, they gave their sympathies to the both of us for what we are going through. Some even commented on how brave Liam was for transitioning given his background in the military. They asked questions like, "Would he like it if we sent him care packages containing makeup or small items of women's clothing?" or "Does he want makeup tips? I'd love giving some makeup advice!" Others took a different, more clinical approach and said things like, "I find that so fascinating. Does he want someone to talk to? I know a woman who transitioned a few years ago and she does a little counseling," or "I feel for both of you – this is a stressful situation – but kudos to him for braving the consequences and being true to himself." Some people were just curious and asked, "How does the transition work? Does he see a psychologist first or is he going to just start transitioning?" What it came down to was that my friends weren't judging Liam. They were trying to understand. And that meant the world to me.

Every supportive comment lifted an ounce of weight off of my shoulders. Every person who accepted the situation and showed some semblance of understanding of the pressure that both Liam and I were under, or didn't question our decisions and took an interest in the transition, made me feel a little less alone. The most simple and supportive comment I got was, "Wow. Poor Liam. That is quite the uphill battle. He's lucky that he has you still." It wasn't much, but even a little recognition of the fact that Liam was still lucky to have me was nice to hear. It felt good having someone recognize all of the effort I was putting into helping Liam.

I wasn't sure why, but it felt like I'd been in a constant defense mode since Liam had come out. Between his parents, his friends, his job, and any close-minded strangers we'd come across, I felt like I was always defending my position and his decision. Finally, I sought help from a couple of therapists. I just wanted help with forgiving Liam for all the times that he'd hurt me or let me down so that, with those feelings of betrayal cleared from my mind, I could move on from the pain I was feeling and focus on helping him. I was very straightforward with what I wanted to achieve in therapy. I was clear that I wanted Liam in my life going forward and that I wanted to figure out how to be okay enough to support him through the transition. Instead, all of the therapists told me that the only way I'd be okay would be to cut him out of my life altogether. They didn't even try to understand Liam or the stress he was under, and that really pissed me off. And so I stopped going.

The most difficult questions to hear came from people who were even less understanding than the therapists. I had several people ask me, "So, if he's coming out as a woman now and dating men, what does that mean about your relationship? Was any of it real? That must be tough for you."

Those questions stung. I understand why people might wonder about that – I can't say that I haven't wondered that too – but it isn't a question that other people need to ask. They shouldn't have asked me that, it wasn't their business and it wasn't easy to explain if they didn't know Liam or if they didn't know us together. I know that Liam loved me, and still does (just in a different way), and I have been trying really hard to trust in that. I've been working really hard to remember all of the good times and not the bad. I've been focusing on the trust that Liam needed to have in me to come out to me. And the trust he needs to have in me to let me help him through the transition. But it's an ongoing battle and, when people ask me questions like "Was any of it real?" they plant seeds of doubt in my mind that I don't need. I may know that those questions have no merit, but that doesn't mean I am emotionally strong enough to ignore them over and over again. It's exhausting.

Finally, one day, I had been asked one too many times about the legitimacy of our relationship before the transition and I caved. While we chatted on Skype, I asked Liam, "Liam, did you *really* love me? Or was it more like how you'd love a friend?"

He looked hurt. "I can't believe you need to ask me that," he said. "Of course I really loved you. I loved you more than I've loved anyone before. You're my best friend."

"Was it just that?" I asked. "A friendship-kind of love?"

"No. You are my best friend, but I also think you're the most beautiful woman in the world. I'm both turned on and in complete admiration of you. Things changed towards the end, but our love was real. It still is."

"Do you think at least part of that love was about wanting what I had for yourself though? Do you think you loved me, in some small way, for looking the way that you secretly wanted to look?"

Liam thought for a moment before he spoke again. "Maybe subconsciously that's partly what attracted me to you at the start, but that's not why I fell in love with you. I loved you because of who you are, and those are the reasons that I still do. I loved you for how you loved me. You're the first person who made me want to be better. You're the first person I've ever trusted so completely. You made me want a life with you. You made me want to laugh and hold you every day, even when you frustrated me more than I can even describe. I still love you more than anything for those reasons and more. I still love you for how much you still love me through all of this." He paused and looked upset. "I wanted to be the man you deserved. I always told myself that when I found a girl like you, I wouldn't have these feelings of wrongness anymore. I told myself that it was the quality of girls that I was dating and the lifestyle that I was leading that made me feel like I wanted something different. When I met you, I fell completely in love with you. But I still had those thoughts and feelings, and that tore me apart. That's largely why I got so angry sometimes. I hated myself for ruining what we had, and I still do. That's something that I'm not sure I'll ever get over. When I couldn't make those feelings subside, I knew I was going to have to make a change. That was the toughest realization for me. When I first realized that what I wanted to do was transition, I wasn't scared to tell my family or friends. Honestly, it didn't even really cross my mind. I made peace with the fact that I'd probably have to leave the military. I was scared of losing you, Kara. I can't live without you in my life, Kara. I *need* you. I *love* you. And it breaks my heart that I can't be the person you thought that I was, and that I've given you any reason to question the love we shared."

I cried then. I still don't have all the answers, and I still can't use the *her* pronoun to refer to Liam when I'm thinking to myself or talking to my friends because it still doesn't feel real to me, but his reassurance gave me the fuel I needed to continue helping him fight his battle.

Thirty-One

After a little under two months of stressful waiting, Liam was called in front of his supervisors on the ship. Liam already knew that he was going to be kicked out of the Navy. He didn't believe that a transgender woman, one who tested positive for marijuana, would be allowed to stay on the ship; especially one who had already been kicked out of the SEAL training program for abusing alcohol. In the eyes of the Navy, no matter how hard he worked to fix it, his reputation had already been tarnished.

Liam was discharged with an "other than honorable" status, citing marijuana use. His immediate superior was very supportive of his transition and had thanked him for his hard work. "You would have made one hell of a soldier," he told Liam. "But I have a feeling you're still going to be a soldier, in your own right, with the battle you're off to fight now. Good luck."

The more senior officers hadn't shown as much affection, or any at all for that matter. Instead, they were clearly fulfilling an order from above them and, if anything, were slightly annoyed at the unexpected hassle that the situation had created for them.

While it was difficult to leave the life he had worked so hard to build, Liam also found his discharge liberating. In his mind, the biggest hurdles were behind him now. Yet, in the back of his mind, he still regretted that he would never become the Navy SEAL that he had set out to be. Driving the truck he'd no longer be able to pay for, with the bed loaded down by bags of the SEAL training gear that he was allowed to keep, Liam's heart had mixed emotions but for once, his head was clear. Though he didn't *feel* entirely like a woman yet, the thought of both looking and feeling like one in the near future was calming.

In an unsuspected act of excitement and support, Liam's mother greeted him happily at the door when he got home. "Elly!" she yelled as she rushed down the stairs to give him a hug. "Elly, it's so good to have you home." While she and Liam's father had been struggling to cope with the news of his transition and of his discharge, she wasn't able to confront him about it. Long gone was the mother who saw it as her job to mold her son into a "proper" man. Instead, she now looked at him as a grown man who she was proud to have raised. Because of that, she decided not to acknowledge any of the difficult issues in Liam's life when he returned home. She thought that, with time, it all would just go away and Liam would return to being the kind of man she wanted her son to be. So she planned to treat him exactly as she had before – and to pretend that his transition into a woman wasn't real.

Liam, on the other hand, only noticed how feminine his mother's nickname for him sounded. He'd never realized it until then. He liked how it felt when she called him that, so he smiled and hugged her tighter. "Thanks, mom," he said.

As if she'd known what he was thinking, she straightened herself and said, "There's some food in the fridge for you, Liam. I know my boy likes his steaks, so I have one marinating for you in there."

Just as quickly as the warmth of his nickname had washed over him, it was replaced by that old feeling of yearning – for acknowledgement, for recognition, for acceptance. Liam didn't want to be her *son* anymore. Going forward, he wanted to be her *daughter*. So, instead of sitting down to steak with his father, he went out to the McDonald's around the corner for a salad and then to the nearest Target to start changing his wardrobe.

* * *

While Kara had, on some level, known that the relationship was doomed, accepting that fact was proving to be more difficult than she had wanted. The only things that were able to draw her from her shell were her retired competition horse, Moon (short for Moonshadow), and yoga classes. After 15 years of partnership, riding Moon often felt more comfortable than walking for Kara. Normally antisocial with humans, Moon would let Kara sob into his neck for hours on end. The end of her visits often left stains his neck from tears because that's where she felt safest to let her true feelings show. He'd nuzzle his nose into her waist while she cried and would patiently wait for her tears to run out. Then, while riding, he would make her laugh by taking off at a gallop at the most unexpected times. Yoga had given her a place to meditate and would exhaust her body so that, when night came, she was mentally relaxed and physically exhausted enough to fall asleep. The beauty of both of those activities was that, in either place, she wasn't required to speak to anyone. She didn't have to explain her actions. She didn't have to provide updates on Liam or herself. No one asked her about her relationship, no one asked her about work, no one asked anything of her. She was able to be alone without ever being truly alone.

After Liam was discharged from the military, he and Kara still talked almost every day. Sometimes it was because one had wanted to check in on the other or had something to say, and sometimes it was out of habit. Whatever reason they had for calling each other, it almost always ended in a fight now. While Liam had become used to living at home, he'd also become more focused on himself than he'd been before. He was starting his new life out with renewed vigor and Kara didn't always fit in the way she used to. As a result, he often forgot to ask Kara how she was doing and Kara was too hurt and angry about his transition to tell him when he didn't ask. She was still trying to be supportive by discussing topics like hair, makeup, and boys. She also sent him small gifts, like necklaces and clip-on earrings. But, whenever they'd speak, there was always a period where she couldn't help but cry. In truth, she almost appreciated that Liam wouldn't ask how she was doing because being angry about it was easier than trying to describe her feelings about their situation. She still wasn't sure how she felt so she didn't know what to tell him. And while support from family and her own friends had helped, she'd wanted her and Liam's mutual friends to know too. Aside from his military friends, no one from their life in San Diego knew about his transition. They all thought that the two of them were still dating. She wanted someone who had known them together to find out because, in her mind, they would understand the shock she'd felt better than anyone else.

Michael had texted her sporadically a few times since graduation, but Kara had always been short with him to avoid talking about Liam. She hadn't quite figured out how to tell their mutual friends why the relationship ended, or that it had at all, and wasn't sure whether it was her story to tell yet.

Finally, Michael texted her about a month after Liam had moved home and said, "Hey pretty girl, how's it going up north?"

Before replying, Kara called Liam. After chatting about Liam's new nail color and improving manicure skills, Kara became serious.

"Liam, our friends in San Diego are reaching out to me. How should I respond to them?"

"What do you mean?" he asked.

"Well, Talia sent me a text a while ago asking about me and us and how you were doing on deployment. I didn't tell her anything about your experimenting or anything, I'd just said that you were doing well. I think she knew something was up because I had a bit of a meltdown before I left San Diego and told her that you had a lot of things to work through, but you were still figuring things out then so it wasn't my place to say anything more. Michael and Franceen have asked about you recently too and, well, what should I tell them? Do you want them to know?"

Liam paused. "I don't give a fuck what they think. Go ahead and tell them."

Kara recognized his defiant tone and knew that he was prepared for a fight. "Are you sure? I mean, they are your friends too. I think they'll understand."

"Kara, if they don't understand, then they aren't my friends. But, they're going to know sooner or later because of the photos I'll be posting on Facebook, so go ahead and tell them now," he said. "You know how to explain it well. I trust you. Just, if you don't mind, could you make it clear that we are still friends? I don't know why, but it matters to me that people know that you haven't rejected me because of this."

Kara smiled. It also mattered to her that everyone she told knew that they were still friends. She wanted everyone to know that they had been a strong enough couple when they were dating that they would make it through this tough situation together as friends.

"Do you want to tell Michael at least? Would you rather it came from you or me?" she asked.

Liam paused before his voice took on a softer tone. "I don't know. Maybe I should tell him." He paused again to think. "Yes, I want to tell him. He was my buddy. It should come from me. Let me call him now."

So, Liam called Michael and told him about his transition. About 20 minutes later, Michael texted Kara again.

```
"Hey, lady. Liam just told me what happened. I
have to admit that it's pretty crazy news. How are
you feeling about all of it?"
```

Kara smiled. It felt good – liberating – to have Michael know. He knew Liam, he knew Kara, and he'd known them together. Because he knew their past and how they were together, it felt comforting to have him know about Liam's transition. In that moment, Kara knew that she wasn't going feel alone anymore. Even though she was relieved, she still wasn't sure how to respond.

After a moment, she typed, `"I'm okay. It hasn't been the easiest, but I hope he can be happy."`

```
"Ya. Me too. But, honestly, it's kind of fucked
up isn't it? Like, did you know?"
```

That was what Kara had been afraid of happening. She had been hoping that Michael would've been the one person who wouldn't need to ask that question. He knew the same Liam that she knew – albeit in a different way – but he knew him well enough to know that it would have been a shock.

```
"No, I didn't know. I knew he wasn't happy, but I
didn't know that this was why."
```

"I don't get it. I mean, it's pretty weird. I'm sorry. It must be tough to wrap your head around. Liam said you guys are staying friends though?"

"Yep! I still love him. Even if we aren't together, I want him in my life and I want to be in his."

"Wow. I don't know if I could do that, Kara. That's pretty… unique. Are you sure you'll be okay with all of that?"

Kara read the message and felt a lump start to build in her stomach. While his words had been kind, she was able to sense the skepticism and uncomfortable undertones. There was also a hint of judgment, which she hoped would dissipate with time. It was that same judgment that planted seeds of doubt in her mind about her and Liam's future as friends, and her ability to shape it into a positive one. This time, though, the comment hurt her more than anything. She felt the same defiance that she'd heard in Liam's voice build inside of her. She readied for a fight that hadn't yet started, and may never start, because it was her go-to reaction. It was then that her feelings about her relationship with Liam became clear to her. Yes, she was heartbroken. Yes, she had lost her first love. Yes, her mind had been completely blown and she was having trouble processing her new reality. But, most importantly, she was proud. She was proud of Liam for coming out and she was proud of herself for standing by his side, no matter how difficult she found it. So, as tired of defending their choices as she had been, she was going to do it again. She felt that if she could stand by Liam, then everyone else should be able to as well. If they didn't, then they would offend her too. She realized that it wasn't just Liam's battle anymore, that it was hers too.

In response to the text, Kara struggled to maintain her calm while trying to explain Liam's decision to Michael and her support of it. She pleaded with Michael to not think too hard about the "craziness" of the situation but simply to be a friend – to both her and Liam – by supporting them.

"I know. It's tough so far, but it'll be fine in the end. No way I'm ditching him just because he wants to be a woman. So, how are things in San Diego now?" Kara tried to change the subject.

"Ah, things are okay. Not sure if you heard yet, but Franceen and I broke up. I just couldn't handle her shit anymore."

And, just like that, the topic changed and Kara's heartbeat returned to normal. She also thought it was karma that Franceen, after all of the times she had hit on Liam and all the times she had boasted about the superiority of her relationship with Michael, was alone. After several subsequent conversations with Kara, Michael seemed to accept Liam's decision. He returned to being the warm and supportive friend that he'd been in San Diego, and eventually, Kara planned for Michael to visit her in Canada.

"We're both in need of a fun weekend. Let's get silly and blow off some steam," he had texted her.

Kara couldn't wait.

Thirty-Two

While Kara had found comfort in telling Michael, Liam had not. He'd only found nerves and an uneasy feeling. Michael hadn't been rude, but he clearly hadn't been comfortable with the news. The lack of support in his response had affected Liam more than usual, and he'd gone out hard – he drank a lot of alcohol and smoked a lot of weed. Kara called later that night to check in on him since she hadn't heard from him after he'd talked to Michael, but Liam didn't pick up.

Liam

I was on my fifth beer when my phone started buzzing on the bar. Kara's smiling face lit up the screen and looked at me. It seemed wrong that she would look at me as I drank while sitting in a dark room that smelled of stale ale, cigarettes, and desperation. So, I ignored my phone and let it go to voicemail.

Her face was stuck in my mind, though, and I thought about the day I'd taken that photo of her. It was a great day. We'd gone hiking in Cuyamaca State Park, and she'd looked so good all sweaty and tanned in her workout clothes, her hair pulled off her face in a ponytail. We'd taken a wrong turn early in our hike and ended up doing an eight-hour expert's hike up the mountain instead of the two-hour beginner's walk that we'd intended to do. After a couple hours of hiking up the steep, rocky paths, we'd reached our first peak. She was panting lightly and her leg muscles were swollen from effort. She'd sat down on a log to drink some water and I'd joined her. "What a great view, eh?" Kara had said. I'd put my arm around her shoulders. "Ya, sure is, baby." She'd looked up at me, then, and I'd snapped the picture. I had never been happier. We'd fought earlier that day – a big, screaming fight in the middle of the parking lot of our apartment building. I don't even remember what it was about, but I remember that we were both really mad. Then, as we'd started hiking, whatever it was that we were angry about was forgotten.

As we'd sat admiring the view, she looked back at me and grinned. "See? You love me. You'll never leave me." I'd laughed. She'd gotten me. Right then and there, I never would have let her go.

But things change.

We've come a long way since that time, I thought to myself as I looked down at my painted fingernails. I thought about the lacy panties I had on under the new form-fitting jeans that one of my new friends had given me from her closet.

"That your lady?" A deep, gravelly twang broke through my thoughts. "You dun see that kind o' girl 'round here too offen."

I looked to my right and saw an old man, toothless and dusty, with a fat wad of dip in his lip and a glass of whisky in front of him. His eyes looked blurred from the drink so he didn't seem to notice that I didn't look like every other man in this place.

"Yeah," I said.

It was easier to lie than to explain the actual situation. I don't like to admit I let her go because, even though I want to be a woman and date men or transgender women, I'm still angry at myself for letting her go. Part of me still wants to date Kara too, though I would never admit that to her. It would only break her heart. So, I just told him that she was still my girl.

"Y'all fightin' or somethin'? If she was callin' me, I'd be pickin' up on the firs' ring," he said to me, a horny grin on his face.

"Naw. I just need my space right now," I told him.

"Ahhh, I hear ya." He laughed and then digressed into a coughing fit. It made me think again that I should really quit smoking. "I need that too, sometimes. My missus liked to talk a lot. I don't." He paused. "That's why I'm drinkin' alone e'ery night now. I don't got no one to go home to anymore."

With that last remark, the man struck on one of my worst fears – that I'd end up alone. I've given up everything to be a transgender woman and the enormity of the sacrifices hadn't hit me until right then. The white picket fence lifestyle that I'd always seen for myself – wife, children, a play set, and maybe a couple of dogs – would be almost impossible for a trans woman to achieve in Tennessee. Kara has been by my side every step of the way so I guess I never really thought of her as single until right then. I knew I was single, and I've liked that, but it hurt to realize that Kara was single too. That meant that she could leave me at any time, that she could get angry and give up on being friends, and that she could start dating someone new and not have time for me anymore. She has no obligation to me anymore. I gave up a future with her for this change and I guess I haven't been coping with that as well as I thought. Maybe that's why Michael's lack of understanding was so much tougher to take. It just reminded me that my life really won't be the same anymore and that the people in it won't act the same with me anymore. I hadn't really slowed down to think about it until I was sitting in that bar. I'm single in terms of the physical side of relationships, but she's still my rock. I haven't met anyone new who actually cares about getting to know me, nor have I met anyone that I really care about knowing that well. I'm somewhat of a novelty to a lot of people that I meet and I'm still exploring my new boundaries. Kara is still the only person I have an emotional connection with. But, when that old man mentioned how he didn't have anyone to go home to anymore, it hit me that I don't have her anymore. Not really. It hit me that she could find a real partner that gives her everything all at once, without any of the drama that I've given her.

That guy meant well by giving me advice, but all he did was stress me out more. He didn't get it. No one gets it. *I'll call her tomorrow*, I thought. I meant it. I just couldn't promise that I'd still mean it tomorrow. I know that she hates it when I ignore her, but I don't like talking to her when I'm upset because it just makes things worse. I can't call her right now either because she's already concerned about my drinking. She'll worry that I'm going to drive drunk.

I told myself that I couldn't go back on my decision to transition. I told myself that this was who I was now. I reminded myself that I was definitely happier now. Doubts have to be natural, right? I am giving up a lot. I know that I've hurt a lot of people. How could I not doubt my choice? I'll be okay tomorrow. I just need some space tonight.

As I was driving home, I considered whether or not I was too drunk to drive. I'd only had six beers and a shot, and a few hits of a joint, so I thought I was fine to make it home. I felt fine and I only had to drive one exit on the interstate. I just needed to not get pulled over. Unfortunately, I must've had a little too much because all of a sudden there were bright lights heading right for me. I was blind. I didn't know if I was in my lane, his lane, or the shoulder, but he was coming right for me. At the last second, I swerved right and felt a crushing impact as my truck was folded up. My head was smashed against my window as the silent country air was pierced with the blaring sound of metal crunching metal. I should've been knocked out, but I wasn't. I was awake when the backseat windows shattered, when the doors folded into the middle of the vehicle, when the lights kept pushing right through me. It was a transport truck, and it didn't stop on impact. It just pushed me out of the way and continued on down the road. I should've gotten the license plate. I should've reported him. He didn't even stop to see if I was alive. But without insurance and with several beers in me, there's no way I would've come out on top. So instead, I called a friend to come get me and I sat down on the side of the road. While I waited, I called Kara back.

Several hours later, while she was sound asleep, Kara's cell phone buzzed over and over again. Usually a light sleeper, she normally kept the ringer on low so that she'd wake up to a phone call, especially on nights when she hoped to hear from Liam. But today she had been so exhausted from the stress of telling Michael about Liam, and Liam subsequently ignoring her worried phone call, that she slept right through.

Kara

When Liam ignores me because he's stuck in his head, I can feel myself slipping away from him. It scares me. And it hurts me. It doesn't matter that, in my heart, I know that he loves me and that he considers me his closest friend. It doesn't *feel* like it. I don't have that confidence right now. I feel abandoned and like a failure all at once. I feel like I'm not doing enough to help him. I can't get through to him and he doesn't want to always turn to me. So instead, he abandons me because he doesn't feel like he should need me anymore. And all of this makes me feel so incredibly alone. I don't want that to be our relationship. I don't want that to be my reality.

Sometimes I get frantic when he doesn't answer my messages and call him over and over again.

"Relax, girl," my friends tell me. "He just needs space. That doesn't mean he doesn't care."

UNSEALED

My head understands what they're saying but my heart just can't always believe it.

It gets even tougher when I talk to our mutual friends from San Diego. All of his SEAL friends are long gone. Aside from a few snide or fishing comments, there is radio silence from everyone that he used to work with. Our mutual friends from outside of the military, mostly from my program, are still around though. Talia is supportive and Michael still checks in on me every now and again. It's tough talking to them without being *with* Liam. I don't feel whole. Because we still talk about him and reminisce, I feel both single and taken, alone and not alone. It's an odd situation.

Franceen, well, she's just as self-involved as always. Once everyone else knew about Liam, I expected her to call. Yet, she didn't. It took her a couple of weeks to make contact. I guess I could have called her about her break up but, quite honestly, I didn't care. My mind was too busy trying to process the extremity of *my* break up.

Eventually, Franceen called on Skype and interrupted my day with a conversation that went like this:

"Hey Franceen, how are things?"

"Oh they're okay," she said with red-rimmed eyes. "How are you?"

My eyes looked the same and, frankly, I didn't have much sympathy for what had caused hers to look that way. My situation had more cause for red-rimmed eyes and tearful calls. Looking back, maybe it was wrong, but in that moment I could not care about anyone else's problems. I was still having a hard time participating in conversations that didn't revolve around transitioning. "I'm alright. Have you heard about Liam and I?"

"No… what happened?"

"Well, we broke up. You know how he seemed to be struggling with something after getting dropped from the SEAL program? I never told you, but he'd been struggling with some real big stuff. Anyway, he's decided that he's going to transition into a woman."

"What??" she asked, her eyes wide.

"Ya. He came out as transgender."

Franceen paused and looked shocked for a split second before her face became bored again. "Well, you had to have seen that coming, right? He's always been a little bit off. You'll never guess what happened to me though. Michael broke up with ME. Did you ever think *that* would happen?"

My heart pounded at the insensitivity of her response. Shocked, I spat back the only words that had come to mind. "I know. He told me. We've been chatting a lot. He actually wants to come visit me to help me through this very shocking and difficult break up I'm going through. Thanks for your concern, though."

She started to weep, and then I hung up the call, blocked her number, and deleted her off of all my social media accounts. Maybe it was extreme or maybe it was something that I should have done a long time ago but I've felt so heavy for so long now and making the decision to cut her from my life lifted a massive weight from my chest. I had enough to deal with without having the additional stress of a toxic friendship with Franceen to maintain. I only needed to surround myself with people who cared about Liam and I.

Less than a week later, Michael called me. He was angry and yelled at me for throwing our friendship in Franceen's face. Apparently, I had touched a nerve with her and she'd been calling him non-stop. Not only that, but she had started to randomly show up at his apartment trying to catch him with a new girl because, after learning that he was coming to visit me, she decided that he must have been cheating on her and had only broken up with her to sleep around. Angry, jilted, and self-involved is a dangerous combination – she'd been threatening to ruin all future relationships for him by destroying his credibility with any girl she found out about. The stress of all of her unannounced visits and her endless phone calls that always ended with her crying hysterically had built up and Michael broken down and sought someone to blame. Unfortunately, I was the target of his frustrations. On one hand, I do regret saying what I did because I knew Franceen would react poorly. But on the other, I'd kind of wanted that. I felt like I'd gone absolutely crazy trying to cope with my situation with Liam and her reaction was so apathetic that I wanted her to feel some of what I felt, and what she'd made me feel for so long now. I didn't really think about how it was going to affect Michael. And for that, I feel a little bad.

"Michael, do you know what she said to me about Liam?" I asked when he called.

"I don't care," he said. "Do you know how much of a living Hell you've made my life?"

"Michael... Come on. I'm sorry that she's driving you crazy but this isn't my fault. You dated her even though we all warned you that she would act like this. That's on you. I've got a lot going on over here too, remember? I can't be perfect. I'm not at my best right now. I snapped at her, but she deserved it," I told him. I was contemplating telling him exactly what I was dealing with. My stomach flip-flopped as I thought back to the text that I'd received earlier this morning. Liam had sent me a photo of himself in a stuffed bra, captioned: *I'm growing into this like an actual girl.* I couldn't ever, and wouldn't ever, actually share something so private and intimate with Michael, or anyone else. I just wish Michael was able to understand how tough all of this is on me.

"Be mad at her, don't be mad at me, please. She's the one who won't leave you alone. I just told her the truth." *She'd minimized how fucking awful I felt. I couldn't even talk to her about it. She was just so selfish that I needed to hurt her back in some way. I'm in so much pain and I'm tired of no one acknowledging that. I hoped that you would've understood what Liam and I are going through. You acted like you did, anyway. You were his friend but you were mine too, so I thought that you would've been the person who understood what this is doing to me. Can't you see that?* I thought, but I didn't say any of that either.

Michael paused before replying. "I know. I am mad at her. But, I really wish you hadn't said all of that too. Did she really need to know that I wanted to come visit you? What purpose did that serve? That hurt her and now she keeps calling me. She sends messages to all of the girls on my Facebook account, asking whether or not they're dating me now or if they've hooked up with me recently. It's so embarrassing and exhausting. I've told her that I'm not seeing anyone new. I've told her that I just want to be single. I've told her that you and I are just friends. She doesn't believe me though and it's really frustrating. Please just don't say anything to anyone anymore?"

"I'm sorry. I promise I won't say anything anymore. Have you talked to Liam recently? He's really going full force into this transition. I'm not really sure how well I'm doing at supporting him either. Can I still say 'he'? God, I don't even know. I feel guilty saying it because I say 'her' and 'she' to him now, but I just can't bring myself to say it to you." I wanted to change the subject and remind him of the kind of things I was struggling with.

UNSEALED

"Uh... No, I haven't. I don't really know what to say anymore, to be honest. I'll talk to him soon, I'm sure. Sorry, Kara, but I have to go to work now." And with that, Michael hung up the phone.

Thirty-Three

Liam

I'd say I'm living as a woman... or, I guess, my real self... about 70% of the time now. I recently started taking estrogen and testosterone blockers, and I'm really noticing a difference. I've started off on a fairly low dose because I'm doing it myself. Growing up in the country, I learned how to take care of myself and to not rely on doctors for anything, unless it was something life threatening. We just deal with things ourselves out here. Aside from the mandatory check ups I had to go to while in the military, and the times my parents took me as a kid, I've never gone to a doctor voluntarily. I drained my own wound when a brown recluse spider bit me as a teenager (their bites can cause severe reactions, including death) and when I had that staph infection after Hell Week, I cut it out myself. I sleep off any cold or flu – or at least let it run its course. I know how to set broken limbs and what to do with sprains. When I cut myself and need stitches, I either do it myself or I super glue the gash together. I basically know enough first aid to help myself with almost anything, and can do it at a fraction of the cost of a doctor or hospital can, so why would I entrust that care to anyone else? I deal with my own problems – always have and always will – transitioning included.

Besides, I don't need a doctor to help me transition. I've done my research. I know the good drugs from bad ones, and I know the correct dosages for someone my age and size. If I had gone to a doctor first, I would have had to go through months, possibly even years, of therapy before I'd have been prescribed hormones. Plus, if I went to a doctor first I'd have to live as a woman for a year without taking hormones to show them that I was serious about transitioning. If I had gone through the entire process, I would've been several years older and that would've been enough time for my body to settle into its masculine form, which would ultimately make it harder to change my appearance. At 24, I'm on the edge of malleability. I've read that hormones have a much stronger effect on men before their mid-to-late 20s. I don't want to waste time with doctors; especially because they, given where I live, may not even be open-minded enough to even want to help me. I know what I want and I know how to get it. So, I found an online store that sells all kinds of hormones and other items for anyone who is transitioning – women transitioning into men and men transitioning into women. I did my research, picked the best affordable brand, and prescribed my own dosage.

At home, my parents are still in denial and they make a big fuss about my clothes and hair whenever we go out to family functions or anywhere where they might run into friends from work. I think they're ashamed of me. It's kind of funny, in a tragic sort of way. My parents get really worried and embarrassed, but my grandparents (who are 94, and conservative, and who I expected to be completely unsupportive) don't seem to care at all. They asked me a few questions about the change in my appearance after I went to their house with braids in my hair and makeup on, and I tried to explain that I was just wearing whatever I wanted to wear. Afterwards, they just moved on. When I asked why they seemed so accepting of my new appearance, they said, "By our age, you learn not to spend your last years worrying about another person's clothing." I wish that kind of attitude was more widespread. Maybe it'll happen one day. But at least I can be comfortable at their house for now. Because of my parents, I haven't been totally comfortable in my own home. The discomfort is all over their faces pretty much anytime they see me now and, instead of being excited about their child being at home with them, it stresses them out. Plus, they constantly stare or ask me to cover up, and I don't want to cover up. I want to be free in my own home. There are enough of these battles to fight in the outside world. Home needs to be my safe place. The way I see it, I see my mom in her nightgown all the time. My dad occasionally wanders around in his boxers. Why can't I wear the pajamas I want, too?

On top of all of that, I've been looking for a new job. So far, it's been pretty difficult. I don't want to lie about who I am in interviews, but I really need to work somewhere else. I had found contract landscaping work through a friend on Facebook when I was released from the Navy, but they only hired me because I looked like a man. I showed up to work with makeup on once and they sent me home and told me that I wasn't allowed back until I'd "washed that shit off my face." So, I've been presenting myself as a man when I'm there. I can't really afford to not work. But the longer I go, the harder it is to hide. I mean, I've been massaging my chest to increase the fat in it (I saw the technique on a YouTube video about Male-to-Female (MTF) transitioning). It's only been a few months, but I already have to wear a thick bandage around my chest now whenever I'm just in a t-shirt because it's starting to look more like I have breasts than pectoral muscles. And, my hair is growing out. It doesn't look too feminine unless I style it, which I don't for work. But, in combination with all of the other changes happening, it's enough to raise some eyebrows. So, now I'm looking for a new job where I can comfortably transition. It makes me so tired to have to lie to all my coworkers. Plus, it's a little bit scary. I know I'm tough, but I haven't been working out in an effort to slim down on muscle and I already feel a lot weaker than I was in the SEALs. A lot of these guys are strong. They're strong and they're narrow-minded. I mean, they make fun of one guy just for being Mexican. They call each other "fag" all the time, and it's definitely meant to be derogatory. When you're someone like me, that's not a great environment to be in. Bad things can happen.

    I haven't gotten many callbacks from anywhere else I've applied at, though. I even asked my mom to help me find a job in retail, maybe even at her store, but she wouldn't. She said they weren't hiring, but I insisted that I would take any job – even janitorial stuff at night. She said didn't feel comfortable asking for me because of how I look now. My dad said that he couldn't help me because he works in a corporate environment and I have no professional skills. I guess that's a fair statement. I don't. But, he did say that he had advice for me. Do you know what it was? He said, "Son, maybe you should just wipe that shit off your fingernails long enough to get a job. Folks'll judge you for that around here, you know. Can't you see how people look at you for it?"

Thanks, Dad. Like I didn't know I was being judged already. I'm trying really hard to ignore the stares and whispers and how people are flat out rude to me, and you just brought it right back up. I'm just trying to be me and not let all these people rule my life, like I've let their beliefs rule me for the last 24 years. But thanks for pointing that out to me.

I couldn't be too mad at him though. I think he's finally starting to try. I was looking for a pad of paper to write on the other day and I had gone into his home office to see if he had a spare. On his desk, I saw a stack of Psychology and Health textbooks, all about transgender studies. At first, I didn't know what I was seeing. But then I realized what it meant - he is finally trying to understand me, even if it isn't explicitly to my face. When he's being hurtful, I need to remind myself that he *is* trying. I can't rush people into acceptance. It's something a lot of people here haven't ever had to deal with or haven't ever tried to understand. This whole transitioning process is foreign to him, so I can't blame him – or anyone – for struggling. I just wish it were more innate for him. My mom is another story. She won't help me get a job, she cries several times every day, and she still calls me "son" and "my boy." She posts photos on

Facebook of my cousin and I with captions saying things like, "Look at these handsome boys! So glad Liam is home and I can have all my family together." It hurts. Not only is she not accepting that I'm transitioning, but she's embarrassed by it. She hasn't stopped loving me though. She lets me live in her house rent-free and she still cooks me dinner sometimes, so I shouldn't complain too much. I know there are a lot of people who have had it a lot worse when they've come out. It's just frustrating. She's trying to override what I'm doing with my life by sharing photos of the person I don't want to be anymore. She's using social media so that she can feel like the whole world will still see me exactly how she wants me to be seen, not how I want to be seen, and that hurts.

After seeing one of these photos online, Kara asked me, "Doesn't that make you angry? That isn't right."

"Ya, it does," I said. "But it's my mom. What am I going to do? I want her to love me and if this is how she's going to do it, I have to let her. I don't want to lose my mom over this. If my parents kick me out or if they decide they can't handle it, I don't know what I'll do. I need my family. I just have to let them adjust at their own speed."

"But, your mom should be someone you can turn to," Kara argued. "You should tell her how all of that makes you feel."

"Maybe one day, but not right now. She's not ready. Right now, I'll just focus on me," I replied.

Kara

Now that all of my friends know about the change in my relationship with Liam, some of my less understanding friends and acquaintances are asking, "So, it's been a while, when are you going to get back out there?"

I don't even know how to respond. It hurts me, like a deep gash in my heart, to hear people ask me that. First of all, I still feel so broken, both mentally and emotionally. I've only just recently started spending time with my friends regularly and I still struggle to immerse myself in their conversations. A part of my mind is always going over what's happening with Liam – what he looks like now, who he's hanging out with, and everything that we've been through. I don't ever feel truly present in any situation. That's probably why I haven't been able to find a full-time job. All I can manage are part-time jobs. I'm still living at home because the pay isn't enough and I just feel like I don't have the energy to go out and get interviews, or to be charming on the ones I have gone to. I feel like a large part of my brain is still processing Liam's transition, and an even larger part is still coming to terms with the sadness and anger I've felt since Liam told me that he was going to go down this path. That's a large part of me that cannot focus on caring about other people or caring about mundane work that, in comparison to what I'm feeling, doesn't matter to me at all. So, I walk dogs, groom at horse shows, and do some writing for local small businesses to make some spending cash. Right now, I'm comfortable living at home with my family and staying in almost every night. I don't want to date right now. I just want to be around people who support me. And I want to sleep. Somehow, this doesn't make sense to people when I explain it. They just think I'm being dramatic. Am I? Maybe I am. Maybe I have been horribly slow at getting over everything that's happened. But, I feel confident that none of these people who are judging me for not moving on in an "appropriate amount of time" have ever experienced this kind of break up or have tried to stay by a loved one while they transitioned into another gender. So what right do they have to judge me?

    I think the hardest part for me in this entire process is all of the anger. I'm so angry all the time. I just can't completely forgive Liam for all the times he's let me down or put me in bad situations. I can't. I tell myself that I have, but I know that I really haven't yet – not fully. I am completely empathetic to his situation. I can now understand part of the turmoil he was going through and I don't think I would have handled the same situation any better. I feel sad that he had to struggle with so many internal demons just to try and find peace and happiness. But none of that makes it any easier to let go of the anger I feel because of how he treated me. Sometimes, I feel like I have forgiven him because I can kind of understand why all the bad stuff in our relationship happened and I feel sympathy for who he was at the time. But then something little happens – he forgets to call me back or doesn't text me back when I know he's out at a bar – and all those feelings come rushing back. I start to shake, tears spring to my eyes, my stomach becomes nauseous, and I get angry that he's let me down again. There's no reason for me to feel this way, especially when he doesn't text me because he's out. I know that. It's such an extreme reaction. But I don't know how to stop reacting that way.

    Being so angry is starting to affect other areas of my life though. Anytime someone lets me down, intentionally or not, even in the smallest way, I've started to have the same reaction. It can be a store clerk telling me they're out of stock of whatever I'm looking for, someone taking my spot in a busy parking lot, or someone making a rude comment while I'm at the gym. In every one of those situations, I have the same physical reaction to feeling let down. I've tried going to new therapists because I don't like these changes in myself and I need guidance on how to get back to who I used to be, but they've all said I should be able to react normally again when Liam stops having an influence on my life. They, too, want me to cut him out of my life completely. But they're wrong. That would be the biggest regret of my life. I know this anger will go away when I learn how to forgive him and to move past the pain. I may be sort of empathetic right now because I feel for him, but I can't fully understand what he's going through. I don't understand him and his current situation more than I can remember the bad memories. Until I can do that, I don't think I'm going to be able to get over everything that's happened. Since none of the therapists could help me, I guess I'm going to have to figure out how to do that on my own. Writing my feelings down in a journal helps, but what I think will help most is talking to Liam. Instead of lashing out at him, or just focusing on the transition, I'm going to start asking Liam to explain more about how he's feeling and how he felt during our relationship. I want to know everything about what he's thinking and how he's feeling – good and bad. I feel like if I can know the ups and the downs then I can really start to see what it is he has been going through. He's not going to like it and he may not want to tell me, but I'm going to try. I have to. I can't feel this angry anymore. In my heart, I know he doesn't deserve my anger. But I need to start moving on and living my life again and this is the only way I can think will help.

Thirty-Four

After over two months of avid searching, and increasingly terrible interactions with his landscaping coworkers as his changing appearance became harder to hide, Liam finally found a job as a hostess at a local steakhouse called Jimmy's Bar and Grill. The hiring manager looked past the chin-length, braided hair and the five o'clock shadow poking through the heavily applied foundation, and welcomed Liam to the join the team.

On top of that, to further show Liam how much more positive the work environment would be than his landscaping position, the manager asked, "How would you prefer to be addressed? Do you have a preference for 'him' or 'her,' 'Liam,' or something else?"

Liam smiled at the question, his body warming all over with gratitude. Kara had asked once for his preference and she'd been using feminine pronouns almost consistently since, but she had been the only one to ask. Liam hadn't realized how much he had wanted someone to ask and consider his wishes on the matter, especially a stranger. He finally felt like the rest of the world was really seeing the changes in him. Until that point, Liam had taken the philosophy that others should call him by whatever pronoun they'd felt comfortable with. As the manager waited for Liam's response, Liam realized just how much it meant to him that others try to see him how he saw himself – as a woman.

"If you wouldn't mind, I'd prefer 'she,' please," Liam responded. "But, Liam is my name. Feel free to refer to me by that. I still like my name."

The manager smiled and nodded, making a note on her clipboard. There was no sign of judgment or unease with Liam's answer. In fact, it was the opposite. Liam thought she looked as if this was as normal as discussing pay – like it was something she did every day.

Working as a hostess was never something Liam had imagined doing growing up. He, or "she" as Liam now preferred to be called, liked to be outdoors and work doing physical labor. However, she'd also never expected to be in the state she currently was in. Above all, she didn't expect to enjoy acceptance as much as she did. So, Liam started working at Jimmy's, surrounded by open-minded and accepting coworkers, and she officially presented herself as a woman to the rest of the world.

Around a month later Liam couldn't wait to call Kara to tell her something that happened at the restaurant, even though it was 1am in Canada and Kara wouldn't check her voicemail for a few hours.

"Hey Kara, guess what! This guy came in to the restaurant earlier today and he kept looking at me, right? He kept looking at me, but not in the way that most people look at me now. You know what I mean? He looked at me like guys look at you. It felt really, really good. The best part was that he left me his number. On his bill, he wrote, 'Call me, sexy girl – (615) 555-1982.' I can't stop smiling! It doesn't even matter that I only made about $20 all day today. That note made everything worth it," Liam spoke excitedly to Kara's voicemail.

Too happy to go home, Liam sat down at the bar after her shift ended, helped herself to a drink, and looked at the number scrawled on the bill. She wanted to call him, but a part of her feared that she had misread the situation and that the man was actually trying to set up an opportunity to hurt her because of her identity. She'd heard of that happening to other trans people.

Sitting with the bill in one hand and her phone in the other, her coworkers started asking questions and making comments.

"Who's Mark?"

"Are you gonna call him?"

"Ohhh! Hot stuff, girl."

"Look at you go!"

Appreciating their support, Liam just laughed. "Oh, I don't know. He was cute, that's for sure," she said, smiling shyly.

"Why not call him? A bunch of us are going to the pub down the road now. You can tell him to come there so you won't be alone."

Liam nodded. *That's a good idea*, she thought. *It's safe that way and I still get to go out on a date with someone who actually likes me as a woman. I've wanted this for so long.*

In the end, she went on the date while her protective coworkers kept an eye out for any signs of a sinister plot. A few minutes before they were ready to leave work, Liam called Mark while she pictured his tall, burly frame and scruffy beard, and smiled.

"Hey," she said. "I got your note. It's me, Liam, from dinner." Her voice oozed calm confidence as she stretched for a higher octave than her voice was used to using. No one listening could tell that her heart was beating faster than it ever had when calling a potential date.

"Yeah, I remember you. I'm glad you called," Mark said, his voice gruff and deep. "Whatcha up to, pretty lady?"

Liam grinned. "Well, a few of my friends and I are going down the road to the Street-side Pub. You should stop by if you're in the area," she said with sweaty palms.

The voice on the other end paused and Liam's heart thudded against her chest. "Sure. I should be able to stop by. I'd like to see you again," he said.

The relief was easily seen on Liam's face. "Great. I'll see you soon, then," she replied before hanging up the phone.

Liam

I did it. I met a guy. He didn't pick me up at a gay bar, I didn't meet him online, I didn't even meet him through friends. He saw me, dressed in a jean skirt with my hair tied back in a half-pony tail and wearing gold, strappy heels and he wanted me. He liked what he saw. It was entirely superficial and that felt great. I feel like someone finally saw me as the woman I am and not just as someone who looks like a guy dressed in girl's clothing. It's *me* he wanted, the real me, and that feels *so* good.

About an hour after I called him, we met at the Street-side Pub down the road from work. It gave me enough time to have a few drinks with my coworkers to ease the nerves. I wasn't overly nervous, but I was definitely more nervous than I had been for any date in the past. It was a new experience, and a pretty exciting one for that matter. I'm glad that a few of my coworkers came, though. Having them there looking out for me let me focus on having fun. Being trans in Tennessee doesn't make dating easy and it makes sense to be weary of people's advances. There's so much hate towards anything outside the norm that, sometimes, people pretend to like you just so they can beat you up. That's why it's best to meet people who run in the same circles as you or to get set up by a mutual friend. However, I'm determined not to let my fear of those situations ruin dating for me. I'm a tough chick and can handle myself in a fight, probably better than most of the people who'd want to hurt me, so I take comfort in that.

Sometimes, I have friends who ask me, "How do you stay so calm and positive as an openly transgender woman in Tennessee? Don't you get angry about all the hate?"

Quite honestly, no, I don't. That isn't to say that all the looks and whispers don't hurt me. I see the way that more conservative customers look at me, and how they try to distract their children from even looking at me. I also hear all the confused and judgmental whispers, like, "Hey honey, look at that she-male over there. Can you believe she's allowed to work here?"

Once, a little boy came running up to me when I left the women's bathroom and said, "Hi. I'm just wondering, are you a boy or a girl? My parents say that you are a boy but you look kind of like a girl to me."

I wanted to explain to him, as simply as I could, that he was right, but that his parents weren't wrong and that they must've known me before I started transitioning, only I didn't get a chance.

His mother came running up to him, grabbed him roughly by the arm, and pulled him behind her. "Get away from my son, you sick fuck. You shouldn't be allowed near children. They're very impressionable. I don't need you spreading your abominable lifestyle like the disease that it is. You should be ashamed of yourself. I'll be filing a complaint with your manager." With that, she stormed off in a cloud of haughty superiority.

All of these situations hurt me, but I have a choice. I can let them make me angry, which will eventually make me sour and bitter. Or, I can force their words to roll off my shoulders and try to focus on being happy. If I let them get to me, I'm letting them do exactly what they've set out to do – make me ashamed and embarrassed of who I am. I've never let anyone do that to me before, so I'm definitely not about to start now. The way I see it, I can't stand there and argue with that person until I change their mind. First of all, neither of us have time for that. Second of all, it's an impossible task. I will never be able to change someone's mind unless they want to change and, frankly, if someone sets out to bully someone like me they are not going to be receptive to anything I say. Bullies generally don't want to change. But, if I go about my life happily and act like they have no impact on my life, my happiness, or my success, then they get frustrated and I win. When that woman complained to my manager, the response she got was a perfect example of this kind of frustration.

My manager told her, "Well, if you feel that way then I suggest you find another restaurant that is more aligned with your beliefs. Here, we offer an inclusive, family environment and do not tolerate discrimination. We reserve the right to deny service to any person and will do so if you continue to discriminate against our employees or our clientele."

The woman was furious at the manager's response. She yelled at her, she yelled at her waitress, and then she tried to yell at me again. I met her rage with a smile and wished her a wonderful day. Her child even waved goodbye to me. *That* is a win. That is why I don't let myself get angry. If I did, I'd just be stooping to her level and I'd much rather spend my time enjoying my life.

Anyways, Mark turned out to be a nice guy and I didn't have to keep my guard up. He genuinely liked me. He was interested in me, he listened to me talk about the Navy and football, and he still thought my pink nail polish was "cute." He told me that I had nice legs, pretty eyes, and a great ass. I felt confident, truly confident. We laughed, we drank, we smoked a little bit out back, and then he asked me back to his place. I felt nervous, but I trusted him. It paid off. I had a great night. He made me feel beautiful and the way he treated me gave me hope that I can still have a normal love life without having to leave my hometown.

The only thing that was a little weird was that he asked me about my name.

"So, what's your girl name going to be?" he asked as we cuddled.

"Huh?" I said, having a flashback to the 101 discussions I'd had with Kara on the same topic. I thought it was just her that would want to know.

"Well, you can't be 'Liam' forever, can you? It's not exactly a feminine name. What about something like, 'Lacy' or 'Elizabeth'?"

"Uh, I'm not sure," I said. "Those are nice names but I'm just not sure they're *me*, you know?"

"Yeah. Well, just throwing ideas out there. You'll find a perfect one that just suits you." He smiled and kissed the top of my head.

I smiled back, but didn't really mean it. The only name that suits me is Liam because that's my name. That's who I am. That's who I will always be.

Kara

It's getting really difficult for me to wrap my head around my relationship with Liam right now. Sometimes, he still treats me like a girlfriend. Well, not a girlfriend per say, but as someone to fill the role of a girlfriend when he's lonely or unsure of himself. I get flirty (and sometimes dirty) texts when he doesn't have someone else to send them to. Then, at other times, he wants to talk about boys and people he's hooked up with. I'm still also the only one he talks to when he's sad or uncertain of himself. I'm his shoulder to cry on. It's an extreme change from what we used to be – a young man and a young woman, in love, and planning to be married. I can't handle it but I can't find it in myself to tell him so.

When he texts me flirty texts, he isn't acting like the old Liam. It isn't a man hitting on a woman. It's not like he's trying to get me back. He's practicing feminine flirting. He acts feminine, which makes me so uncomfortable. It's one thing to be supportive of the physical changes, but another to be there for the changes in sexuality when they're being practiced on me. I don't know if I can do that. It's too conflicting for me. But, I also can't *not* do that for him because he seems so vulnerable when he texts me in those moods. If I don't respond within a few minutes, he asks, "Are you okay? Are you there? Do you have time? Am I doing something wrong?" Liam has never been one to show insecurity so now that he is, and now that it's so often, it must mean that he is feeling hugely insecure. I don't want to meet that insecurity with rejection because I want him to feel comfortable while he figures himself out, but I also don't want to read the texts. So, I've started opening them and trying to reply with smiley emojis so that I don't have to think about the message long enough to figure out how to properly respond. I feel guilty for doing this, and for not setting boundaries for myself, but I just don't know what else to do.

I think that I need some space from being on the romantic side of Liam's life. After pretending to be his girlfriend well after he came out to me, and now receiving these texts, I feel like *I need* some space from the romantic side of his life. However, whenever I get any space from him, I freak out, but in a different way. Every time I hear a story about how he's met some new guy or about how someone checked him out, it cuts a little deeper into the giant wound that's been left on my heart. It makes me feel like we're drifting even farther apart and that, one day, he won't need me at all anymore. It's stupid, but I can't help it. Plus, I feel like I haven't really registered that we're broken up still (somehow) and I feel a little bit betrayed every time he goes out with someone else.

He can't win and I can't find peace. So instead, we fight. We fight about him going out with other people. We fight about him drinking too much. We fight about him not making plans for his future beyond working as a hostess. And we fight about him not seeking support from a therapist or support group, or really anyone else outside of me. Well, maybe "fight" isn't the right word. It's really more of a heated lecture by me and a pained and defensive reaction by him.

We continued on like this until one day Liam excitedly told me that he'd ignored my calls the night before because he had been on an amazing date with some guy named Mark. Unable to help myself, I'd launched into a mini-tirade against him that consisted of me calling him a "slut" in between sobs. During this, Liam seemed to figure something out.

He said, "Kara, I think I finally understand what you're struggling with."

I stopped crying and sniffed. Somewhat sarcastically, I replied, "And what is that? Moving on from you? I know. That's pretty clear."

He didn't laugh. "I'm serious. I watched a YouTube video by a very intelligent woman who had transitioned. She transitioned from being a man, and a loving husband, and said that she watched her ex-wife struggle in much the same way that you are. She also said that she watched her friends react in a completely different way. So, she came up with an analogy to try to explain it to other people going through the same situation. She said, 'Be respectful to your loved ones as you go through the transition. I thought I was, but I actually wasn't. I was focused on *my* fight and didn't try to show them appreciation for their help; my focus was almost entirely on my struggles and my future. I used to get mad when they weren't reacting the way I wanted them to and I took their attempts at support for granted. You shouldn't do that because they're going through something big too.

I compare the experience to a kind of death. I understand that people who transition are still alive and it is by no means as final a goodbye as actual death, but I find that this is the easiest way to describe the experience of watching a loved one transition. When you transition, the old version of yourself (the version they have always known and loved) dies. For some people, it's a quick death. When I came out to my friends, it was just that – a quick death. I could see it in their eyes. Once I'd told people that I was going to become a woman, I was dead to them. Our relationships were never the same. Sure, I have rebuilt relationships with some of them, but they have never been the same as they were before I transitioned. Then, you get people like my wife who are there for you non-stop. They vow to stay by your side as you transition and to help you through everything. They try to keep things as normal as possible and as your transition progresses they keep trying without acknowledging their own feelings. Those are the people who are watching a slow death and watching the old version of you slip away, and it can sometimes drive them a little bit crazy. They're watching the person they once loved disappear, little by little, until there's nothing left.'"

I listened carefully. I had to admit, it made sense. "I'm a little uncomfortable with the 'death' analogy," I responded. "You're not dying. You'll always be here."

"Yes, I will. And we will always be friends. But, I'm not going to be the person I used to be anymore. I'm changing already. That's what she means by 'dying.' The man you fell in love with *is* dying because I will never be him again."

I paused for a moment. I felt both guilty and relieved. "I mean, I guess that makes a lot of sense. I am sorry for all of the extra stress I've been putting on you. That isn't at all what I want to do or mean to do. I just don't like seeing the old you disappear. We had this whole amazing life planned together and now that's all gone. I guess I'm just having trouble letting go."

"It's okay, I know you're trying. And maybe I don't tell you enough how much I appreciate that you're trying. I just need you to know that your support means the world to me. I'll try to be more respectful about what I put on you from now on and I'm going to try to be there for you too, but I might mess up sometimes and I'll probably be a little selfish sometimes. But, whenever that happens, just remember that you are my girl. You are my best friend. And I would be lost without you. I love you, Kara," he said, his voice soothing, like it used to be when he needed to make me feel better while we were dating.

"I can't think of you as a woman yet," I blurted out, maybe in the spirit of mutual support and understanding, but more likely out of pure guilt.

"What?" he asked, sounding shocked.

"I'm sorry. I am happy to call you a woman and use feminine words to your face but, when I think about you, I just can't. I've tried but my brain just cannot process you as anything other than a man."

He chuckled, deep and low. He wasn't using the feminine voice he'd been working on for the last several months. "Darlin' don't worry about that. That's all part of what we just talked about. You haven't resolved who I used to be with who I'm becoming in your mind yet, so how could you possibly only think of me as a woman?"

"You're not mad?" I asked. "I almost feel like I'm lying to you every time I call you a woman to your face."

"Ha - no, I'm not. It just means that you're still trying to accept me, which I deeply appreciate. That's all I can ask of you."

"Thanks." I smiled. "Are you planning to change your name any time soon? Have you had any thoughts on what you'd like it to be? It might make it easier for people to think of you as a woman all the time, not just when they remember that they should."

He took a moment to respond. "You are the second person to ask me that in two days, you know that? Mark asked me that last night too."

I was a little uncomfortable with his comment, but I laughed. "So, are you?"

"No," he replied simply. "No. Liam is my name. I don't want to call myself anything else. Everything else seems fake. I am Liam – always have been, always will be."

"Don't you want a name that is, you know, societally accepted as feminine for when you're farther into the transition since you want people to accept you as female?"

"The name doesn't make me male or female, it's just something to call me by. I don't care what people say about it. That's my name and I don't want to change it. And, to be honest, I don't even know if I want the surgery. People are always so curious about it and seem to think it's the obvious end goal, but I don't think it is. I like my body the way it is. Sure, there are things that can be toned down and other things accentuated, and the hormones are helping with that, but I don't want to really *change* anything. I like my body and I like my name. Anyone who doesn't think I'm doing this transition right can shut up. I like me the way I am."

I'd just gotten schooled. I couldn't argue with his logic or sentiment.

Thirty-Five

After about a year of separation with Kara living in Canada and Liam living in Nashville, Kara flew down to visit Liam. Apprehensive, she fiddled with her dress on the plane, bit her fingernails, and walked up and down the aisle several times to use the bathroom over the course of the short 90-minute flight.

"What's wrong, dear?" asked the 50-something year old woman next to her as she sat crumpling her sweater in her hands after her third trip to the bathroom.

Kara looked at her sideways. "Oh, just flying to see my ex-boyfriend. I guess I'm a little more nervous than I expected."

"How long ago did you break up, sweetie? I'm sure he'll be thrilled to see you. You look fabulous." She smiled kindly.

"I don't know... 10, maybe 11 months ago?" Kara couldn't think clearly. She was thinking more about who was waiting for her upon landing.

"Are you thinking about getting back together?" the woman asked. "Sorry if I'm being nosy. You just seem so nervous! Maybe it will help if you talk about it."

Kara smiled wryly. "I'm not sure about that." She laughed humorlessly.

"Try me. I've raised four daughters and two sons. I've heard every story in the book," the woman replied with a knowing smile.

Bet you haven't heard this one, Kara thought. "Well, no. We aren't getting back together. You see, we met while he was training to be a Navy SEAL in San Diego. We fell in love. We lived together and planned to be married. But, he had some issues that he hadn't dealt with and, well, he is now a woman in Nashville and is working as a hostess." Kara summarized the story in the way she had done with so many strangers. After the initial wariness of telling new people, she'd learned to appreciate the shock value it could bring. The more blunt she was when she told them, the less likely people were to react poorly because they were simply too shocked to say anything.

The woman's eyes widened. "Well, I guess I spoke too soon. I definitely haven't heard that one before."

Kara smiled dryly. "I know. It's a unique situation, that's for sure. That's why I'm so nervous. We talk on the phone all the time, but I haven't actually had to see him – or *her*, rather – since our break up. I get photos somewhat often, but I'm nervous about what it'll be like in person," she confided.

"I can't imagine that it will be easy at first. I mean, I've never had that experience, but if you were both so in love, then I would guess that it'll get easier as time goes on. Maybe seeing him, or her, for the first time will be difficult. But, you'll get to talking and then I bet it'll be just like old times. Well, maybe not *just* like old times, but easier," the woman advised, though she didn't sound convinced.

"Thanks, I hope so."

"You're doing the right thing though. You're doing a nice thing. I just think you should know that," the woman added.

Kara genuinely smiled at this comment. "Thank you."

Liam picked Kara up from the baggage claim and, true to Kara's fears, it was difficult for her to see Liam dressed as a woman in person. Trying hard not to stare, Kara chattered on incessantly as they drove off. She asked about Liam's family, friends, job, clothes, love life – everything. While she did care about Liam's answers and listened intently, Kara feared any silence between them now. She feared that silence would reveal her discomfort to Liam; she feared that silence would make Liam feel awkward and unsupported. Most of all, she feared that silence would make both of them feel that being friends, real friends, was impossible in their situation. So, she went on about anything and everything that entered her mind.

Eventually, Liam interrupted her. "Girl, I love that you're here and I have missed your voice so much. But, if we're going to talk about all of this, I'm going to need some food. How about we stop for a bite to eat?"

"Sure. I could go for some fried pickles." Kara grinned at Liam. She loved fried pickles even though Liam had never understood her taste for them.

"Oh lord, you and your pickles. I swear that's the only reason you ever came to the South – the fried pickles."

"Maybe," she replied teasingly.

"Well, Old Joe's has some pretty good pickles and it's right near where we are, so let's go there. We can go to the Street-side Bar for your favorites another day."

"Alright."

So, they went to Old Joe's and were seated by a hostess who eyed the two up and down, lingering on Liam a little longer, before turning around.

"This way," she said.

Kara followed Liam inside. She watched as Liam tucked a small purse under her armpit and walked ahead. Kara saw how much tighter Liam's jeans were now. They were actually women's jeans with rhinestones on the back pockets. Liam swung her hips in an exaggerated motion, her one hand tucked under her purse strap and the other swaying with her hips. While it may not have looked too extreme to anyone else, it looked overly exaggerated to Kara and it made her stomach lurch as reality hit her. Liam's hair was long – her bangs were almost down to her chin now. Having only known Liam with a shaved head, even the longer hair was a big change. To keep it off her face, Liam had clumsily braided most of the bangs back with just a few strands pulled loose to frame her face. While still fighting off shock and sadness at the changes, Kara's heart swelled at the effort Liam was putting in to learn how to do things that Kara had learned as a young girl. The image of Liam struggling in front of a mirror made her both a little sad and very inspired.

When they reached their table and the waitress put down the menus, Kara hugged Liam from behind.

"It's really happening," she said, more to herself than Liam. "You look great." She smiled.

Liam patted her forearm. "Thanks, Kara. Thanks."

Kara sat down across from Liam. They ordered food quickly and, while they waited, Kara stared at Liam while Liam talked, taking in all the changes in her face and features.

Liam's face grew serious. "How's it feel seeing me like this?" she asked.

Kara took a moment before responding. "It's pretty crazy, to be honest. I kind of feel like my brain is going to explode trying to take it all in."

Liam smiled sadly. "I thought so. I look pretty different, huh."

"Ya, you do. You look great though. You look happy, finally. And you're getting good at your makeup and hair! I'm really impressed," she complemented, truly meaning it.

This time, Liam smiled. "You really think so?"

"I do. Honestly."

Again, Liam smiled. "It's really good to see you," she said, her voice thick with emotion. "Thank you for coming to visit."

With that, Kara's nerves didn't quite go away, but they were overridden by a feeling of gratitude. Seeing Liam in person, seeing the reaction she gave to Kara's presence and words, Kara felt thankful to herself for standing by Liam, and thankful to Liam for letting her, despite all of their difficulties.

"Of course. I've missed you after all this time!"

As they ate, they chatted about a variety of things – work, friends, family. With every passing minute, it became easier for them to speak without having to ward off their emotions about being together again.

Liam felt more confident in her new body and new wardrobe after seeing that Kara could be okay with it, and Kara felt more at ease as she saw how truly happy Liam was.

After lunch, they went back to Liam's house where they socialized with Liam's parents for a while before going to meet some of Liam's new friends at a nearby bar. As Liam went inside to help his mom with something, Liam's father turned to Kara with a serious face.

"He still loves you, you know," he said.

Kara looked up at him with her eyebrows raised. "As a friend, yes. I know."

"No, as more than that. I can see it in the way he looks at you."

Kara noted that Liam's father hadn't yet switched to feminine pronouns either and wondered whether or not he had tried to use them when Liam was within earshot.

"I'm not sure about that. He's really happy right now. That's all I see."

"He's happy because you're here. You should talk to him… please. I just don't know if transitioning is the right decision for him. I still can't really believe that this is what he wants. I never once suspected it when he was growing up, and he still seems like the old Liam in so many ways. Plus, on some level, I know he still he loves you. Doesn't all of that count for something?" Liam's father paused. "I just want him to be happy and fulfilled in his life, and going down this path in this town…" His voice trailed off.

Before she could respond, Liam came through the door with a tray of drinks and her mother behind her. Fighting the tears from her eyes,

Kara smiled and reached for one. *God, I hope it's merrier at the bar tonight*, she thought.

It was.

Liam's new friends were warm and accepting. They were definitely an alternative crowd – piercings, dark clothing, tattoos. They were smokers and drug users and at first Kara was nervous. She was polished, proper, tanned, and fit. She was entirely lacking of any tattoos, experience with (or willingness to use) drugs, and the only piercings on her body were on her ears and which were usually filled with fake pearl earrings. Kara worried that this group would judge her just like she was mildly judging them.

Instead, they accepted her just like they had accepted Liam. They poked fun at Liam for saying or doing things that were silly without fear of offending him, and Liam never seemed to take offence.

"They keep me on track to be a proper woman," Liam said, laughing. They were discussing one particular incident where the group had teased Liam heartily for wanting to purchase a particularly inappropriate outfit for her age and body type that she'd seen online. "They said they'd help me look like the woman I want to be. And, man, is there ever a lot to learn!"

Kara laughed and looked around at the people who she had so often been jealous of because Liam spent so much time with them and talked about them so fondly. Instead of jealousy, she now felt gratitude. Liam was happy and supported with them around. As she realized this, Kara felt the weight on her shoulders getting lighter.

Eventually, the group dispersed. They had only gathered for a couple of hours to meet Kara and to have a few drinks. By 10pm, Kara and Liam were alone again. Moving from their booth, they went to the bar to chat with the bartender, another one of Liam's new friends.

After ordering another couple of beers, Kara asked, "What's that smell?" She smelled something familiar. She sniffed herself to see if it was her lotion that had simply wafted up to her nose, but it wasn't and she couldn't figure out where the familiar scent was coming from.

Looking up, Kara saw Liam blushing and, before she could say anything, the big man on the stool next to Liam who looked more like a homeless drunk than a paying patron, said, "It smells like something a fuckin' faggot would wear. It's comin' from this dude here and, judgin' by those heels he's wearin', he is a fuckin' faggot."

Kara was shocked into silence for a moment but soon opened her mouth and tried to find something to say in response.

Liam just shook her head at Kara. "Ignore it," she whispered.

"But, that was so fucking ignorant and rude," Kara said loudly, hoping that the man would overhear.

All the man did was grunt and continue to sip his drink.

"It isn't going to change his mind. He's drunk and small-minded and will probably start a fight. I don't want that tonight. I just want to hang out with you." Liam smiled reassuringly at her.

Kara opened her mouth to argue but shut it as she recognized the scent she had smelled. "That's my perfume!" she exclaimed, louder than she intended. "Ralph Lauren's Romance!"

Liam looked down and blushed a bright crimson red. "I... I hope you don't mind. I mean, I didn't buy it because I wanted to copy you. I just really liked it when I smelled it at the store and I only realized later that it's the one you wear. Maybe I liked it because it reminds me of you? It just smelled like the ultimate feminine scent and I had to have it. I hope you're not mad..."

Kara's heart swelled and she wanted nothing more than to hug away Liam's nervousness and uncertainty, though her mind did slightly reel as it tried to understand that her ex-boyfriend now wore her perfume. But, she was more concerned about making Liam feel comfortable, so she hugged her tightly. Squeezing Liam against her, she laughed. After pulling away, Kara grinned openly at her. "Hey, it's a great perfume. Wear it all you want. Imitation is the sincerest form of flattery, right? So consider me completely flattered."

Liam grinned back at her. "It is! I just want to be half as sexy as you. Take that as a complement."

Kara just laughed.

Kara

I'm happy that I went to visit Liam. I was so close to canceling the trip because of my nerves, but it wasn't nearly as awkward or sad as I thought it would be. Liam is happy. But it was definitely shocking to see him in a dress with cleavage, a purse, and a feminine strut. While we were out I couldn't stop looking at the tattoo on his shrunken forearm and thinking about how I used to trace it lovingly in the car or while it rested on the table when we were together. I also saw the familiar freckles all over his shoulders when he wore just a tank top. I saw all these pieces of the old Liam, but it was as if they were planted onto someone new. His face has become leaner and his hair is longer than I've ever seen it. It's down to a little past his chin now, while I've only ever seen him bald before. He's also practiced using a more feminine voice and softer movements. My brain still feels swollen as it tries to reconcile all the familiarities with all the new.

What's most important, though, is that he's happy and that he's still the same person he's always been deep down. Once my initial shock at his new appearance dissipated, it became easy to talk to him again. We laughed and joked. I teased him and he teased me back. It still stings when he introduces me as his ex-girlfriend, but that must be a natural reaction because it feels normal when he calls me his friend. Now that I can see all of the changes he's making, and how happy they're making him, it's becoming easier to process. He's surrounded by really good friends now. They love him for who he is, regardless of whether he's a man or a woman. They aren't trying to change him or undermine me. Instead, they welcomed me with open arms. I don't feel jealous of them anymore. It actually makes me happy that Liam has found a group of people who accept him and seem to care about him like I do. It makes me feel less alone.

Most importantly, though, I think I can finally start to let go. Now that I've seen him happily living his new life, it's a lot easier for me to really *understand* the fact that the old Liam is truly gone. I can even feel my brain starting to accept him as a "she." Maybe now it won't be long before I can think about him with female pronouns and have it feel natural.

Thirty-Six

Kara, with her heart becoming lighter every day after her trip to Nashville, finally found the energy to find a full-time job that not only paid her bills but that also held her interest. Excited to finally be moving forward, she was ready to start the next major step in her life. She went in early one morning to sign a contract and, afterward, signed a lease for her own place. Then she called a friend she who she had previously interned with to tell him that she would be starting soon. They went for coffee, they chatted, they laughed, and it wasn't until she met her parents for a celebratory dinner that Kara realized that she hadn't called Liam first. It had been a long time since she hadn't called Liam immediately with good or bad news. When she realized that, a wave of sadness settled over her.

"What's wrong?" her mom asked.

"Oh, it's nothing. I just realized that I didn't call Liam first with the news for the first time in a long time," Kara replied.

Her mother nodded knowingly. "That happens sometimes," she said. "Relationships evolve."

"I know," Kara said. "I think I knew he wouldn't always be my number one, but at the same time I don't think I really expected it, if that makes sense." Her eyes welled up. "I feel a little bit guilty – like I'm betraying him by not acting like I always have. I don't want to hurt him."

"You shouldn't feel guilty. These kinds of changes are natural. They're a part of all friendships and relationships, and you two have broken up. Your relationship *is* changing. But it doesn't mean you'll hurt him. Does he still call you immediately about everything in his life? Do any of your other friends call you immediately with any news? Do you call anyone else consistently with news?"

Kara thought about it. "No, I don't," she answered. Looking back on their conversations over the past few months, Kara saw a trend too. Not only was she usually the one who called Liam first, but she was also the one who asked, "What's new?" or, "How's work?" If she hadn't asked, she likely wouldn't know any of his more exciting updates. "I guess Liam doesn't either," she said. "He really only calls now to check in."

"See?" Her mother smiled. "It's okay. You guys have been through a lot together. You know Liam will always be there to listen when you call, and he knows the same about you. It's okay for relationships to evolve. It's part of moving on."

Knowing that there were no more words to say on the subject that Kara needed, or wanted, to hear, her mother just hugged her tightly. Kara was confused about how she felt. One part of her felt relieved and free. The other part of her was sad because, with this change, it became clear that their relationship had really changed. Their romantic relationship had truly transitioned into the past while Kara was too focused on other things. With the realization that she and Liam had truly become just friends, Kara began to mourn the relationship in a way that she hadn't yet.

In Nashville on the other hand, Liam didn't slow down to think about her life and her changed relationships until almost four months later. By that time, she'd quit Jimmy's after growing tired of hearing excuses every time she asked for a reason that she hadn't received a raise or promotion, even though she was one of their most hardworking employees. While the company had always protected Liam's right to life as she chose to live it, the battle was becoming more difficult, and more costly, than the managers had anticipated. Just as Liam had grown tired of the whispers amongst customers and complaints to the managers, the managers had grown tired of defending Liam against those complaints. Eventually, Liam was urged to "dress more like a man" for work hours and was provided a locker where she could keep her female clothes to change into after her shift ended. Jimmy's was no longer the safe and supportive environment that it had been when Liam started working there.

With feet dragging, long naps taking up large portions of her day, and little energy left to interact with other people, Liam started to fall into another depression. Whether it was the repression of her identity and the constant battle Liam had been fighting at work and at home that had led to it, or some new personal turmoil, Liam wasn't sure. Every night, she had nightmares that left her feeling heavy, tired, and at odds with her body again. Struggling to make sense of it all, she'd ultimately quit her job at Jimmy's because she didn't feel comfortable in the environment anymore, she didn't feel at all challenged, and she didn't have any desire to work in the industry anymore. She craved the outdoors and the physical labor that she was used to, so she'd found work as a landscaper once more.

She enjoyed working outside again. Her muscles craved the attention and her mind enjoyed the male humor. On the first day, she worked with dip in her lip, ate fast food for lunch, and went home so physically exhausted that she didn't have any desire to go out to the bar. It also stopped bothering her that she had to tape down her chest, hide her long hair under a ball cap, forgo makeup and nail polish, and revert back to her natural deep and gravelly tone of voice while at work. In fact, it started to feel right.

One day after work, Kara called Liam for the first time in four days to catch up, which was a new standard for them.

"Don't you feel like a phony again?" Kara asked. "You're hiding everything you worked so hard to let out."

"No, I don't at all, actually. I feel good again."

"Really? But, it's like you're going backwards. You're hiding this new you. And doesn't it bother you how often they use homophobic phrases? I can hear how often they say things like 'fag' whenever I talk to you over lunch."

"Honestly, it doesn't. I mean, do I wish they didn't say those things? Of course. Does it make me feel angry or insecure at work? Not at all. They're not targeting me, or even intending anything negative by it. It's just the way these people are, especially in this industry. And, on the whole, I've kind of missed it. I don't even really hear what they say anymore. I'm too happy to be working with my hands again. I like fixing things and making things, it feels natural and right."

"What about the hiding part? Why do you want to go back to hiding who you are?"

"I'm not hiding. This feels right for me right now. It feels good to be using my muscles again and to build things. I love going home physically tired. I feel comfortable in my old clothes, even though they're a little extra baggy now. I don't feel like I'm hiding because I'm just nurturing a different part of me."

"Okay," Kara said, somewhat skeptically. "As long as you are happy, I guess."

As time went on, Kara heard Liam talk about how she dressed up in women's clothes far less often and started wearing her old clothes more often, even when not at work. She'd spend less time talking about dating men and women's fashion styles and more time talking about lifting weights and meeting attractive girls, and always using her velvety deep, natural tone of voice. One day, Kara asked her about it again.

"So, are you transitioning back?"

"I don't know, Kara. I don't know. This is just what I want right now. I miss the old me, the guy version of me. It doesn't feel right to put on my girl clothes and to use the higher voice to go hit on guys right now."

"Have you stopped taking your estrogen pills and your testosterone-blockers?" Kara asked, trying to clarify the changes she was hearing about.

"Yeah. I stopped those a while ago. I didn't want to change anything too much or have anything work less if I wasn't 100 percent sure, you know?"

"That makes sense. What about testosterone? Are you going to take that?"

"Nope. I don't know what I want, so I'm just going with what feels good at the moment. And, at this moment, I like to wear my old clothes and use my old voice and work landscaping. Plus, I'm moody as hell and I think my body needs to balance out. I don't know what I'm going to want tomorrow or next week or next month, so I'm just letting my body rest while I figure it out."

"So, how should I refer to you then?"

Liam laughed. "God, I don't care anymore. Call me whatever you want – he, she, it, that… anything. You can call me fucking 'Sparkles' if you want. I'm tired of that question. I just want to be me. Whoever that is to you, call me that. I won't be offended by anything you say."

Kara laughed. "You'll always naturally be a 'he' to me. I hope that's okay. You're never offended by anything I, or anyone, says. How is that? How do you stay so calm? I think I get more offended over things than you do."

With that, Liam laughed even harder. "I don't know. You've got some anger bottled up in you from everything that happened with me, so maybe you just need an outlet? I'm much more zen than you, I guess."

Kara could imagine the grin and toying wink on the other end of the line. They both knew that, while Liam was most often levelheaded in his interactions, he had a temper that made him anything but "zen."

Kara giggled. "Maybe," she said. "But, I still feel so protective of you. I know you think that I don't need to be, but I am. And I might still be angry at you deep down, but I love you much more than I'm angry or hurt by you. I hate it when people don't understand you and are rude about it. It hurts me. It's almost like they're talking about a part of me or are trying to attack me because I care about you so much. I can't even imagine what it must feel like for you when those comments are directed at you, along with everything else you've been going through. Are you sure it isn't that you just grew tired of the fight? I mean, life was not easy for you as a woman. It seems like it's a lot easier when you're living as a man." Kara held her breath, hoping that she hadn't pushed her point too far.

Liam paused. Kara could hear the seriousness in his voice when he started to respond.

"Honestly Kara, you're right. It wasn't always easy. I haven't told you about half the things that have happened since I transitioned into a woman. For example, about halfway through my time at Jimmy's, some Latino guys cornered me in the bathroom while I was on shift and were whispering things like 'queer' and 'fag' to me. One guy even came up so close behind me that I could feel the wet heat from his breath on my ear. He asked me how much I liked to bend over. He told me he'd make me bleed from my asshole until I didn't want to get fucked by anyone anymore. The manager saved me when she came into the bathroom after a customer reported seeing the men follow me in. They got kicked out and I went back to work. But they didn't go away. They met me outside when I had finished my shift. They'd waited for me. The same guy who had whispered in my ear in the bathroom threw the first punch. But I threw the last. I was in fucking four-inch stiletto heels and a mini skirt, but you know that would never stop me. Heels or boots, I can still throw down. At the time, I still had some of my military muscles, so I picked up one of those metal newspaper boxes with the free newspapers inside and chucked it at him. After that, the rest of the guys scattered. I thanked God that night for putting me in BUD/S before transitioning. I had it easier than many others going through the same kinds of changes because I could protect myself better. That was a seriously dangerous situation and I don't know what would have happened if I hadn't gotten the training I did. It probably wouldn't have ended the way that it did."

"Oh my god!" Kara exclaimed. "Did anything else happen? No one actually ever hurt you, did they?" Kara asked.

"No, I never got hurt. I've been really lucky. There have definitely been a few sketchy times, like going on blind dates with guys from dating websites who I'm fairly certain were baiting me, or when I'd go to a bar far out in the country and the hicks couldn't contain their hatred, but every situation worked out okay. Like I said, I'm lucky because people may initially think they want to get into it with me but when they do, they realize their mistake."

"Oh, Liam…" Kara was at a loss for words.

"People made their views known in other ways too, like 'donating' their bibles by leaving them on my parents' doorstep with hateful notes tucked inside or bookmarks in passages some might have deemed applicable to my decisions. I've also lost friends and jobs, and I've been shouted at and leered at more times than I can count. I know I've talked about how accepting people have been here and how amazing it felt to come out and to be seen as a woman, but that's only because that's what I'd chosen to focus on. If I had stopped and thought about all the negativity, it would have taken over my life and erased all the good things I was experiencing. That kind of angry and bitter life is not one that I wanted to lead, you know? So I brushed off all of those bad situations and I focused on the good ones."

"Liam…" Kara started to speak. She had so many questions she wanted to ask him but wasn't sure how to get them out.

Liam continued, "I want to be happy. I want to feel accepted and loved. Anyone who doesn't put good into my life deserves to be forgotten. I can't fight all of them. I have to fight some because, well, I need to stay alive and I want to stand up for myself too. But, for all of those people who had said hurtful things, it was just talk. At the end of the day, it didn't matter what they'd said because I was happy with who I was then, and for who I am now. It doesn't matter to me if I'm a man or a woman anymore. I want to be happy, and that's that. I can't fight everyone or be offended by everyone because then I won't have any energy left to enjoy the life I've fought so hard to live. I wouldn't have any time left to be happy. Because of all that, I hope you can see that I'm not going to transition back because I'm scared. I'm not returning to living as a man because all of the negativity finally got to me. I'm not scared at all. I'm a warrior and I will fight to the death to stay who I want to be. Living as a woman was exhausting and, at times, nerve-wracking, but it was so worth it because that was what I had wanted. I felt *good* and *whole*. I just don't feel the same way anymore. If I've learned nothing else from all of this, I've learned that I need to focus on staying true to myself and, right now, that means I live and look like a man. If I ever get those urges again, you can bet your last dollar that I won't shy away. I'll jump right back in. It's just not *me* right now."

Liam's speech was met with silence. Then, tears started to roll down Kara's cheeks as the reality of Liam's life hit her. "I'm so sorry Liam. I had no idea all of that was happening to you. Why didn't you tell me?"

"It's okay. I didn't want you to know because I didn't want you to worry. I know you worried even when I only told you the good things, so you'd have been a fretful mess if you'd known everything that was going on. You had a lot to deal with too, so I didn't want to put more of my stuff onto you. That wouldn't have been right. I just wanted you to be able to move on and to be happy." Liam smiled into the phone. "Plus, I had made some new friends who kind of made it their job to protect me. This guy I worked landscaping with in high school started working with a biker gang here in Nashville after graduation. He's got the leather and guns and knives... all of it. They're a tough-ass crowd."

"You're not making me feel much better," Kara interrupted dryly even though she couldn't help but laugh to herself while the tears dried on her cheeks.

Liam chuckled and continued, "They're tough, but they liked me. They saw me throw down with those Mexican dudes outside of Jimmy's. Apparently they respected the hell out of me for that because, after that, my old buddy approached me and asked me to hang out with them. I didn't hang out too often because, well, those guys are a little intense even for me. But they were friendly and accepting, and they know how to throw one hell of a party. It was fun and they made me feel safe. When I went out, one of them was always around. I would see them seated at the bar while I was working, I'd see them in the corner of any pub I went to, and I even saw one of them outside of the gay dance club when I went with some other friends. The gang basically adopted me into their group and looked out for me when I needed help. It was pretty great actually. They always had my back. If someone ever looked at me wrong, messed with me, or even said something too rude behind my back, one of them would step in. It often wasn't even violent. Their mere presence was intimidating enough to keep me safe. I'll tell you – a lot of people hated me for my appearance, but not many hated the sight of me enough to take on that group of guys."

"A biker gang in Nashville, Tennessee adopted you, an openly transgender woman, as a friend?" Kara asked incredulously.

"Yeah!" said Liam. "I was shocked too, to be honest. But, it goes to show you that you can find support in weird places if you let it happen. I mean, they probably made the biggest difference for me down here. I could go out and feel safe, so I got to be myself but without the fear. I did have some bad experiences so I needed some pretty thick skin. But, I think I handled it all pretty well. I had a good set up. I was safe and, if I'd wanted, I probably could have found work with them. They have their fingers in a lot of pots down here."

"Did you ever have to, you know, do anything for them?" Kara asked. She'd watched enough crime shows to know that a gang's friendship often didn't come for free.

"No, not at all. It wasn't like that. They just really seemed to like me. I think I was a novelty for them. I could throw down with the best of them, but I looked unique. I looked soft. They respected me for that and then, after hanging out with me, they ended up liking me for *me*, without getting caught up in what I looked like. We shot pool, we drank... it was all very relaxed. I have to say that I'm pretty happy it's over with them though." He laughed. "I was always a little nervous that they'd ask me to do stuff for them in exchange for their protection. It just seemed too good to be true. They didn't though. Thank God that I got out before that changed and they decided to make use of me, but, if I wanted to go back to that life, I could easily start hanging out with them again if necessary."

"No kidding," she said. "I'm speechless, Liam. That whole story is pretty unbelievable – from SEALs to being a trans woman to socializing with biker gangs. You are one cool dude... or chick... or person," Kara stumbled over the descriptions. "I watched you live it and it's still doesn't sound real. Are you considering doing counseling or volunteering or something? There are so many ways that you can help others with your attitude and experiences. You could show kids that you don't have to fit in with societal norms to just be who you are."

"Oh hush, girl. Don't overreact, and don't be so cheesy." Liam chuckled. "People are people. I'm nothing and no one special. No one needs to hear my story – they're all out living their own stories. I can't teach anyone anything and I shouldn't pretend that I can. I'm still trying to figure out my own life. There's no lesson for me to talk about and there's no way I could help anyone else figure out their own problems."

"That's the point, though! You're still figuring it all out and you're okay with that! I think that's a message people can learn from and I can't think of anyone better to show them." Kara was eager to convince him. "You're wasting your talents and your experiences by keeping them to yourself. You could make a difference," she said.

Liam just chuckled in response. "Oh, girl. What am I going to do with you…" he trailed off. He didn't see himself the way Kara did. He just saw himself as the same as everyone else – on the lifelong journey of figuring out how to be happy.

Epilogue

Over the next few years, Liam worked primarily as a site foreman for a construction company and as a bartender near Music Row. Since transitioning back to life as a man, Liam reconnected with a couple of his old friends. Never speaking about the time when Liam lived as a woman, their relationships appeared to return to exactly the same relationships they'd had before. And despite feeling more guarded against each other, they refused to let it show.

In construction, Liam took over the responsibilities as site foreman for a well-respected company in Murfreesboro. During this time, he worked with some very wealthy and stereotypically conservative bosses and clients who, with his charm and military-style appearance back, always trusted him. Wanting to return Nashville, Liam eventually turned to bartending as a way to incorporate his love of the city's nightlife into his work, as well as a means of letting him return to his hometown.

While bartending somewhat near several recording studios, Liam met singers from every level of stardom – from newly signed to seasoned veterans looking for an escape. Never caring enough about celebrity gossip or status to gawk at them, the musicians found it easy to chat with him as he poured their drinks in a particularly unsuspecting venue.

One particularly hot and sunny day in early summer and only days from the four-year anniversary of when he came out as transgender to Kara, Liam sat alone in the late afternoon during one of his day shifts. He'd wandered to a small park near one of Nashville's many recording studios to enjoy some fresh air. He breathed in deeply, relishing the quiet after a long day that kept him engaged in endless chatter by customers. He heard someone sit near him and breathe a sigh of relief. Too tired after a long night of partying and an early morning start for a construction job, Liam didn't open his eyes to see who had joined him.

The two strangers sat in silence for several too-short minutes before Liam's cell phone rang. He knew it was Kara without opening his eyes because it was the chorus to "Cruise" by Florida Georgia Line that played, not his standard ring. Liam had assigned Kara a personalized ringtone after, on one too many occasions, his current girlfriend had thrown jealous fits over Liam checking his phone while they were together and seeing Kara's face on the screen. With the personalized ring tone, which he claimed he had assigned to a friend from the Navy based on an inside joke, he could avoid those kinds of fights and unnecessary stress. Since he didn't need to open his eyes to look at his phone, he kept them shut with his head against the trunk of the tree and simply reached for the phone, but only after the third ring. He hadn't talked to Kara in several days since he had been staying at his girlfriend's apartment because it was closer to work, so he was excited. He missed her, especially with all of the thoughts and urges of being a woman flowing back into his mind recently. He was so tired though and sitting in the shade quietly was very appealing.

"Hey Kara," he answered, finally. "How are ya?"

Kara smiled. "You finally picked up!"

"Hah – I did. Sorry girl, I've been busy the last few days. I'm here now though." Liam chuckled.

"And, what were you busy doing? Amber-Lynn? You can pick up my phone calls when you're with your girlfriend, you know. We're just friends now," Kara said, trying not to be annoyed.

"Take it easy, girl. I've been sleeping there, but I've also been working a lot and going out a lot, so I'm just real tired."

Kara smirked into the phone. "Sure. You just don't feel like chatting with me anymore now that you have a girlfriend," Kara said, poking fun at an old and stubborn insecurity of hers that had taken several years to resolve.

Liam groaned. "Kara, darlin'. That will never happen, you know that. You're my girl! You are my beautiful, sweet, kind, and generous best friend." Liam had learned early in their friendship that, if he excessively upped his flattery of Kara when she least expected it, she'd giggle and forget that she was annoyed with him. It was a good trick that he still employed out of habit when Kara teased him with her mock jealousy. "I've just been blowing off some steam… Work has been crazy busy and I've just needed some time to let go. I'm here now though. What have you been doing?"

"You bet I am," Kara said with a smile.

While she and Liam had left their relationship behind and reached a comfortable level of friendship, she knew that her long-living insecurity, which had become a bit of a running joke between them, was based in a very real insecurity. While resolved in her mind, Kara still had some open emotional wounds that caused her to fear that all they had gone through together would be forgotten and Liam would forget about her. She had always known that Liam placated her to get through some of her most emotional moments, but the fact that he cared enough about her as a friend to placate her reminded her that she mattered to him. And it still soothed her.

Kara and Liam chatted for a few more minutes. Liam had thought about bringing up his new thoughts to Kara, but then remembered that there was a stranger sitting nearby and didn't want to risk the wrong person hearing his revelations, which could potentially result in the loss of his current job. To prevent that situation from arising, Liam let Kara tell him stories from her day. In an unusually high-energy mood, Kara chattered so quickly about a variety of topics that she had Liam distracted from his fears and laughing heartily, even though he could barely follow her stories because of the speed with which she spoke. Then Kara hung up to get back to her job at a magazine, and Liam, now awake, was left to decide what to do with the rest of his lunch break.

"Y'all sound really happy," said a deep, drawling voice behind him.

Liam turned to look to his left and saw that the stranger had sat down a few feet away under the next tree over. It was then that he noticed who had come to share the shade with him – a new-to-the-scene country singer who had broken into the Nashville bar scene around the time that Kara had visited Nashville for the first time. Kara had adored his voice and bought his demo CD after his performance ended, praise gushing from her lips. They had listened to the demo on repeat as they drove back to DC for Kara to catch her flight back to San Diego.

Never one to raise a fuss about celebrities or possible future-celebrities, but always one to give credit where he felt it was due, Liam grinned easily at him and answered honestly. "She's a great girl. She can drive me a little bit crazy sometimes, but she makes me laugh. She's the only one that makes me laugh like that these days. And, on top of all that, it doesn't seem like there's anything I can do to get rid of her. I'm not a perfect guy, but she's just always there saying she isn't going anywhere. I've never experienced that before." Liam paused before adding, "By the way, we saw you play at Melodee's quite a while back and you're really talented. It was a great show and she played your CD on repeat for hours afterwards."

"Keep her around. That's the sign of a *great* girl." The singer grinned in thanks. "But honestly, she sounds like the best kind of girl – the kind that accepts you and supports you. The kind who, with all of the relationship stuff stripped away, is still your best friend. It's tough to find that." The singer paused and looked introspective for a moment. "Do you have a pic of y'all together? I saw her face light up your phone. She looks like a pretty girl."

"Of course! I love showin' my girl off." And he did, despite their current relationship situation. Like the man had said, she was still his best friend. So he took out his phone and found a photo of them together.

"She's a beauty. Sweet smile. Y'all look real happy. How long have you been together?"

Liam hesitated before answering. "Uh… Going on almost six years, I think." He didn't feel like he was lying. They had known each other for over five years, and had been big parts of each other's lives the entire time. He felt a pang deep in his stomach with the realization of how much had happened in those five years.

"Jesus! That's a while. Is there a ring on her finger yet?"

"Naw – not yet. You know how it is, right? Life gets complicated. She's in Canada and I'm here. She's got her own life up there and I've got… stuff… going on here." Liam thought about the familiar stresses that had been seeping back into his mind, pushing him to party harder than his grueling work schedule should have permitted. He also realized how hearing Kara's understanding and friendly voice for even those few minutes had calmed his stress level a little bit.

"There ain't nothin' too complicated to sort out if you love her. Trust me. I've wasted too many opportunities in my life because things were complicated or I was busy or I needed to focus on my music and now all I can do is write songs about the people I've lost and the memories I've missed out on. It's good for this job, I guess. But it also means that I don't have anyone to share my successes with or to cheer me up after every rejection. My bed is cold every night and my closest friend here is my dog, and that can get pretty lonely."

Liam smiled back, a touch of sadness in his eyes. He was sentimental at the loss of a future like the one being described, but thankful that he would never have to feel so alone. Swallowing his thoughts, he replied, "We'll figure it out. One day we'll get to where we each need to be and we'll be happy. We've got time."

In his experience, artists were generally more likely to be open-minded towards LGBT individuals, but Liam still didn't want to get into the truth about his relationship with Kara – it was too complicated and too delicate a situation to explain to someone who didn't know their history, and who may want to impose their discriminatory views on him.

After a few minutes of sitting in contemplative silence, the singer stood up to leave. "I've got to get inside, but I hope you and your girl figure things out. You guys look and sound too happy together to waste time on issues that don't matter."

"Good luck in there," Liam said in response.

Before Liam went back to work, he quickly called Kara to tell her about the exchange. He knew she'd be excited to know that he'd both mentioned her name and shown her photo to the singer.

"Why didn't you just tell him that I'm your friend or your ex-girlfriend? You have a current girlfriend now and we've been just friends for quite a while now," Kara said.

"I don't know. It just seemed easier."

"Why is it easier to lie and say we're together? I mean, you don't seem to have a problem anywhere else. When I came down last, you always introduced me as your ex-girlfriend," Kara replied.

"I don't know Kara. It was just easier to lie today. Our situation, my situation, is so messed up that it's just easier to lie. It felt right to lie."

"Are you okay, Liam?" Kara asked. She knew him well enough to recognize the signs when his thoughts were stressing him out.

"Yeah. And no. Just have a lot on my mind, is all."

"I haven't really asked how everything is going with you recently. I mean, you know, with your thoughts and urges and everything. How are you doing?"

"Well, they're still very real. They're very much a part of my life still and I think they're getting worse."

"Have you told anyone? I'm here if you need, but I think talking about it with people would probably help."

"Thanks, darlin'. I actually told my mom yesterday and we talked a little bit about it."

"Really? How did that happen? Did it go well?" Kara was both surprised and happy, but also nervous. His mother had avoided acknowledging the topic of Liam's transition ever since he had returned to living as a man.

"She asked," Liam replied. "We were driving to my grandparents' house for dinner and she asked if I ever thought about being a woman again. I don't know what prompted the question. It seemed so out of the blue. I was so surprised at first that I couldn't speak. But it was just the two of us in the car and I'd been alone with those thoughts for so long that I really needed to let them out, so I finally told her that some of those old thoughts have come back. I told her that the urges are getting stronger again and that I'm trying to work out what that means."

"And... how did she take it?"

"It was fine," he said. "She handled it well, actually. She listened, and then asked a few questions. She didn't say much else, but I think it was because she didn't know what to say and not because she didn't want to hear what I was saying. You know what I mean? It felt like things would be different than they were last time if I went down that road again – or any other road. She wanted to know how I was feeling, so I told her. And we were *good* in the end. I felt supported."

"That's great. I really hope that continues," Kara replied with both hope and skepticism. She liked his mother, loved her even, and believed that she wanted to support him. *What mother wouldn't want to help her baby?* Kara thought to herself. However, she still found herself very protective of Liam, especially with anything relating to his transition. "Have you told anyone else? Your dad or Billy?" she continued.

He laughed. "Kara, if I hadn't told you, do you really think I'm going to be telling my dad or my cousin or anyone else? I only told my mom because she flat out asked me. I don't want to stress my dad out again until I completely understand what's going on in my head. He tried hard last time but I know the whole situation wasn't easy on him, so I want to be sure of what I want before I go changing myself again. And I enjoy being friends with Billy again. I like feeling like we're the same kind of buddies we used to be. I don't think he could handle me coming out again. I think that'd be it for us." Liam paused. "If I tell anyone but you and my mom about what I'm thinking and feeling, things will change. And I'm happy with things the way they are. So, no, I haven't told anyone. I'm keeping this very quiet until I know exactly what I want."

"Well, I'm always here if you need to talk. You know that right? I'm here. No matter what's going on in my life, whether I'm dating someone or not, or whether you're dating someone or not, I'm here."

"I know, thank you." Liam paused. "There is something you could do for me…" he said, letting his gruff voice drift off into sheepishness.

"What's that?"

"You could, you know, maybe send me some things to wear?"

"What?" Kara asked, her mind reacting to the news a little more slowly than it used to. "Like, clothes?"

"Yeah," Liam giggled slightly in excitement. "Anything you have – clothes, swim suits, make up… anything. I just really need some of that in my life."

Kara giggled along with him. "Are you going to start dressing up again? Don't you have anything left from before?"

"I think I want to start again. I don't know if I'll go anywhere, but I want to wear stuff in my room at least. I want to start dressing up a little, and it may as well happen soon. I threw out everything from before. It was probably a little rash. I regret it now. But now I can get some new pretty things!"

"I'll take a look at what I have and see if any of my friends are doing a closet clean-out soon. In the meantime, why don't you go to Target or Walmart and buy a few things?"

"Oh, no. I couldn't do that. Could you please just send me something?"

"Why can't you do that? You go to Walmart all the time for other things, just pick up a t-shirt or something and pretend it's for your girlfriend. Or don't you have anyone that lives closer to you that can donate a few items to you?"

"I'm not ready to go buy anything. That's too much. I need to start small and buying clothes to wear doesn't feel small. And I guess I could ask someone else to help me but I don't really want to. You're my go-to girl. You're my style icon and transition-helper. I need you, Kara!" Liam was talking quickly now, aware of the fact that he was almost back on the clock.

Kara smiled to herself. "Of course, sweetie. I'll find you some clothes, and maybe some make up, and I'll send the care package out next week."

"Thank you, darlin'. You're the absolute best friend I could have," Liam replied, and meant it.

"Oh stop. You're just using me for my closet," Kara teased.

Liam grew serious. "No, I mean it. Sometimes it's really hard for me to realize that you're dating and moving on while still talking to me all the time. It can be hard because I miss you and I miss us, even though that relationship is not what either of us wants anymore. But you are the best thing that has ever happened to me. I want you to know that. Regardless of whether I'm dating or what I wear or how grumpy I might be, I am thankful for you every single day. I hope you know that."

Kara smiled. "I love you too," she replied, tears springing to her eyes. While she was moving on with her life in a job that she liked and with a boyfriend she cared deeply about, Kara missed their relationship too. It wasn't a longing to have it back, but rather a nostalgic memory with wounds that hadn't fully healed yet. Deep down, her emotions were still raw so, when it came to honest moments with Liam where she recognized real emotions, she felt like the rawest parts of her soul where the wounds were still very open were being touched, and it almost always brought her to tears. She wiped her eyes and focused on her computer screen, forcing her mind to return to work. She couldn't help but smile though. It was nice to feel appreciated after all of the turmoil and pain.

In Nashville, Liam attempted to focus on work and to forget the call he'd just made. Surrounded by dozens of patrons, many of which were rough around the edges, he tried to forget the excitement he felt about Kara's care package. The other bartenders wondered why his mood seemed to have shifted so drastically from annoyed and exhausted to light-hearted and joking, but Liam would simply shrug his shoulders and wink because they would never understand.

Kara

It feels unbelievably good to hear that Liam appreciates me and that he still considers me his go-to person for the really big things. He doesn't always show his appreciation, or even that he really cares, especially when he's going through hard times. In response, a part of me has had a tough time letting go of the anger and hurt, and I think I'm still a little more overly sensitive than the logical part of my brain knows I should be. I know he cares, but sometimes I can't help but take his shutting me out personally, which makes me upset and hurt and angry. So, when he told me that he appreciates me and recognizes everything that I've done, I was so touched that it brought tears to my eyes. Still. Even after all this time. A part of me wonders if that feeling will ever stop, if that part of me will ever fully heal.

Because he means a lot to me and because of all we've been through together, I still constantly worry about him. I wonder if he'll find the right partner, if he'll find a good career, and what his future looks like. I worry about his health and about him not talking to a therapist, and then I worry about what would happen if he did start to see one. His most recent girlfriend, Amber-Lynn, wasn't right for him and they broke up. It's better for him that they're not together, but I don't like that he feels guilty about the relationship not working out. I don't want him to feel guilty anymore. I want him to feel good about himself and with where he is. And with who he is. When they'd parted ways, I'd told Liam to focus on sorting himself out rather than worrying about letting potential relationship partners down, which brought back a lot of bad memories for me. That feeling of being let down has stuck with me in many ways. But talking to Liam about his break up also made me realize that Liam doesn't really need me to worry about him. He acknowledged that he shouldn't be dating seriously yet because he couldn't give enough of himself to a relationship until he figured out what he wanted. He learned from us. He learned from our pain and our mistakes.

It's not easy becoming friends with an ex, especially when neither of you takes any space before the transition. Liam and I went from being very much in love to platonic friends in what felt like one night. Because of this, we both had to deal with points of extreme emotions and the repercussions of those outbursts. Now, enough time has passed that we have a better understanding of one another as friends. When Liam feels overwhelmed and stressed out he takes a break from technology and takes some time alone; however, when I feel overwhelmed and stressed out I need to communicate and talk through my problems. We're still working on our friendship but we communicate our needs to each other in a much healthier way now.

Realizing all of this has helped me to come to terms with the fact that the Liam who made me cry is not the same Liam in my life now. I've also realized that the Liam I met in that bar so many years ago now is also not the same Liam in my life now. Well, he is and he isn't. At his core, he is still the same person and always will be. But all of that surrounding stuff – how he relates to me, how we interact, and how he interacts in the world – is all different. The Liam in my life now is my friend. The Liam of the past is gone. Understanding this and reconciling these different versions of him has helped me to realize that we are going to be okay. He'll be the same caring and giving person he has always been, regardless of what path he decides is right for him. He's ready to get to know himself. He's ready to let himself be happy now. Once I thought about that and believed it, I felt ready to move forward. And I did. I let go of the hurt and the anger, I let go of the worry, and I held on to my favorite memories. I held onto the love. I let the romantic relationship move into the past so that my friendship with Liam could move into the present and future. I felt light again. I found the energy to be passionate about work. I fell in love again. And, most importantly, I started to truly appreciate the people who have been there for me throughout all of the highs and the lows. I found myself happy again.

Liam has changed a lot over the years; he's grown up a lot. Despite the fact that things are still hard for us sometimes, I know that Liam is trying really hard to be the kind of friend I want him to be, not just someone who is there when it's convenient. I need to remember to thank him more for that, and to let him know that I really do appreciate him. I may have supported him through some of the most difficult times in his life, but he has never stopped being there for me. I've promised myself to remember that in those times I'm trying to cope with the effects of some long-buried pain or memory because, at the end of all of this, I'm nothing but proud of us and of him. He has never let the stress, discrimination or judgment stop him from living his life and striving to be happy, and I believe that he never will. I'm going to keep sending Liam clothes and nail polish when he asks. I'm going to try to remember to ask him more often how he is doing, and I'm going to really try to be there for him this time around if he decides to transition again, or if he wants to explore new paths. Friends listen and support one another, without judgment. I'm going to be there for Liam, without asking him to define himself or what path he's going down, because he's Liam. And I love every aspect of him.

Liam

Amber-Lynn broke up with me. I'm upset, but also relieved. I thought what I had with Amber-Lynn could have been real and lasting; I've been with plenty of girls since Kara but Amber-Lynn was the first one to make me feel like being a boyfriend again. That was, until I didn't.

When the urges to start dressing up came back, I had asked Kara to send me care packages. I got them and then started staying home more, telling Amber-Lynn I was too tired to go over, and then dressing up in my room. Because of the stress of the urges combined with having a new girlfriend and a heavy work schedule, I started to have trouble sleeping and started drinking more.

One day, after a particularly long week filled with 18-hour days, I was really tired and told Amber-Lynn that I couldn't go over. She'd called me right as I tried to go to sleep. She'd told me that a man was outside her door and that she was scared and needed me. Wanting to protect her, I'd rushed to her house. Only, when I got to her house, there wasn't a man there. Amber-Lynn lied to me to get me to come over and met me at the door completely naked and reeking of alcohol. I was so pissed at how she exploited the responsibility I felt for her as her boyfriend that I just lost it. I don't have the capacity to feel responsible for anyone, let alone have it exploited like that, regardless of her motivations. So I screamed at her and cussed her out and then left. I was so tired by the time I got home that I passed out and ended up sleeping until 5pm the next day.

When I woke up I felt better than I had in weeks. Amber-Lynn had left me 10 texts and had called me 15 times. It was too much pressure and I didn't want to deal with it, but I felt bad about how much I had screamed at her the night before and decided to try to make things work. So I called her and apologized. After that night things were always a little tense with Amber-Lynn and I. And I didn't have the energy to fix it at the time.

What finally ended my relationship with Amber-Lynn, though, was a fight we had over me missing an important party that I didn't know was even happening. She had texted me asking me to come over one night after work, and I really did plan on going over, but I really needed to sleep and decided to take a nap before I headed to her house. I set an alarm but was so tired from working long days and not sleeping enough that I didn't wake up until the next day. I slept right through my alarm. When I called her to apologize she told me that she had invited her friends and family over to meet me, and when I didn't show up she decided that she didn't want anything to do with me anymore. She said I wasn't worth the pain and effort, so she wanted to end it.

I do feel mostly relieved that we're not together anymore. I mean, her words stung but I've been thinking a lot about it and I don't think I should be in a relationship right now, not with everything going on inside of me. I need to figure out who I am and what I want for myself again before I can be with someone else and try to consider their needs and desires. If I learned anything from my relationship with Kara, it's that I need to be upfront and honest about my thoughts and feelings, and that I shouldn't get into relationships without knowing first what I want.

I'm nervous about all of these urges getting stronger again. I'm more than a little tired of this constant internal battle and I just want to be happy. I'm tired of repressing parts of myself all of the time. I'm tired of listening to people's opinions about my past and present choices. For as long as I can remember I've always had to repress part of myself; as a man I repressed the feminine urges and as a woman I repressed the male urges. Honestly, now, I don't think that I have ever really felt *whole* in either gender. I just don't know how to reconcile the two different parts of myself and trying to figure it out is exhausting. As much as

I thought that being in a relationship would be good for me, I've realized that I just need love and support, and I have Kara for that. She's the only one who knows the real me, every confused and uncertain part. And she still loves me. She makes me feel understood and, living and transitioning in the South, having her support and understanding means the world to me. I can rely on her when I feel like I can't rely on most people. My feelings are so difficult to figure out, and I have so much inner turmoil, that having Kara be a steady presence in my life makes all of it seem a little more manageable. Man or woman, employed or not, dating men or women, she's always there. Nothing scares her away and it gives me hope that no matter what I decide to do that I won't be alone and that things will be okay. It doesn't matter that our relationship isn't romantic anymore – I think it's actually better now. I don't know where I'm going or how I'm going to get there, but I know that she'll be there and that is more than enough. Sometimes, one good friend is all you need.

Acknowledgments

I'd like to say a big thank you to my family – Sandy, Ed, and Tom – for the endless love and support you gave to me throughout the process of writing, editing, and publishing this book (and throughout my entire life). Mom and Dad, your constant encouragement has been invaluable and is more deeply appreciated than you can ever know. Thank you for raising me to dream big, to work hard to achieve those dreams, and to believe in possibility.

I am also forever indebted to my friends for their willingness to give feedback on section after section, draft after draft, and for championing my ability to tell this story. I am so lucky to be surrounded by so much support.

Cory Visser, you have been selflessly supportive in so many ways, not least of which has been your dedication to learning about formatting novels so that you could take on the role of interior designer for this book. I cannot thank you enough for your constant and unwavering encouragement throughout the writing, editing, and publishing process.

Thank you to my wonderful editor, Jessica Wright, for your commitment to making this story stronger and clearer with every edit and to my talented designer, Warren Keefe, for designing a cover that I absolutely love.

I would be remiss not to mention my animal babies – Shadow and Sully – who kept on loving me throughout the period of shortened outings and diminished play times when I was too involved in writing to take much of a break. Though they will never read or understand this, for their role in helping me write this story, they deserve to be acknowledged too.

All of you have helped me in your own way to achieve one of my life's goals by completing this book, and for that I thank you.

P, you have been such an inspiration to me and I would not be the person I am today without having known you. Thank you for being so unapologetically you.

CPSIA information can be obtained at www.ICGtesting.com
Printed in the USA
LVOW07s2011071016

507895LV00003B/5/P

9 780995 303805